OUT OF VIRGINIA

OUT OF VIRGINIA

Black Americans' Search for Freedom in Nineteenth-Century Liberia

Joseph P. Stinnett

RIVANNA BOOKS
University of Virginia Press
Charlottesville and London

The University of Virginia Press is situated on the traditional lands of the Monacan Nation, and the Commonwealth of Virginia was and is home to many other Indigenous people. We pay our respect to all of them, past and present. We also honor the enslaved African and African American people who built the University of Virginia, and we recognize their descendants. We commit to fostering voices from these communities through our publications and to deepening our collective understanding of their histories and contributions.

RIVANNA BOOKS
An imprint of the University of Virginia Press

University of Virginia Press

Printed in the United States of America on acid-free paper

First published 2026

9 8 7 6 5 4 3 2 1

LIBRARY OF CONGRESS CATALOGING-IN-PUBLICATION DATA

Names: Stinnett, Joseph P. author
Title: Out of Virginia : Black Americans' search for freedom in nineteenth-century Liberia / Joseph P. Stinnett.
Description: Charlottesville : Rivanna Books, An imprint of the University of Virginia Press, 2026. | Includes bibliographical references and index.
Identifiers: LCCN 2025039113 (print) | LCCN 2025039114 (ebook) | ISBN 9780813954677 hardback acid-free paper | ISBN 9780813954684 paperback acid-free paper | ISBN 9780813954691 ebook
Subjects: LCSH: American Colonization Society | African Americans—Colonization—Liberia | African Americans—Virginia—Piedmont—History—19th century | African Americans—Liberia—History—19th century
Classification: LCC DT634 .S85 2026 (print) | LCC DT634 (ebook)
LC record available at https://lccn.loc.gov/2025039113
LC ebook record available at https://lccn.loc.gov/2025039114

Cover art: Thoughts of the Future (Thoughts of Liberia, Emancipation), Edwin White, 1861. Oil on canvas, 18 × 21 in. (The Robert L. Stuart Collection, The New York Historical, S-200)
Cover design: Elke Barter

For James, Jack, and Elliott

For James, Jack, and Elliott

CONTENTS

PREFACE

While researching the end of slavery for a newspaper series about the Civil War, I read in the Oct. 19, 1865, edition of the Lynchburg *Daily Virginian* that a large group of local formerly enslaved people—172 total—were emigrating to West Africa. Eight had signed a public letter to the newspaper announcing their intentions. These few inches of type intrigued me. Why had I never heard of these people? Why were they leaving Virginia immediately after gaining their freedom? I'm a journalist, retired editor of the Lynchburg and Roanoke newspapers, and familiar with the history of Piedmont Virginia. I knew that some Southern enslaved and freedmen had been sent to Liberia, where malaria killed many of them, but nothing about these local emigrants.

Although the 1865 emigration made national headlines at the time, over the years these 172 migrants were almost forgotten. Two local historians I spoke with had never heard of them. But fortunately, their story was preserved in the records and letters of the very group that wanted them to leave Virginia and the United States: the American Colonization Society (ACS).

Significantly the 172 men, women, and children from Lynchburg and surrounding counties were among the largest single groups of emigrants to Liberia from the US in the nineteenth century. They were among about 374 people who emigrated from and through Lynchburg between 1829 and 1865 via the American Colonization Society, an organization abounding in conflicting motivations but dedicated to moving Black Americans out of the United States. Some were free Black men and women who went willingly to seek a better life and citizenship in a new land, but many were freed only on the condition they emigrate to a region of West Africa that was already home to an estimated 250,000 people, many different ethnic groups and languages, and multiple cultures. To these Black Americans, this was an alien world.

I had a hard time reconciling the inherent racism and victimization of the colonization movement with the willpower asserted by some emigrants as they decided for themselves to go to Liberia and fought to survive once there. Then I realized that this ostensible contradiction was *the* story. John McNuckles, the leader of the 1865 expedition, and Levi Norvell who helped plan it, acted on their own to leave Virginia despite their emancipation. A free Tennessee minister and his family spent 1830 marooned in Lynchburg working to get to Liberia. A semi-independent carpenter enslaved by Lynchburg's wealthiest citizen was among the most influential advocates of Liberia in Virginia in the 1840s and 1850s whereas two Bedford County women resisted colonization for nearly ten years and when forced to Liberia in 1859 began planning their return before they even landed in West Africa. These intrepid Black Americans showed foresight and fortitude, acting to build a better future for themselves and their families. This makes their remarkable story worth telling, in all of its complexity.

It's also a much-needed corrective to stories about the nineteenth century that dominated Virginia until very recently. Like other students growing up in Virginia in the mid- to late twentieth century, I was taught in segregated public schools that Black people were inferior to white people, and that after the Civil War, they were too ignorant to handle their freedom. Lasting for nearly a century, these were bald-faced lies inculcated into Virginia textbooks and society soon after the war ended and renewed around 1900 as part of the Lost Cause movement that aimed to deny the facts of the Civil War and Reconstruction and restore elite white men to a position of legal and economic superiority over everyone else in Virginia. Colonization supporters loved to compare Liberia to the Jamestown colony; a more appropriate analogy might be the drama of the Lost Colony on Roanoke Island in North Carolina. In the end, the Roanoke colonists marched off into the unknown to live among the Indigenous people. No one knows for sure what happened to them.

The Lost Cause movement, on the other hand, is well documented. Believers generally subscribe to an interpretation of the Civil War best described by historian Caroline Janney: 1) The war was caused by secession, not slavery. 2) Black people were loyal to their enslavers and as an inferior race could not handle freedom or responsibility. 3) The South lost due to the overwhelming numbers and resources of the North. 4) Confederate soldiers were heroic and saintly. 5) Robert E. Lee was the most heroic and saintly of all. 6) Southern women remained loyal to the cause and in turn were sanctified by Southern lives lost in battle.

Once set in motion, southern schools, newspapers, churches, and other institutions, not to mention southern families themselves perpetuated this Lost Cause interpretation of the Civil War. That's why it remains so powerful among Virginians of my generation. Southern slavery was not that long ago in generational terms. Most of the teachers I had in elementary school during the 1960s had likely known an old Confederate veteran or had one as a family member or had family members who enslaved people. It is still hard for me to acknowledge that one of my great-grandfathers, a Confederate sergeant wounded in Pickett's Charge, was fighting a war to perpetuate slavery, whether or not he believed that himself. Or that another great-grandfather, a farmer, enslaved a family of four.

As a child, I was curious about slavery and asked one grandmother if she remembered it, not realizing she was born long after 1865. She said no, but that slavery "wasn't so bad." I read a book about Robert E. Lee in elementary school and asked my other grandmother about him. As if talking about a Biblical figure, she replied, "Oh, Robert E. Lee was a great man." Her father was a Confederate soldier.

It wasn't just my family. Lynchburg's immersion in Lost Cause mythology was deeper than I realized. In fact, people from Piedmont Virginia came up with and marketed the very concept. Edward A. Pollard is credited with inventing the term with his widely read 1867 book, *The Lost Cause: A New Southern History of the War of the Confederates.* He grew up on the Oak Ridge estate in Nelson County and died in Lynchburg. Confederate Gen. Jubal Early spent the last 20 years of his life in Lynchburg working to perpetuate white supremacy and market the myth that the war had been about the rights of the states, not slavery. He and Pollard described it as a constitutional struggle between two philosophies of government and culture, the Southern one warm, refined, Anglo-Saxon and agricultural, the Northern one cold, base, foreign and industrial.

Early, an attorney, was a dominating personality hailed as the savior of Lynchburg when he and his troops repelled Union attackers in 1864. After the war, he enlisted other former Confederate officers in his Lost Cause effort, carried out via the innocently named journal *Southern Historical Society Papers.* One of his acolytes was US Senator John Daniel, "The Lame Lion of Lynchburg," a wounded Confederate veteran who helped disenfranchise most Black voters as an influential member of the 1901–2 Virginia Constitutional Convention. Daniel, in turn, was a mentor to Senator Carter Glass of Lynchburg, another powerful advocate for disenfranchisement, proclaiming it would eliminate four-fifths of the Black vote in the state via "discrimination." He also owned the Lynchburg newspapers until he died in 1946, and the papers continued to discriminate against Black Americans until the early 1970s.

Reading Pollard and Early and Confederate President Jefferson Davis while working on this preface, one thing stood out. Confederate veterans and their followers did not consider enslaving people, whipping them, and selling their children, a problem in the sectional disputes over slavery. "The question of the right or wrong of the institution of slavery" was not involved, wrote Davis in his influential 1881 book, *The Rise and Fall of the Confederate Government.*

Davis's book was dedicated to the women of the South. As more and more Confederate veterans died toward the end of the nineteenth century, the United Daughters of the Confederacy redoubled their efforts to push the Lost Cause. This was the era that generated Confederate statues and monuments at courthouses across the South. Black children still pass them on their way to school. The biggest one in Lynchburg was dedicated in 1900 to Early and his troops and contains a poem titled (upsettingly to modern ears) "The Nation's Ward, A Nigger," which remains embedded in a time capsule in the cornerstone.

Part of the tragedy of slavery was white Southerners' purposeful reduction of the enslaved to a faceless mass, not individuals, while the slaveholders' lives and genealogies were studied as if they were saints. Although our history is no longer taught in these stark terms, the culture war over school textbooks and critical race theory shows that these same forces are alive and well. *Out of Virginia* aims to not only explain local aspects of the Virginia colonization movement, but also to document and remember the emigrants to Liberia, to give them back their individuality, and to illustrate how Southern colonization functioned on a personal, small-town level. It also shows how the nineteenth-century colonization movement was a key part of the national concern over slavery, opposed by many, supported by some, but always stimulating questions about freedom, liberty, and enslavement.

Why did the 1865 group want to leave America now that they were no longer enslaved? How did they fare in Liberia? Why did free families decide to go to Liberia in the early 1830s? Why not go to Ohio, where a brother of Lynchburg's founder had helped establish another, free Lynchburg? Why did some people freed by their owners' wills choose reenslavement in Virginia over liberty in Liberia? The answers have roots entangled with American history, Piedmont Virginia, and West Africa, and perhaps a more basic question: Who were all these people? *Out of Virginia* is their story.

ACKNOWLEDGMENTS

When I decided to write this book after a long career in journalism, I thought to myself, how hard could it be? Plenty hard, I soon discovered, so hard I could not have done it without help from many people, as well as the ever-growing body of work on Liberia and colonization from scholars and historians. I was first guided by the database of early Liberian emigrants at the University of Virginia's Institute for Advanced Technology in the Humanities, developed by historians Marie Tyler-McGraw, author of *An African Republic: Black and White Virginians in the Making of Liberia*, and Deborah Lee. The database provided names, dates, and county of origin for emigrants from Virginia through 1865 and enabled me to compile a spreadsheet of those from Lynchburg and surrounding counties. Lee also pointed me toward the Library of Congress's ACS records which include thousands of letters to and from emigrants and colonization officials. Their work, and that of Claude Clegg in *The Price of Liberty: African Americans and the Making of Liberia*, was crucial in my early research and provided a foundation for the rest.

I presented a paper based on my early research to the Sphex Club of Lynchburg. After that meeting, one of my fellow members, Tom Tiller, a longtime University of Lynchburg professor began encouraging me to write this book. Ken West, another University of Lynchburg professor and Sphex member, also provided me with much good advice, and both Tom and Ken read each chapter as I went along and offered valuable suggestions. As I got further into the book, I began discussing it with old friend Howard Meissel, a retired teacher with a deep knowledge of American history, and a talented editor. He read each chapter, and his advice is reflected throughout. Howard, Tom, and Ken saved me from many mistakes, and I alone am responsible for any that might remain. Former colleague David Poole suggested that the 1865 emigrants lead the book, not simply take their place in chronological order. Another former colleague, Dwayne Yancey of Cardinal News, published an excerpt from the book and tipped off my editor at the University of Virginia Press, Nadine Zimmerli, to expect my proposal. I deeply appreciate Nadine's faith in the book, as well as that of UVA Press editors Mark Mones, Ellen Satrom, and Wren Morgan Myers, who helped guide the book toward publication. Former colleagues who encouraged or inspired me included Caroline Glickman, Jon Ness, Mark Bailey, Suzanne Ramsey, Beth Macy, and Mike Allen. My indexer, Amaranth Tupelo, made many valuable suggestions.

I am also grateful to Nancy Blackwell Marion, who published an early excerpt from the book in her *Lynch's Ferry* magazine, and the late Jane White, a community activist and author who encouraged me throughout the process. Others who encouraged me were Lynn Rainville, Billy Giles and the BG Hilltrippers hiking club, Worth Proffitt, and Hermina Hendricks. Chuck Bradner of Jones Memorial Library in Lynchburg always greeted me with a smile and a wisecrack as he awaited my next question about a book or document. I found many out-of-print, old books about Lynchburg and Virginia that I used in my research at the Givens family's independent bookstore in Lynchburg. And it's impossible to write accurately about Lynchburg history without referring to S. Allen Chambers' pioneering work, *Lynchburg, An Architectural History.* Several anonymous peer reviewers also contributed valuable suggestions, which enabled me to broaden my themes and to include some recent historiography.

But mainly, I thank my wife Ellen, who with my sons Drew and Patrick, provided much encouragement. I would never have been in a position to even attempt a book without Ellen, who keeps me anchored, takes care of all our obligations, most of which I either ignore or forget, and brings me back to current reality after I disappear into my basement office and start writing.

NOTES ON TERMINOLOGY

Throughout this book, I have tried to use words that stress the individuality of the people involved. For that reason, I prefer to use "enslaved" for those held in bondage, because it implies a condition to which they were subjected. I sometimes use "slave" to indicate how white people viewed those they enslaved.

Americo-Liberians:	This term refers to Black settlers from the US and their descendants, as opposed to members of West African ethnic groups who had lived in Liberia for centuries. Most of today's Liberians descend from West African ethnic groups, not the US settlers.
Emigrant:	Technically the people who went to Liberia from the US were "emigrants" from America and "immigrants" once they arrived in Liberia. I refer to them as "emigrants" for the sake of simplicity.
Freedmen:	This was the commonly accepted term for Black people of both genders released from bondage. I use it to denote to people freed at the end of the Civil War. African Americans who had been free prior to the Civil War, sometimes for generations, are referred to as "free" men or women. These terms are tricky because many emigrants were released from bondage only on the condition they go to Liberia. The colonizationists claimed they only sent free people to Liberia, but many were enslaved until the moment of emigration and did not receive free papers until they boarded the ships.
Indigenous:	This is a collective term for all members of the diverse West African ethnic groups who lived in what would become Liberia. I use it when necessary but try to specify their ethnic group or refer to them as "West Africans."

Liberians: I use this word to denote people who lived in the colony, then country of Liberia, regardless of their heritage.

Liberty: More than simple freedom, I use "liberty" to mean the status of being able to vote, own property, testify in court, marry, and enjoy other rights of citizenship. Although Black men received some limited voting rights in Virginia in 1867, African Americans were not full citizens of the United States until ratification of the 14th Amendment in 1868—and thereafter their rights were curtailed again under Jim Crow.

Recaptures/recaptives: This is a period term for more than 5,000 Africans from other parts of the continent who were rescued from slave ships by the US or British navies and dropped off in Liberia, with no attempt made to return them to their home regions. Americo-Liberians called them "Congoes" although not all were from the Congo River area.

The West Africans

The history of the peoples who live in Liberia is long, rich, and complex.[1] Linguists divide West African languages into three or more groups. Each language group includes various ethnic groups with languages of their own. Today's Liberia includes about twenty different languages and sixteen official ethnic groups. Prior to colonization, as many as 250,000 people lived in the Liberia region. They had well-established cultures and polities and had interacted and traded with Europeans for centuries. Here are some of the groups who welcomed, resisted, traded with, and intermarried the nineteenth-century intruders sponsored by the ACS.

Bassa: Bassa speakers began trading pepper and enslaved people to Europeans centuries before the American colonists arrived. One Bassa sub-group, the Queah/Kwea, lived around Careysburg, the destination of the 1865 Lynchburg emigrants. Agriculturalists, they grew sugarcane for their own use and for trade. They were friendly to the emigrants and assisted, worked with, and married some of them.

Condo Confederation: A loose alliance of several ethnic groups led by the Manding, formed to control trading in enslaved people and commodities between Liberia and the rest of the Atlantic world.

Dei/Dey: The Dei lived in the Cape Mesurado region and along the St. Paul's River and ceded coastal land to the American Colonization Society in 1821. The Americans initially had to employ Dei brokers to trade with the Manding, who controlled access to commodities from the interior.

Gola: The Gola are thought to be the earliest inhabitants of the Liberia region. Oral tradition in West Africa indicates they established the Poro (male) and Sande (female) semi-secret ritual societies across all Liberian ethnic groups, which brought young people into adulthood and influenced political, judicial, and religious matters.

Grebo: The Grebo lived mostly in the southeastern area of Liberia, around Cape Palmas, originally a colony of the Maryland Colonization Society. The Maryland colonists united with the rest of the Republic of Liberia after 1847, prompting the formerly friendly Grebo to burn part of the settler town of Harper in 1856.

Kru/Kroo: Often the first West Africans the Americans encountered, the Kru had interacted with European ship captains and traders for centuries and were skilled boatmen and dock workers in addition to their traditional activities of trading, farming, and fishing.

Loma: The Loma people lived in northeast Liberia, in a region rarely accessed by outsiders until the later 1800s. They produced valuable trade goods like cotton cloth and gold rings.

Manding: Also called Malinke, or Mandingo, the Manding lived farther from the coast than some of the other groups and controlled trade access to the resource-rich interior of Africa via their town, Bopolu, which was also the headquarters of the Condo Confederation.

The Manding were Muslim, some could read and write in Arabic, and many were living throughout Liberia by the time the Americans arrived.

Vai: The Vai were also mostly Muslim, converted by traders from northern Africa over the centuries. They developed a written language in the 1820s and 1830s and established a school to teach it.

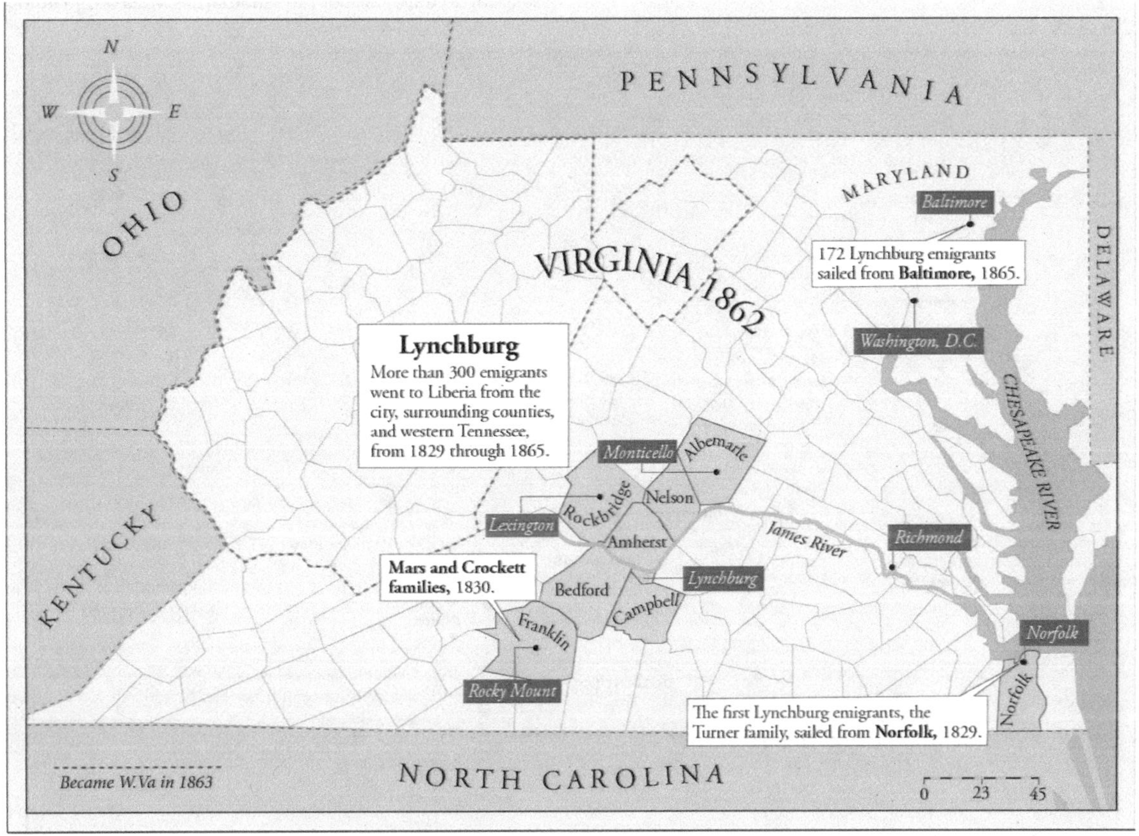

Home regions of emigrants to Liberia from Piedmont Virginia. (Map by Jon Ness)

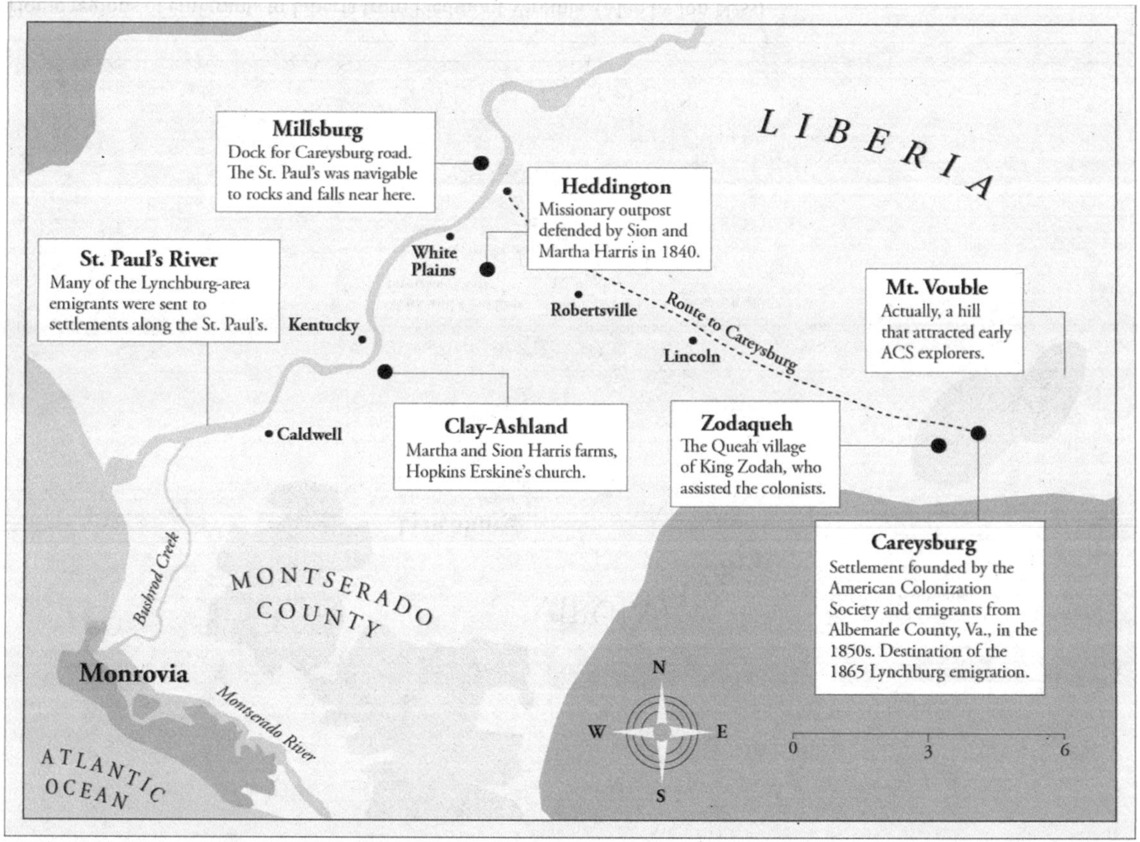

Some of the early settlements in Liberia. (Map by Jon Ness)

OUT OF VIRGINIA

INTRODUCTION

The American Colonization Society was established in 1816 to remove African Americans from the United States of America. Free Black families began going to Liberia from Lynchburg, Virginia in 1829 and 1830, followed by enslaved people coerced to emigrate. In 1865, freedmen in Lynchburg organized themselves, seized their own destiny, and formed the first large group to emigrate to Liberia from the South after Appomattox, 172 strong. About 200 Black residents from the Lynchburg area had already emigrated to Africa, beginning in 1829. Based primarily on original research, this book is a narrative of these Piedmont Virginia emigrants' lives, adventures, triumphs, and tragedies amid the limited success and ultimate failure of the colonization movement.

Out of Virginia approaches the story from the emigrants' point of view. While advocating opportunity for Black Americans and using them to convert Africans to Christianity, ACS records show that the organization's day-to-day focus was moving as many Black Americans as possible out of the United States. That included spending limited resources on more emigrations instead of supporting emigrants who were already in Liberia. About half of the Piedmont Virginia emigrants died within a few years, mostly from malaria. The most detailed information about them comes from records preserved by the group trying to get them out of the country. The ACS kept a voluminous archive of letters written by the formerly enslaved themselves, with other records including thousands of names and family relationships for these Black Americans, thus documenting their lives and labor.

That's important because the enslaved built Virginia, and their labor was the foundation of its prosperity. Piedmont Virginia was not the Deep South, with vast cotton plantations worked by hundreds of enslaved men and women. But some of those cotton field workers had been shipped South from Lynchburg, where the enslaved were whipped, beaten, separated from their families, and bought and sold like livestock. Many white Americans, both in the North and South, had come to believe that treatment like this had so degraded Black Americans that even if they were free, racial distinctions meant they should be physically separated from the white population. In the 1800s, a broad consensus was developing across the Atlantic world that the concept of a "nation" involved people with a shared race, heritage, culture, and values. In Virginia, this concept was even more exclusionary, ruling out not only Black Virginians but also immigrant laborers like the Irish Catholics who "ranked just above blacks" in Lynchburg's social order.[1]

The colonization movement defies easy explanation, but most of its Virginia supporters believed slavery was wrong for economic, not humanitarian, reasons and some simply thought the state had too many enslaved people and needed to expel them. Some Northern supporters of the Society believed slavery was morally wrong but also believed the two races could never live together in harmony. Such thinking resulted in a variety of nineteenth-century colonization schemes to push Black Americans out of the United States to places ranging from Haiti to the unexplored Northwest, to Mexico, or to Central America. The Grain Coast of West Africa, which became Liberia, eventually attracted the most attention thanks to the efforts of the ACS. A letter Thomas Jefferson wrote to Lynchburg's founder was one of the seminal documents of the American Colonization Society. Jefferson said colonization was a good idea and mentioned its likely "civilizing effect" on native Africans. He also said Africa was the country of the slaves' origin, even though by the early 1800s most Black Americans had been born in North America, not Africa.[2] The third president was well-acquainted with Lynchburg, storing and selling his tobacco there, and his Poplar Forest retreat was nearby. Jefferson was ambivalent on slavery, recognizing it as a malign practice but unwilling to advocate for immediate abolition, sometimes offering support for the idea of colonization if not the reality. His writings were cited by both friends and foes of colonization.

The American Colonization Society (ACS) was founded by Northern clergymen, Southern enslavers, and lawmakers. The clergymen and the early emigrants believed that the only way Black people could enjoy their full humanity was in another country, while the enslavers wanted to remove all free Black families so they couldn't influence the enslaved with ideas of freedom and liberty. The lawmakers wanted to make the United States a country for white people only. As a result, the ACS established a colony in West Africa in 1822 and named it Liberia; the first family of freemen from the Lynchburg region emigrated to this new African colony in 1829.

While they wanted freedom and liberty, most enslaved and free Black Virginians had no interest in leaving the Commonwealth and saw colonization as a white scheme to prop up slavery. They insisted that they too were Americans. Still, as scholar Wilson Jeremiah Moses writes, emigration was not necessarily a surrender to white supremacy: "There was a variety of heroism in the decision of a few adventurous souls to brave the dangers of an ocean voyage, the ravages of malaria, and the hardships of a frontier society to seek their fortunes in Liberia."[3]

By 1820, Black people comprised about 40 percent of Virginia's population, and white Virginians thought that was too many. In 1825 a dozen of Lynchburg's leading white citizens, led by a Methodist minister and nearly all slaveholders themselves, formed a local colonization society affiliated with the ACS, declaring colonization the solution to the economic and moral questions raised by slavery. The Lynchburg-area emigrations began with a free Black family from Bedford County influenced by and aligned with Richmond's free Black community. They determined for themselves that they would have a chance for a better life outside the United States. But in Lynchburg—as in the South more generally—colonization almost

Mary Brice was enslaved at Point of Honor, a prominent Lynchburg house. This photograph, ca. 1853, is a rare image of an enslaved person taken during enslavement in Lynchburg. Like most African American people there, she did not emigrate to Liberia. (Photograph by Peter E. Gibbs; Library of Congress Prints and Photographs Division, Washington, DC, LC-DIG-ds-08056)

immediately expanded to include those who had been freed, often when their enslaver died, on the condition they emigrate to Liberia. This was a far-less voluntary choice—while they weren't exactly forced to emigrate, they had to go somewhere because a state law, passed in 1806, said they couldn't remain in Virginia, supporting the Black belief that colonization was a hypocritical attempt to avoid abolition and emancipation.

Local societies like Lynchburg's ACS chapter attracted white men who saw membership in the seemingly high-minded colonization movement as a social and civic steppingstone, with Lynchburg often involved in national controversies over slavery, abolition, and colonization. Lynchburg Quakers, including the city's founder, had freed all their enslaved laborers by the mid-1780s. This came at a high cost—they were unable to compete agriculturally with planters using enslaved labor, and many of them left the faith or left Virginia. By the 1830s, slavery sustained the region, both via enslaved labor and via the sale of enslaved men, women, and children to cotton plantations in the Deep South, and abolitionist William Lloyd Garrison often blasted Lynchburg in the *Liberator.*

White disdain for Piedmont Virginia's Black Americans only got worse in the months after the Confederate surrender in 1865 as farmers and plantation owners colluded to essentially re-enslave the freedmen, declaring they were not citizens, merely ex-slaves. At the same time, the ACS was desperate to revive itself. It therefore welcomed letters from two freedmen, John McNuckles and Levi Norvell of Lynchburg, describing their intentions to leave the United States. Norvell, a minister who also worked in a tobacco factory, wrote, "Now that the fetters of degradation are burst asunder . . . we are willing to venture upon the land of Africa and there put our trust in Almighty providence."[4]

So after centuries of oppression in Virginia and a bloody war which freed them but did not elevate them to citizenship, the group of 172 Black Americans from Lynchburg took matters into their own hands. Long experience had taught them waiting for Southern white people to help was futile. Their leadership was determined to establish a new community in Africa, where they could enjoy the rights of citizenship, educate their children, farm their own land, and determine their own future.

1

From Many an Ancient River

1865

> I was very glad to hear that we could be transferred to Liberia. . . . I have been an advocate of this cause for 15 years.
>
> —Mack Nuckles, Lynchburg, 1865

> Here are many anxious people to reach that old world . . . we desire to go and teach and be taught, and so Excell in life, and fit our souls for heaven and immortal glory.
>
> —Levi M. Norvell, Lynchburg, 1865

THOUSANDS OF people, Black and white, gathered in Lynchburg at the Orange & Alexandria Railroad depot on a chilly October night in 1865, a few steps from the James River. Nearby, the city's slave markets were finally out of business. Thanks to tobacco grown and processed by enslaved laborers, and its location at the intersection of river, roads and rails, Lynchburg had become a prominent Southern city before the war and one of the largest in western Virginia. In 1863, another crowd here had watched the coffin of Confederate hero General Stonewall Jackson lifted from a canal boat and paraded through town. Many enslaved men and women worked in the leaf factories scattered on the hills rising from the south bank of the James. Others labored in the tobacco and wheat fields. Like that of Thomas Jefferson, who warehoused his tobacco here, Piedmont Virginia's prosperity had been based on Black enslavement through the antebellum years. But in late 1865 the region was rotten with contempt for the freedmen, and many white residents were anxious to be rid of them. Despite the end of slavery, white Virginians vowed to perpetuate the racial discrimination they had relied on for centuries to justify it. A bronze Confederate soldier still faces south above downtown Lynchburg today, straight up the hill from the old depot.

But more than 170 Black people from Lynchburg and surrounding counties had decided to leave for Liberia on this Halloween night rather than endure virtual re-enslavement in the foothills of the Blue Ridge. Union troops occupying the city mingled with onlookers there to say goodbye to friends and neighbors they would never see again. Others would see off people they had enslaved, employed, bought, sold, and fathered. About 43 percent of the population of Lynchburg and its three surrounding counties, which totaled about 65,000 in 1860, was Black, all but about 1,300 enslaved. After Appomattox, local white residents continued to deny them their rights. Though free, they were not yet citizens of Virginia or the United States. They were going to Liberia to get their "full civic growth" and "all that the heart could wish in freedom," their leaders wrote. They needed their own land. They went "for the good of their rising generation," and nearly half of them were eighteen or younger, many under twelve. Once they'd reached the Baltimore wharves, they would board a chartered ship and sail to Monrovia, the capital of the Black republic, then travel up the St. Paul's River to remote Careysburg.[1]

LYNCHBURG HAD been the crossroads of western Virginia since the 1700s, with roads leading north to Charlottesville, east to Richmond, west to Bristol, and south to Danville and North Carolina. The James River and Kanawha Canal, and multiple railroads, enhanced its central location and the riverfront was a busy place. Leaf tobacco packed in hogsheads and plugs of chewing tobacco manufactured in Lynchburg were shipped nationwide and to Europe, along with commodities like iron and wheat brought down the canal from the west and loaded onto trains in Lynchburg. An old wagon bridge spanned the James but the newest tracks, the Orange and Alexandria's running north to Washington, crossed on their own bridge upstream. Two other railroads converged here connecting western Virginia with Richmond and the rest of the world. The depot was adjacent to the canal, and upstream, one rail line paralleled Blackwater Creek which flowed into the river near an engine roundhouse, a machine shop, and a mill. Downstream, tenements, bars, and gambling houses lined the river in Buzzard's Roost. When he surrendered in April about twenty-five miles east of Lynchburg, Gen. Robert E. Lee had been trying to reach Confederate supplies stored in the city's warehouses.[2]

Influenced by the location of Virginia on the map, poking up into the free states from the South, support for Southern secession had been weak because of the city's trade ties with northern cities like Baltimore and New York. But Lynchburg's prominent white citizens became virulent supporters of the Confederacy after Virginia left the Union in 1861. Two Confederate generals from Lynchburg were killed in battle, and an infantry unit from the countryside was on the front line of Pickett's Charge at Gettysburg in 1863, when the rebels who survived clambered over a stone wall and reached what would be memorialized as "the high-water mark of the Confederacy." The city's sheltered location in western Virginia, surrounded by hills and mountains, meant it was only attacked by Union forces once, unsuccessfully, as part of Gen. David Hunter's 1864 march through western Virginia when he burned Virginia Military Institute in Lexington.[3]

Hunter had hoped to destroy the multiple railroads that made Lynchburg important to the Southern war effort, first as a mustering location from soldiers from all over the South headed to the Northern Virginia battlefields, then as a hospital and prisoner of war center, and finally as a Confederate supply depot. More than 10,000 Union prisoners of war were brought to the city between 1861 and 1865. At first, they were confined on the city fairgrounds without much food. That improved, but conditions remained so bad in the camps that military physicians eventually opened Lynchburg's 30 Confederate hospitals in tobacco factories and warehouses to sick and wounded Union prisoners as well. Convalescing Confederates helped defend the city during Hunter's Raid, and a local physician later recalled seeing a pile of amputated arms and legs four feet high outside a Union field surgery. Local white women helped care for both Union and Confederate patients, but the bulk of the hospital workers were Black. Records list 474 "attendants," Black orderlies, in spring 1864.[4]

Surviving Hunter's Raid, the city was threatened again in March 1865 as Gen. Phillip Sheridan's federal cavalry captured Charlottesville, with units led by Lt. Gen. George A. Custer ransacking the countryside and railroad tracks north of Lynchburg. By then, enslaved people were running away in increasing numbers as the Northern lines drew closer amid shortages of almost everything. In the weeks after the surrender, starving stragglers from Lee's army and soldiers from the hospitals looted the supplies Lee had been trying to reach in Lynchburg. Chaos reigned, with poor white people, soldiers, and freedmen joining the plunder before things calmed down as occupying Union troops imposed martial law. "A few days after the town formally surrendered, the black community congregated at the Fair Grounds—the place where the militia had once

This map, by Jedidiah Hotchkiss, shows the region's hilly terrain, and the downtown area along the James River where the 1865 emigrants would depart for Liberia. (Library of Congress Geography and Map Division Washington, DC, 2005625265)

paraded—to celebrate," writes Steven E. Tripp in *Yankee Town, Southern City*, the most detailed account of the city just after the surrender.[5]

At this moment, had the freedmen not achieved what they'd been dreaming of for generations? At least a few hundred in Lynchburg, like Mack Nuckles, a respected craftsman, and Levi Norvell, a minister who also worked in a tobacco factory, weren't so sure. Nuckles had wanted to emigrate to Liberia for years. Both men realized that the Civil War had ended slavery, but not racism and discrimination in Lynchburg. They planned to emigrate to Liberia with their families and urged other freedmen to go with them, making the first leg of the journey north to the Baltimore docks on the same tracks that had brought the wounded into town earlier in 1865.

By this time, the ACS had been recruiting and distributing information and disinformation in Lynchburg for decades, and about 200 local people had already gone to Liberia, mostly in small family groups. The official goals of the ACS were to send free Black Americans to a land where they could prosper; to help prepare the way for gradual abolition of slavery in the US; to help abolish the slave trade; and to uplift Africa through the spread of Christianity. Some white members viewed colonization as a way to expel Black Americans from the US, and it was derided by most Black commentators and abolitionists as a white alternative to emancipation.

Emigrants from Lynchburg and around the South soon began to include the enslaved who were encouraged and coerced to emigrate or were freed on the condition they emigrate. An estimated 12,000 Black Americans were transported to Liberia prior to the war and more came from Virginia than any other individual state, in part because of the 1806 law requiring newly freed Black people to leave the Commonwealth. Virginians formed the core of the early leaders of both the colony and the Republic of Liberia, which became a sovereign nation in 1847.[6]

The 1865 group was organized by Lynchburg African Americans themselves. They used the resources of the ACS to get to Liberia and were the first from the South to leave for West Africa after the war. Wrapped in blankets, the departing families gathered at the train station in October 1865 cried, sang hymns and prayed. A reporter asked who was more to be pitied, those who were leaving or those who were staying? One newly married couple from the country was so inspired by the scene they joined the emigrants, who had a variety of nineteenth-century occupations: tobacco factory workers, domestics, blacksmiths, shoemakers, tobacconists, carpenters, a butcher and a baker, homemakers, farmers and laborers. About 40 percent were women and girls, and many were children. The ACS would give each family ten acres of land in Liberia and food and shelter for six months. After that, they were on their own.[7]

The ACS corresponding secretary and day-to-day manager, William Coppinger, traveled to Lynchburg twice to assist the 1865 departure. Leading the group was Nuckles, a skilled bricklayer, plasterer, and carpenter, who had been one of the most valuable enslaved people in the city. But he quickly shed the hard shell of enslavement, changing his name to John M. McNuckles. "He could do as well here as any of his race, but he long sighed for a country and nationality of his own, where he might help to elevate his brethren according to the flesh," reported the always-upbeat *African Repository and Colonial Journal*, published by the colonization society. Waiting with McNuckles was Norvell, a literate Baptist who helped organize the departees. Their friend, freedman and political activist John "Jack" Averitt stayed behind to assist a second emigration planned in the spring.[8]

Like many others, McNuckles's family had been scattered by slavery and war. His wife lived in Washington, DC, and he had been unable to talk her into going to Liberia. But his brother, Woodson, who lived in Lynchburg, was also waiting amid the throng at the depot with his own wife and seven children. Some of the women were not anxious to leave their homes in Lynchburg. Levi Norvell's pregnant wife, Nancy, had resisted until a few weeks before when she said, "by the help of God she would try to make herself satisfied," her husband wrote. They took their four young children, along with Levi Norvell's 73-year-old grandmother.

Black family ties like these were of little import to the white elites who had governed Virginia until a few months before. Enslaved marriages were not recognized under state law, and the local newspaper mocked a Northern minister who had come to Lynchburg and offered to legally marry couples in July. In late 1865, the legal status of freedmen was the same as it had been for Virginia's free Black residents before the war, and they couldn't vote or hold political office. Still, most Black Southerners did not want to leave the United States, where they had lived for generations. If forced to leave Virginia, they often went to the free state of Ohio.[9]

By 1865, letters from emigrants and word-of-mouth in the community meant local African Americans were well-informed about the danger of catching a deadly fever in Liberia. They also feared re-enslavement, with rumors that emigrants were actually shipped to the sugarcane plantations in Cuba. Why would they put their faith in a white institution whose overriding goal was to remove Black people from the country? Human nature generally tends to shy away from risk, and there is nothing riskier than moving with your family to a new land you know to be dangerous and where those without skills or money would become worse off than they were in Virginia, at least temporarily.

As was true before the war, in summer and fall 1865 nothing much had changed for Black Virginians in and around Lynchburg despite their emancipation. Still subject to discrimination, abuse and violence, they had almost no rights, little property or money, former enslavers were colluding to make sure they received little or no pay for field labor, and white residents demanded they accept their status or leave town. But this was true throughout the South. So why were these Lynchburg people the only large Black group to leave the country so close to the moment of their emancipation? What made Lynchburg different? Many factors converged for this emigration to achieve critical mass in the summer and fall after Appomattox, including:

URBANISM: A large portion of Lynchburg's enslaved, including multiple members of the emigration, were rented to tobacco factories and had a semi-independent lifestyle free from the day-to-day supervision that farm laborers experienced, and some were paid a few dollars a week for working beyond their allotted hours in the factories. The Black community comprised an under-the-white-radar network of hundreds of adults who lived near each other in the relatively small city where they were a near-majority and shared similar backgrounds and family ties. It was part of the Black "nation within a nation" emerging side-by-side with nineteenth-century concepts of American nationalism for white people only.[10]

LITERACY AND AWARENESS: Some portion of the Black population of Lynchburg was literate despite Southern prohibitions on education. McNuckles, the craftsman, could read. Norvell, the minister, could read and write. Several others wrote letters home after they reached Liberia. Some had been reading the colonization journal for many years via white friends while enslaved. Literacy combined with the urban environment and word-of-mouth in the "nation within a nation" meant ACS information—and disinformation—about Liberia could spread quickly.

FAMILIARITY: Family groups from Lynchburg and surrounding counties had been going to Liberia since 1829. Smaller groups and individuals emigrated almost every year in the 1850s. Pamphlets and books about Liberia circulated in Lynchburg, and after the mid-1830s, colonization was the only form of Black freedom that could safely be discussed. McNuckles told colonization officials he had wanted to emigrate for 15 years.

DISINFORMATION: The American Colonization Society often told emigrants untruths about actual conditions in Liberia and always downplayed the danger of sickness. Some historians view ACS officials as well-meaning but poorly informed themselves, others see the disinformation as propaganda. Coppinger himself must have been aware he was presenting an inaccurate depiction of Liberia when he edited and censored letters from emigrants, including McNuckles's first letter from Liberia, to remove passages about fever and death.

LIBERTY, NOT JUST FREEDOM: Dreams of a better future than what they could achieve in Virginia, especially for their children—40 percent of the 1865 emigrants were 12 or younger—were mentioned by almost every Lynchburg emigrant who wrote or dictated a letter. The right to vote, to educate your children, to join a political party, to own property, to defend yourself in court were all rights that seem an essential part of freedom today. Often unspoken, their need for land ownership was paramount in a culture where subsistence agriculture was the norm for rural people who did not own slaves. Lynchburg's 1865 emigrants understood that freedom in 1865 Lynchburg meant only that they were no longer enslaved. They wanted more than that: they needed "liberty," meaning the same rights of citizenship that white Americans enjoyed.

LEADERSHIP AND ORGANIZATION: The leaders of the 1865 emigrants were motivated and accustomed to working on their own in the tobacco factories or at crafts like carpentry or shoemaking. As a minister, Norvell was adept at speaking to large groups. McNuckles seems to have stepped from slavery to freedom seamlessly, organizing, traveling, and negotiating in the months after Appomattox. He had the wherewithal to travel to the ACS offices in Washington by train, not once but three times, as part of his preparations. At one point in the fall, his leadership group had convinced about 300 people to join them, enough for a second emigration that never happened.

A WHITE GO-BETWEEN: Charles L. Mosby, a local lawyer and enslaver, had been a colonization supporter since the 1820s. He was apparently McNuckles's former owner, vouched for him, and served as the initial go-between with the ACS and the Lynchburg group. He'd pushed colonization as a remedy to the problems caused by slavery since around 1830 and continued to support and communicate with the ACS after the Lynchburg Colonization Society itself withered away around 1840. Long one of the town's leading citizens, Mosby owned 14 enslaved people in 1860, including a man born in 1820, the same year as McNuckles. Forwarding McNuckles's first surviving letter to the colonization society, "written by some Yankee here," Mosby wrote that it was from "my man Mac" with a note: "He is a freed man and they all feel it."[11]

But what else gelled with talented Black leadership, organizational skills, literacy, and urbanism to make this emigration go forward?

PERFECT TIMING: John McNuckles initiated the trip with a query around July 1 to the ACS offices in Washington, DC, just as the ACS was desperate to resurrect itself and export a shipload of American Black people to Liberia. The situation was so bleak for the colonizationists that they had just violated their own constitution, which limited recruitment to American Black people only, sending more than more than 300 Barbadians to Liberia. Many ACS officials believed that finding enough Black Southerners who wanted to emigrate now that they were free would be impossible. ACS officials needed a large emigration and were willing to finance the voyage to revive their movement, which had shrunk to irrelevance.[12]

Other than timing, some of these factors were present in other communities, but nowhere else had McNuckles, who combined leadership skills with a charismatic personality which he used to convince others to follow his dream of emigrating to Africa, nor did they have Levi Norvell, a well-known, no-nonsense Bible preacher and tobacco factory worker. They were independent men who stood up for themselves but also knew how to accommodate white people. They were determined and familiar with colonization and the emigration would not have gone forward without them, and in fact, the second attempted emigration fell through without them.

While enslaved, McNuckles was once valued at $2,200, about twice as much as a regular laborer. Colonization officials cited this as an indication of his intrinsic worth. His craft skills and knowledge likely had helped keep him from being sold south to the enslaved labor camps in the cotton fields. Norvell was a preacher and "a good scholar," but his job while enslaved was working in one of Lynchburg's forty-five tobacco factories, helping process the leaf into plugs that could be chewed. Closed for the last two years, the factories were beginning to reopen in late 1865 but Southern elites were complaining mightily about the supposed unwillingness of the freedmen to work. The reality in Lynchburg was that there were few jobs for them. White people were hired first, and farmers aimed to pay former slaves little or no wages. For a full day's work, tobacco factory owners paid only what the freedmen had received for a few hours extra labor during slavery. Charley Mitchell recalled those days in a 1937 interview with the Federal Writers Project: "I worked in a [Lynchburg] tobacco factory for a dollar a week and that was big money to me. Mammy worked too and we managed somehow to live."[13]

McNuckles and Norvell called their group the "Lynchburg Emigration Society," or the "African Emigration Society." The freedmen initiated their own emigration. The ACS was happy to take credit for it and featured the Lynchburg emigration in the *African Repository,* and stories about it appeared in national newspapers. Misleading information from the ACS touted the country as a near-utopia, at the same time admonishing emigrants they would have to take care of themselves. Norvell seemed to be answering when he wrote, "For god has [told] us that every man shall live by the sweat of his brow or in other words he that won't work shall not eat." He continued, "We desire to go and teach and be taught, and so Excell in life, and fit our souls for heaven and immortal glory unto Jesus Christ our father and brother." He merged the spiritual challenges with the physical dangers: "As our forefathers had to get used to this [Virginia] climate so God I trust will acclimate our nature and spirits too."[14]

Recent histories have stressed how the creation of Liberia, rather than a benevolent project, was similar to other American expansionism at the expense of Indigenous peoples. Americans saw taking over lands already populated by others as a way to solve "the political, economic and cultural crises" of the day, writes historian Brandon Mills. Although the Liberian colony was a quasi-governmental effort, run by a private group, the ACS, it was authorized by Congress, received some government assistance, and aimed at solving the multiple dilemmas of slavery. Black people did not fit into white America's vision of itself as nation united not only by ideals but also by race and culture.[15]

The coast of West Africa had long been the destination of trade routes that extended to and from Europe, the Americas, and the West Indies. In the late 1600s, palm mats from Cape Mount—north of today's Monrovia—were exported to Holland and used as house decorations. Some West Africans themselves had traveled to Europe or the West Indies and adopted Westernized names and European-style clothing. The coastal forest was crisscrossed with trade paths linking the Indigenous people with not only each other but also the African interior, Europe, and the Americas. They were not "uncultivated" as Mosby had declared: Some of their art objects were reminiscent of ancient Egyptian motifs, and two of the major ethnic groups were Muslim. Several ethnic groups had formed a confederation to cooperate on trade and slaving. The trade in human beings had expanded when European explorers seeking gold, and Africans to enslave, arrived in the fifteenth century, then increased dramatically with the demand for labor in North and South America. This ravaged the West African population while anchoring the economy on both sides of the Atlantic.[16]

The commerce and slave trading also meant that the ethnic groups of West Africa were familiar with the unexpected arrival of strangers long prior to colonization. Driven by the continuing desertification of the Sahara, the groups had migrated over the centuries from the northeast as the old trading empires of Mali and Songhai declined. The impact of this migration was a slow-moving transformation of West Africa from subsistence farming, hunting, and small-scale trading to large-scale slaving, more complex social organizations, and new technology, including cotton weaving and iron smelting.[17]

Among the first West Africans encountered by Lynchburg newcomers in 1865 were the Dei, who lived near Monrovia in the Cape Mesurado region, and the Kru, skilled sailors who manned the Liberian docks. American settlers relied on these and other sometimes-hostile West Africans for many staples, finding trading for rice easier than growing their own. Echoing the culture of the American South, the Liberian republic's authority over the ethnic groups involved denying them citizenship until they became acculturated. Self-identifying as Christians and Westerners, the settlers considered themselves "Americans" and members of an advanced culture. For their part, the West Africans found culture more important than skin color and sometimes referred to the Americo-Liberians as "white," telling them they were only liberated slaves, not free men.[18]

Another significant group in 1865 Liberia was made up of so-called recaptive Africans from other parts of the continent. The US and British navies patrolled the Atlantic and intercepted slave ships up and down the West African coast, but any rescued Africans were not returned to their homelands. They were dropped off in Monrovia, sometimes hundreds at a time, and the US government paid the ACS for any resettled from American ships. Called "Congoes," although few were from the Congo, they were often apprenticed to Americo-Liberians, sent to school, and trained to work. Because the Americo-Liberians were unable to turn the Indigenous people into a reliable labor force, the recaptive people filled that role.

An American reporter made them sound like the prewar "happy slaves" in the South: "Along the banks of the St. Paul river the merry song of the Congoes is heard while feeding the steam mills and industriously cultivating the soil." This was something like forced labor, or forced apprenticeship, according to scholar Lisa A. Lindsay, who writes that it may have involved the traditional African practice of "pawning," in which human labor was exchanged for something of value, as when poor people sent family members to work for, be cared for and raised by someone else. American settlers soon adapted the practice of taking Indigenous and recaptive children into their homes to raise and learn Christianity.[19]

The emigrant leaders stressed their belief in missionary Christianity, but a lifetime in bondage had also schooled McNuckles and Norvell in the art of telling white people what they wanted to hear. Writing to the Reverend William McClain, who had been the ACS financial secretary and treasurer since 1840 and who handled finances and provisioned the ships to carry the emigrants, McNuckles stressed his group's social standing and religious motivation. "I was very glad to hear that we could be transferred to Liberia on such reasonable terms . . . I think I can furnish your list with men of all classes . . . some of them have a very good common education." All the prospective emigrants were among "the very first class of colored people." Many were church members, "who could do a great deal of service . . . in bringing the nations to the light of the gospel."[20]

Later letters revealed the Lynchburg emigrants had more immediate concerns. They wanted their own land and farms and the ability to make a decent living for themselves and their families. They wanted education, citizenship, the right to vote, to be treated as equals. There was little prospect of any of that in 1865 Lynchburg. As Ibram X. Kendi writes in *Stamped from the Beginning* about the postwar period in the United States: "Nowhere was opportunity as unequal as in work, where rural Black people's desires for secure land and urban Black people's desires for secure jobs hardly registered in the political discourse." Freedom did not equal liberty. Black Americans were not guaranteed US citizenship until 1868 with ratification of the 14th Amendment, which wasn't ratified by Virginia until the following year. The ACS's Coppinger believed that any African Americans who thought they might prosper in the United States after emancipation were wrong, and stressed the importance of the Lynchburg emigration:

"A failure just now would tell mightily against us . . ." Like many people caught up in a stressful, lifetime occupation, carrying out his mission had become as important as the original reasons for it.[21]

Excited, but cautious, he and McClain devoted much of September and October 1865 to arranging and encouraging the Lynchburg voyage. In Liberia, "The highest social and political standing is open to any citizen," Coppinger had told McNuckles. "You alone have full scope to develop your capacity." McClain wrote, "We will give to each single man five acres . . . and to a man with wife and children, ten acres." To encourage the 1865 Lynchburg emigrants at this crucial moment, the ACS also offered them free passage to Liberia provided they numbered at least 100 to make chartering a ship worthwhile. Freedmen in Georgia, North Carolina, Florida, and South Carolina also expressed interest in emigrating just after the war. The South Carolina group became discouraged by rumors that the colonization society was selling the emigrants back into slavery in Cuba. This rumor had dogged the colonizationists for years and in 1865 Lynchburg was spread by white soldiers.[22]

A belief among freedmen they would receive their own land in America after the Union victory also bedeviled the colonization society. Lynchburg's Charley Mitchell recalled: "After surrender a man calls a meetin' of all the slaves in the fairgrounds and tells us we's free. We wasn't promised anything. We jus' had to do the best we could. But I heared lots of slaves what lived on farms say they's promised forty acres and a mule but they never did git it." This belief was based on fact. As of March 1865, the federal government possessed about 850,000 acres of seized or abandoned land in the South. An original mandate of the US Freedmen's Bureau was to lease forty acres to each male freedman, then allow them to buy it outright after three years. After Lincoln's assassination, President Andrew Johnson, who believed Black people were an inferior race, began pardoning former Confederates and restoring their land. By September 1865, when Freedmen's Bureau commissioner Gen. Oliver O. Howard came to Lynchburg, plans for land redistribution were dead, but not the rumors.[23]

Known as the "Christian General," Howard met in September with Lynchburg's city council, and spoke to a large crowd of African Americans gathered for a church service. He was known for kindly feelings toward Black people, and was later the namesake of Howard University, which he helped found. Howard told the freedmen to work hard or face starvation, to turn the other cheek. They should not expect to be rewarded with land for their lifetimes of bondage. The government had no land to give them,

Howard said, and even if it did, they would not be able to handle it "due to their want of experience in managing for themselves." Howard also told them that the rumor that the federal government would be parceling out Southern land to the freedmen at Christmas was "utterly without foundation." Still, the freedmen continued to hope. The belief that the ex-slaves would receive land on Christmas Day 1865 remained so powerful that Major General A. H. Terry, in charge of the Military District of Virginia, ordered Army officers to hold meetings throughout the state and "explain to the freedmen that the government has neither the intention nor the power to meet these expectations, and to urge upon them the absolute necessity which exists that they should make proper contracts to labor during the coming year." In August 1865, using the only leverage they had, their labor, some of the freedmen in the countryside around Lynchburg said they would not help with the next year's grain crop, pending distribution of local land. The *Daily Virginian* noted that the "industry of the country" would be paralyzed if the freedmen did not work in the wheat. Mitchell said, "We had to go to work for whatever they'd pay us."[24]

McNuckles's associate Jack Averitt, who was to lead the aborted second expedition, later testified to a House of Representatives' committee on Reconstruction about local masters who conspired to pay low wages and increase rents. This collusion was no secret: It was planned in public meetings and reported in the Lynchburg newspapers. Without their own farms, former slaves without craft skills could survive only by becoming hired laborers. The economic prospects for unskilled workers were not much better in Liberia, but each family would have their own land to farm. Telling white people they wouldn't work in the wheat fields, like moving to a new country, was an expression of Black freedom: Not liberty yet, but freedom they'd lacked for generations.[25]

Still, equality of Black and white was an impossible proposition, asserted one of Lynchburg's two daily newspapers. Such statements carried a menacing subtext: If Black people were not content to be menials, their race would disappear. Without slavery, competition for jobs would "result in crowding the negro out of the country or out of existence." That editorial was published on July 6, 1865, the same day the *Daily Virginian* reported the public suicide of a well-known Lynchburg slave dealer who was drunk and despondent over the loss of his business. An Ohio correspondent visited Lynchburg around this time and said nearly all Lynchburg Black people still hoped that land would be distributed to them soon. Many had refused to sign labor contracts. He wrote approvingly of an Amherst County man's suggestion that any Black people who couldn't support themselves as of Jan. 10, 1866, be hired out to the highest bidder. By believing they would be better off in Africa, the correspondent wrote, the emigrants were essentially agreeing with barroom talk that "Virginia is no place for free niggers." The ACS operatives, Coppinger and McClain, never used such words. Their beliefs, expressed in genteel language, were essentially the same as the barroom talk, but at the same time, the responsibility and reliability of the Lynchburg emigrants and their leaders impressed them. This dichotomy was characteristic of colonization supporters' belief that while American Black people, free and enslaved, were a degraded race, they could somehow rise to become religious saviors and lift West Africans to the higher civilization enjoyed only by white people in America.[26]

The emigrant leadership group gathered at McNuckles's house on the second and fourth Sundays of each month to organize and met with Coppinger there in September. Coppinger was impressed and concluded the group would make excellent emigrants. "The male adults are generally young and nearly all good mechanics," he wrote. "Eight are carpenters, seven are boot and shoe makers, three are blacksmiths, two are bricklayers . . . Those that I saw were men of good appearance, nearly all of light complexion, and evincing much practical sense and good judgment." That McNuckles lived in a house large enough to host this many people indicated he was relatively well-off compared to other Lynchburg freedmen. Some lived in shacks and shanties without basic furniture like beds, chairs, and tables.[27]

Coppinger also met with several white people in Lynchburg, including Mosby, McNuckles's white ally, who had spelled out Virginia's stark racial divide many years before: "Let [the freeman] toil from youth to age in the honorable pursuit of wisdom—let him store his mind from the most valuable researches of science and literature—and let him add to a highly cited and cultivated intellect, a piety pure, undefiled, and 'unspotted from the world'—it is all nothing: he would not be received into the very lowest walks of our society." White feelings were if anything stronger after emancipation. The white people didn't even want to attend a local theater production put on by a Northern producer. Coppinger added a harsh PS to an 1865 letter about Lynchburg, providing another glimpse into the reality of the moment: "The feeling is intense against the 'Yanks' as everybody from the North is termed. The 'nigger' is all the talk here, and anything is popular which looks to their removal from the South." The North had won the Civil War, embittering white Virginians and freeing their enslaved, thereby increasing white fear and resentment of Black Americans in Lynchburg.[28]

A few weeks before they departed, the Lynchburg emigrants were encouraged by a letter from the Reverend Alexander Crummell, a Cambridge-educated Episcopalian priest from Boston, a Black abolitionist, and a public intellectual. Originally an opponent of colonization, he had moved to Liberia in 1853 and lived there off and on until he moved back to the US in 1872, became a professor at Howard University, and mentored W. E. B. Dubois, who devoted a chapter to him in *The Souls of Black Folk*. Crummell's attitude toward Liberia was complex—he originally thought it was a distraction from the more important goal of equality for Black people in the US, adding "to the burden of slavery the weight of deportation." Nonetheless, he took up the cause of Liberia, but not necessarily the ACS, as racial attitudes hardened.

In late 1865, he was visiting the US and on good terms with Coppinger and McClain, although they privately expressed frustration with his requests for financial assistance. At Coppinger's suggestion, the leaders of the Lynchburg group, "your unknown friends," asked him to accompany them to Liberia, saying McNuckles would meet him in Washington, DC, to discuss arrangements. Crummell couldn't arrange to go but replied with a poetic letter from Philadelphia that must have seemed inspirational to the newly freed still enduring prejudice and discrimination: "Brethren . . . When you come to think of all the future of yourselves and your children, when you contemplate their temporal status as men and as citizens it seems to me most judicious to set up your homes in a land where you can have no rivalries of prejudice and caste; where you can reach at one bound the full stature of free men; where everything in church and state is your own; where you will rank at once among the upbuilders of a new state; where every avenue of preferment is open before you, according to your mental and moral fitness for superiority . . . we shall meet on the shores of Africa, and I wish you, your wives and children, a very pleasant passage and safe arrival in Monrovia."[29]

McNuckles went to Washington in early October to see his wife, perhaps in a final attempt to convince her to go with him. He also met with Coppinger again at the ACS offices on Pennsylvania Avenue, where they prepared a list of the emigrants and a letter to Freedmen's Bureau

Alexander Crummell was a well-known nineteenth-century minister and public intellectual with mixed feelings about colonization. Nonetheless, he wrote a warm note of encouragement to the 1865 Lynchburg emigrants, promising to meet them "on the shores of Africa." (The Library Company of Philadelphia, 5750.F.122)

commissioner Howard, requesting rail transportation for the emigrants and their baggage from Lynchburg to Baltimore. Freedmen's Bureau teachers in Lynchburg mostly opposed colonization, but Howard received the Secretary of War's approval to pay the cost of the group's train travel to the Baltimore docks, nearly $1,000, an example of US government subsidization of colonization. By now, the colonization society was promoting McNuckles as a near-perfect example of a freedman acceptable to both races. "A great man," McClain wrote. "He has the confidence of all the people of all colors in Lynchburg." Coppinger also wrote a letter of introduction for "John McKnuckles, (colored)" to a Petersburg colonization supporter. McNuckles was coming to Petersburg "to endeavor to obtain possession of two children—relations of his—with a view to have them go with him to Africa." These may have been his brother Woodson's children, because Coppinger would have likely noted if they were Mack's sons or daughters.[30]

With departure only weeks away, the emigrants turned their attention to a fundraising appeal to the white community. In their public letter, they proved adept at targeting a specific audience, and did not mention equal rights, citizenship, or property. Instead, they praised former masters as their "best friends" and said they hoped to help Christianize Africa.[31]

> Lynchburg, Oct. 17, 1865—To Our Former Masters—We, a portion of your former slaves, have formed ourselves into a society, known as the African Emigration Society, for the sole purpose of migrating to Liberia, on the west coast of Africa, to convey the light and civilization that we have received here, even in a state of slavery, to our heathen brethren on that benighted and long neglected continent.—We expect to leave this city on the 1st of November next for our father-land; and leave you all for no reason but the one above mentioned; none of us will carry with us the prejudices and ill-will that might arise from our being held in bondage by you, as slaves. We know that you have been our best friends, and we feel it now the more, though we are free. You all know the particular situation the termination of the late war has left us in, so therefore, we call upon you to aid us in our enterprise. We know that your generous and sympathetic hearts will not let you stand aloof from us in our endeavors to do good for ourselves and people. Some of us are capable of conveying ideas of the mechanic arts; some can unfold to them, in our poor way, the marvelous light of the gospel, and point them the way to God. We are not going to try to elevate the people of Liberia, because, from what we can learn, they are far our superiors in intelligence, wealth and learning; but Africa generally. Some of us have a good common education which we think will be of value to those who have no art.—You know we are very poor; the smallest sums you can afford to contribute to our scheme will be very acceptable to us. We call upon you because we know the kind and generous impulses of your hearts, and you, on the other hand, know our situation and wants. Give us, of the abundance of your wealth, a small sum, and we believe that you will be rewarded by Him who says, 'He that giveth to the poor lendeth to the Lord.'—We think this will be our last request from your hands, so join and help us in our efforts to do good for our race.
>
> We are ever your friends and obedient servants,
> (Signed) Mack Nuchols, Jno. J. Garland, Isam Bourne, Charles Lewis, Wm. Eubanks, Charles B. Loving, George W. Rose, Levi M. Norvell.

The letter was published not only in the two Lynchburg dailies but also the *New York Times.* Whether anyone in Lynchburg contributed financially to the emigration is unknown, although McNuckles later thanked unnamed friends for gifts the emigrants received. By now correspondence among ACS officials, the Lynchburg group, and its supporters was peaking. Coppinger forwarded the letter from Crummell to McNuckles on Oct. 20, the same day Coppinger himself wrote six letters dealing with the pending voyage. McNuckles went back to Washington and Coppinger's office a few days later, on Monday, Oct. 23, and assured him that the group members were busy preparing to leave Lynchburg the following week. Some were so poor they did not have decent clothing or their own mattresses—the emigrants would travel in the ships' hold, not passenger cabins, and use their mattresses as bedding.[32]

Skilled emigrants like Charles Lewis, who signed the open letter, were better off. Lewis, 44, was a shoemaker who could read and write. Liberia had no factories to manufacture necessities so his trade would be valuable there. Emigrating with him were 10 family members, including his wife, Mary, 39; his mother, Millie, 60; Mary Lewis, 39; Squire Lewis, 30; Henry Lewis, 26; Segis Ann Lewis, 18; Elizabeth Lewis, 16; Lucinda Lewis, 9; Haram Lewis, 7, and John W. Lewis, 5. They took enough baggage to set up housekeeping in West Africa, including 180 pounds of soap, 14 large cotton bags, 4 dresses, 4 aprons, an oilcloth bag full of more clothing, two dozen cups and saucers, two dozen plates and dishes, 3 cans of sundries, 2 gallons of kerosene, a large carving knife and fork, a fireplace poker and shovel, a box of sewing ribbons and silk, a box of medicine, and a large cloak.[33]

Family names of the emigrants reflected their roots and connections in the Virginia Piedmont. Another shoemaker leaving Lynchburg with his family was George Rose, 28. Like Norvell, he had learned to read and write despite Virginia's prohibitions on slaves' education. With him were his wife, Louisa, 24; Octavio Rose, 22, possibly his sibling, and three children. Rose family members, Black and white, had been among the first settlers of this part of Virginia, but determining the ancestry of the 1865 Lynchburg emigrants is difficult, since the enslaved were not listed by name in any prewar US census. This was no accident: When the enslaved were enumerated for the first time in the 1850 census, Southern senators made sure their names were not recorded, denying even this basic acknowledgement of their humanity.

George Rose later asked to be remembered to Lynchburg tobacco magnate J.W. Murrell. Rose's mother was Linda Murrell, so both may have been enslaved by the Murrell family. J.W. Murrell's brother, Lynchburg physician Dr. Edward Murrell, had freed Jack, Patience, and Carrell Murrell in 1847 and sent them to Liberia. Others enslaved by Edward Murrell, who lived in a grand house at the corner of Madison and Second streets, had to wait until the end of the war for their freedom. Among them were the Gilbert Dudley family. Now, Dudley, 37, a farm worker, his wife, Jennie, 26, and six children ranging in age from 2 to 12 were headed to Liberia.[34]

Addison Banks, 48, and his wife, along with their seven children were also awaiting the train at the Lynchburg station on Oct. 31, 1865. Banks's occupation was listed as butcher, but he was an experienced mechanic, proficient at skilled work like carpentry and operating machinery. The Lynchburg group was relying on him and the other men to help build their houses, and the ACS to ship them sawmill equipment. His wife, Amelia, was six months' pregnant and likely not looking forward to a rough train ride followed by a month on the Atlantic Ocean. She must have also known that keeping her family healthy would be a challenge. Childhood diseases like measles sometimes spread aboard the crowded emigration ships but the chief threat in West Africa was malaria, the acclimating fever that virtually all emigrants suffered. The ACS always downplayed sickness and misled potential emigrants about the risk. An 1859 pamphlet by a colonization proponent went so far as to say that not a single death could be attributed to fever alone. An Americo-Liberian himself, the writer claimed it was no worse than measles. But he also acknowledged that virtually everyone got it to some degree, and that it consisted of a debilitating attack of chills, then fever, which repeated itself for weeks, sometimes killing the sufferer. Physicians did not know what caused the tropical fever, but the generally accepted belief was that it came from "miasma," dank, invisible vapors carrying tiny particles of decay. (The word "malaria" comes from the Italian for "bad air.")[35]

Earlier emigrants had written back to friends, family, and former owners, and stories of illness and death had circulated in Lynchburg since the 1830s. Amelia Banks couldn't have known the exact figures but the mortality to which she herself would fall victim was horrifying. About 50 percent of the previous nineteenth-century Lynchburg-area emigrants had perished. That mirrored the statistics for all US emigrants to Liberia. Not until 1880 was the real cause discovered: a tiny parasite carried by the *anopheles* mosquito. The 1865 Lynchburg emigrants were bound for remote Careysburg, which was founded in the 1850s to establish an outpost away from the fever-ridden lowlands and swamps of the West African coast. Unfortunately, no one told the mosquitoes.

But all that was in the future. Now it was Tuesday night, Oct. 31, 1865, All Hallows' Eve, the travel moon was nearly full, and the Lynchburg people were ready to board the railroad cars to Baltimore. First, everyone sang and prayed and many wept, both those leaving and those staying. "The emigrants were there, huddled and blanketed for the voyage, and hundreds of their friends were there, also, to bid them adieu. Religious services were held, songs were sung, and prayers uttered for the safety and welfare of those who were about to commit their destinies to the vicissitudes of a strange land and uncertain future. It was an effecting spectacle, the last of the leave taking of those sable friends, between whom the ceaseless surges of ocean will soon sound the solemn elegy of perpetual separation. The adieus were spoken in tears and sadness," wrote the *Daily Virginian's* reporter. Coppinger, who had been in Lynchburg for several days helping the emigrants get ready, said he would never forget the scene at the station, and he gave McNuckles a letter of introduction to Liberian President Daniel Warner.[36]

The reporter wondered about not only the emigrants but also those who stayed to face "a hard and cheerless life" in Virginia. He wrote about the African Americans as if they were wayward children, not responsible adults acting on their own agency. Those leaving were undoubtedly nervous but hoping and praying they were heading for a better life for themselves and their children. They arrived in Baltimore the next day, where five emigrants got cold feet, including the impulsive newly married couple and John J. Garland, one of the original organizers who wrote the open letter to the newspaper. But a few days later, on Saturday, November 4, 1865, the steadfast 172 boarded a schooner at Smith's wharf. After more religious services, the ship was towed from its moorings around 4 p.m. and headed down the Chesapeake Bay. *The Baltimore Sun* reported:

> The superior fore and aft schooner, H.P. Russell, 426 tons, Captain Nickerson, chartered by the American Colonization Society, sailed from Baltimore, on Saturday, November 4, with one hundred and seventy-two men, women, and children as emigrants, for Liberia. They are all of the class known as 'Freedmen,' from in or near Lynchburg, Va. Among them are a number that can read and write, and several experienced mechanics

> and agriculturists. Many are professing Christians, generally of the Baptist persuasion, one of the latter being a preacher. They are a substantial working party, well calculated to give a good report of themselves and the country.[37]

The 1865 emigration and what happened to the Lynchburg emigrants later in Liberia highlighted the end of nearly fifty years of effort to remove Black Americans from Virginia. After a war that ended their enslavement but not their oppression, the 1865 Lynchburg emigrants took themselves out of Virginia, not the other way around. They left the tobacco fields and factories behind. After a mighty struggle, a few found what they were looking for in West Africa.

2

Quakers and Colonizers

1763–1829

> Mr. Jefferson . . . has in truth injured us more, and has been as great a barrier to our emancipation as anything that has ever been advanced against it.
>
> —David Walker, Massachusetts, 1829

UNDERSTANDING THE colonization movement and the 1865 Lynchburg emigration requires understanding how tightly slavery was woven into the region's history. White settlers and the Black people they enslaved streamed into the western Piedmont of Virginia in the second half of the 1700s. They soon quadrupled the population of the Lynch's Ferry region along the James River in the foothills of the Blue Ridge Mountains. A town spread up the hills above the river where growers shipped their leaf downstream to Richmond. Quaker John Lynch built the first tobacco warehouse even before Lynchburg was chartered, and a society evolved around a tobacco economy based on human bondage. Officials at Lynch's Spring Warehouse on the south bank of the river said they inspected more tobacco in 1796 than any other warehouse in the state.[1]

The burden of the tobacco economy was carried on the backs of the enslaved who planted, nurtured, and harvested the golden weed. Black men and women became the region's early industrial workers as warehouses became factories where tobacco leaves were transformed into a product for chewing. "It was in the production of the quid that the first Lynchburg manufacturers were engaged," wrote local historian S. Allen Chambers. African Americans did the work in every part of the process, from raising the plants in the fields to floating the heavy hogsheads down the James to Richmond by bateau. Five more tobacco warehouses were built in the first decade of the nineteenth century, and Virginia licensed some of them to auction the closely regulated commodity. Lynchburg was on its way to becoming a center of the industry in Virginia and the nation.

The tobacco business molded the town into a slave society where men, women, and children were bought and sold like livestock. The prosperous white people maintained their lifestyle via the blood and brine of slavery but considered themselves high-minded and progressive. Evangelical preachers shouting salvation in the afterlife to Black and white rode circuit through the countryside where close to 40 percent of the region's 40,000 inhabitants were enslaved by 1800.[2]

However, Lynchburg's Quaker heritage meant slavery was not ubiquitous in its early years. To avoid banishment from the sect, the region's Quakers—the Religious Society of Friends—had freed their enslaved in the 1780s, resulting in a small but significant population of free Black people. Of the 1,400 people living in Lynchburg town itself in 1810, 135 were free Black people. White people viewed the free people of color as a malign influence on the enslaved, encouraging rebellion amid a growing belief that the state had more enslaved than needed to maintain the economy. Most white people viewed Black people, free or enslaved, as inferior and degraded by generations of slavery. Lynchburg's white elites saw Africa as a savage, uncivilized place, while sometimes acknowledging that the Southern white people themselves had fostered a savage society built on enslavement and torture. They believed that sending American Black people to Africa, their "native land," would help civilize and convert Africans to Protestant Christianity and thereby justify efforts to make sure all remaining American Black people were enslaved, not free. But most American Black people did not consider Africa their native land. Bishop Richard Allen of Philadelphia, a founder of the African Methodist Episcopal Church, wrote in 1827: "This land which we have watered with our tears and our blood, is now our mother country and we are well satisfied to stay . . ."[3]

Allen was speaking as a free man of color in the North. If given a choice, few Lynchburg enslaved would have described themselves as "well satisfied." Raising tobacco was labor-intensive and required almost superhuman effort. One enslaved laborer who might be able to cultivate forty acres of wheat and corn could only handle two or three acres of tobacco, planting, hoeing, pulling sucker leaves, weeding, cutting, hanging the sticky weed to dry in a smoke house, all amid the oppressive humidity of a Virginia summer. Thomas Jefferson visited Lynchburg often and wrote in the 1780s, "It is a culture productive of infinite wretchedness. Those employed in it are in a continual state of exertion beyond the power of nature to support." In nineteenth-century tobacco factories, labor was divided into separating the leaves from the stem, dipping the leaves into sticky flavorings, twisting and forming them into plugs for chewing, and even more strenuous tasks like turning large screw presses to pack tobacco for shipment. By the 1850s, tobacco factory and warehouse workers were generally rented from their owners, and while the labor was preferable to working in the fields, it was so onerous that dippers sometimes had to work naked in high heat near the drying roofs. By 1860, 47 factories in the area employed more than 1,500 enslaved, also producing granulated tobacco for smoking.[4]

Despite sending mixed messages on slavery, Jefferson could not maintain his Monticello lifestyle without it and owned a second plantation surrounding his retreat, Poplar Forest, just outside Lynchburg. A free Boston man, David Walker, targeted Jefferson, who died on July 4, 1826, in a powerful pamphlet that reads like it could have been written yesterday instead of 1829. Citing Jefferson in his *Notes on the State of Virginia,* that Black people were inferior to the white people both mind and body, Walker wrote "Mr. Jefferson . . . has in truth injured us more, and has been as great a barrier to our emancipation as anything that has ever been advanced against it." His *Appeal . . . to Coloured Citizens of the World* mentioned the third president repeatedly and predicted that because Jefferson was so universally respected his ideas would far outlive those of most men. Walker derided colonization, saying that despite the words of its proponents, its actual purpose was to "get the free people of color away to Africa, from among the slaves," leaving the enslaved "to rest in ignorance and wretchedness." He continued, "tell us now no more about colonization, for America is as much our country as it is yours.—Treat us like men, and there is no danger but we will all live in peace and happiness together. For we are not like you, hardhearted, unmerciful, and unforgiving." He said the barbarity of Christian slavery in Virginia and other states was unparalleled in the annals of heathens or devils or Sodom and Gomorrah. The essay was so incendiary that even an abolitionist group declined to reprint it years later.[5]

Tobacco soon turned Lynch's Ferry into a boomtown. In addition to laboring in the fields and warehouses, the enslaved worked as domestics in brick houses built from the region's abundant red clay. Point of Honor on Cabell Street, built in 1815 on the town's dueling grounds, still stands today as part of the Lynchburg Museum system. It's an imposing brick mansion overlooking the James River. Taverns and hotels sprang up all over town, especially on the main road leading west. Looking for skilled labor to construct the first buildings of the University of Virginia in Charlottesville, Jefferson said he had offers from "some of the best workmen in Lynchburg" and hoped to improve on "the barbarous workmanship" of Charlottesville laborers. Jefferson's grandson attended school in rapidly growing Lynchburg in 1817, but his father wrote that the youth "speaks of the inhabitants as a race devoted solely to gain and having no ideas unconnected with money." A sense of entitlement came with the money as austere Quaker influence waned. One young tobacco baron was said "to stroll to his factory on a summer morning like an Indian nabob, clad in spotless white linen, a Negro slave walking beside him and holding a great green umbrella over his head." By 1815, Lynchburg society had advanced to the point that it could host a 300-seat dinner featuring a band of 20 musicians in honor of Andrew Jackson's visit on his way to Washington, DC, following his victory in the Battle of New Orleans. Jefferson was staying at Poplar Forest and walked in an afternoon parade along Main Street with Jackson and other notables including Mayor John Lynch. One account says the revelers drank eighty gallons of wine at dinner. A couple of years later, Jefferson was asked to select the wines for the town's new Franklin Hotel, built by his friend and Lynchburg agent, Samuel Harrison, who had moved to Lynchburg from Tidewater where five generations of his wealthy family had owned slaves. Nominally a Quaker, Harrison freed at least one person in 1792 after the sect forbid its members to own slaves but soon left the faith.[6]

There had always been opposition to slavery among Lynchburg's Quakers, preachers, and traveling missionaries. Wicked Lynchburg (once called "the seat of Satan's Kingdom") had no churches in its early days, and the founding Quakers built their meeting house miles outside the town. Other denominations established themselves after the American Revolution, dropping their early objections to slavery and embracing it, but the Quakers remained steadfast. Sarah Clark Lynch had helped found the South River meeting in 1763. Her son, John, was the farmer, ferry operator and land developer who subdivided some hilly acres on the south bank of the James River to establish Lynchburg. Lynch, born in 1740, was a tall man who looked older than he was and dressed in plain Quaker style with a broad-brimmed hat. His mother and sister opposed slavery. South River, while the largest, was not the only nearby Quaker "meeting," as Quakers called their churches. One was founded on Goose Creek in Bedford County around 1788 on land donated by Elijah Turner, whose mother and uncle were Quakers. Elijah owned young Joseph Turner, who with his wife and children would become the region's first emigrants to Liberia decades later. He and his brother were apparently freed as children after the Quakers began to expel slaveholders from the faith. The Quakers had officially disapproved of slavery for years, but Virginia law had made freeing individual slaves difficult, requiring an act of the legislature for each case, and their free status could be challenged later. The state passed a law in 1782 allowing owners to use wills or other legal documents to free slaves in a process called "manumission." After the manumission law was enacted, Quakers decided that anyone continuing to enslave Black people would be expelled and as a result members of the South River meeting freed nearly ninety people.[7]

In Lynchburg, a reconstructed South River meeting house still stands near the old Quaker cemetery where the Lynches and other Friends are buried, their final resting sites marked by stones that have eroded along with the memory of their lives. The Lynchburg Quakers are sometimes remembered as quaint, old-fashioned even for the late 1700s, "thee" and "thou"-saying curiosities. But they exerted a strong moral force in the late eighteenth century, and local historian Asbury Christian went to great lengths to praise them a hundred years later. He described their clothing in detail but omitted their opposition to slavery, which was so strong that many eventually moved to Ohio where they founded another town, also called Lynchburg. The former Quaker enslaved and their descendants contributed to the numbers of free Black people living in Lynchburg before the Civil War. John Lynch manumitted 14 enslaved, including Peter Hackett, a 39-year-old veteran of the Revolutionary War, in 1782. Lynch's Quaker neighbor, the lawyer Christopher Johnson, manumitted 15 people a few weeks later. Christopher Anthony, one of the Quakers who later moved to Ohio, freed 11 people on the same day.[8]

Lynch's sister, Susan Lynch Terrell, was an outspoken opponent of slavery and was one of the first to endorse the emancipations of the 1780s. "So strongly did she impress her neighbors that many leading men acted on her suggestion and freed their bondsmen," wrote Lynchburg historian Douglas Summers Brown in 1936. The Lynchburg Quakers had close connections to those in Richmond, who organized the Virginia Abolition Society in 1790. It never gained widespread support, but its president, Robert

The old Quaker cemetery and its rebuilt meeting house are landmarks in west Lynchburg. City founder John Lynch and other members of the Society of Friends were buried here, but most Lynchburg Quakers left the faith or moved away as slavery hardened in Virginia in the early 1800s. (Author photo)

Pleasants, freed nearly eighty enslaved, and Richmond would later become a center of the colonization movement. Pleasants visited the Lynch family several times in the late 1750s. While the Quakers, especially women, were concerned about the welfare of the enslaved, part of Quaker opposition was based on slavery's negative effects on society. They believed slavery prevented the South from developing a progressive economy based on industry and manufacturing with a thriving middle class, rather than a plantation economy with wealth concentrated at the top.[9] Antislavery sentiment gained traction in Virginia during the years after the Revolution, with a few planters advancing ideas about colonization.[10]

The Revolutionary manumission movement in Virginia was short-lived. Fear of Black revolt increased following Gabriel Prosser's foiled rebellion in Richmond in 1800, and the Virginia legislature passed a law which benefited colonization, requiring any Black people who were freed after 1806 to leave the state. That same year, the Women Friends of the

South River meeting noted, "We know of non[e] among us who hold slaves." The Quaker refusal to hold, or to even rent slaves, was making life difficult for them in Central Virginia, where enslaved labor was necessary to make large-scale agriculture profitable. Manual labor was disdained by Virginia's wealthy white people. It was one of the signifiers that separated Black from white and contributed to the rise of the racial component of slavery. The Friends were willing to work the fields themselves, but that would have resulted in a loss of their standing in society, and they were on the top rung of old Lynchburg. Many of the local Quakers joined other denominations, and at least 300 eventually left Lynchburg for the free state of Ohio. Founder John Lynch stayed and became a wealthy land developer, but his oldest son moved to Ohio where he helped found the free Lynchburg.[11]

The Society of Friends wasn't the only white denomination opposing slavery in those days. Prominent Presbyterian cleric Samuel Stanhope Smith, the first president of Hampden-Sydney College, and later president of the College of New Jersey (now Princeton University), disagreed with Jefferson about the inferior nature of the Black race, believed non-whites had a right to improve themselves, and advocated that American slavery be extinguished. Born in Pennsylvania and educated at the College of New Jersey, Smith saw Piedmont Virginia's slavery culture firsthand, tutoring young enslaver William S. Crawford, who owned a plantation in the colonial village of New Glasgow (now Clifford) about twenty miles north of Lynch's Ferry. Crawford graduated from the College of New Jersey in 1781 and later became the first lawyer, and the first court clerk, of newly formed Amherst County. Smith apparently had some effect on him, because he named his plantation Tusculum, after the home of the Princeton president. But the Northern influence only went so far: Crawford did not give up his enslaved and owned forty-three people at Tusculum in 1810.[12]

Presbyterian George Bourne, a Baltimore writer and typesetter who grew up in England, moved to New Glasgow in 1810. He only stayed about a year before moving to the Shenandoah Valley where he became a Presbyterian minister, but the plantation life he saw helped make him an abolitionist, and in 1816 he published *The Book and Slavery Irreconcilable.* Historian Nicholas Guyatt says it was "perhaps the most vehement attack on the religious credentials of slavery that had ever appeared in the United States," and along with the Bible, it inspired abolitionist William Lloyd Garrison. Bourne was subjected to a church trial for his views and expelled from the

Presbyterian ministry. An 1837 work by Bourne described in lurid detail the culture of rural Virginia. In *Slavery and Its Effects upon Woman,* he portrayed a depraved society in which both male and female white people cooperated. Black women were raped by masters and their sons and then convinced lonely white women and girls to have sex with the slaves. These women in turn would attract a healthy man from the North into marriage who would come to endorse slavery, while his wife tended to a "harem" of Black women.[13]

Per their doctrine, early Virginia Methodists also opposed slavery, with evangelists preaching to both races. In 1784, Methodists were given a year to free all their enslaved but few did. In 1785, the Rev. Thomas Coke, an associate of John Wesley, the founder of Methodism, passed through the Lynch's Ferry region during one of his first evangelical journeys in America. Parishioners at one area church threatened Coke with 100 lashes for his antislavery message but he persisted, saying the force of his message was acknowledged by New Glasgow slaveholder Samuel Meredith, who was reluctant to heed it "for fear of losing his popularity." With the population of free Virginia Black people growing after the Revolution, the Virginia legislature required them to register with local governments in 1793 and they were issued free papers.

A Quaker missionary from Pennsylvania was appalled at what she found in Virginia a few years later. Mary Robinson Morton visited the South River and Goose Creek Friends near Lynchburg in June 1806 after riding through the springtime countryside from Richmond: ". . . Alas the beauties of nature [and] of cultivation are obscured with a gloomy cloud in this country . . . here in every scene of rural plenty we behold the wretched meagre half-naked Slaves, toiling for the pride [and] avarice of their masters, employed in raising delicacies for their table which they themselves must not taste." She was particularly touched by the plight of "their poor little helpless friendless children, born to no inheritance except slavery, and the complicated miseries included in it." Morton did find some cause for optimism, based on her Quaker faith: "Light has spread, *even here* [her emphasis], upon this subject, many are convinced of the injustice of holding them . . ." Morton continued with an even more hopeful sentence, envisioning not just freedom but dignity for the enslaved: ". . . I can hardly help hailing them as the future lords of the land and owners of the soil." Acquiring their own land was difficult for Black people even after the Civil War, and few white people in Virginia agreed with Morton and her visions of a free country.[14]

As the tobacco industry prospered, the enslaved population of Lynchburg and its three surrounding counties of Amherst, Campbell, and Bedford, increased at a faster rate than that of the white people. Over the next half century or so, it nearly tripled as the white population doubled. By the time of the Civil War, so powerful was Methodist support for slavery that the national denomination split into pro- and anti- slavery branches. One of the leaders of the proslavery faction was Bishop John Early, a Methodist pastor and the first president of the Lynchburg Colonization Society. Born in 1786 not far from Jefferson's Poplar Forest in Bedford County, legend has it he began his ministry preaching to Jefferson's enslaved.[15]

By 1816, the year the ACS was founded, Jefferson was praising Lynchburg's business and society: "I pay three or four visits a year to a very distant possession I have in Bedford, where, being comfortably fixed, I pass a month or two at a time, so that it is almost a second home. it is in the finest part of our state for soil & climate, and near to Lynchburg; now the [second] town in the state for business, and thriving with a rapidity exceeding any thing we have ever seen. when I first visited that place 50 years ago, there was nothing but a ferry house. it may be considered as the out-port of Richmond, receiving all the produce of the S. Western quarter of our state, and of the upper part of N. Carolina, & transmitting it down the river 130 miles to Richmond. it furnishes me therefore good society while in that neighborhood."[16]

One of the founding members of the Lynchburg Colonization Society, Elijah Fletcher, had visited Jefferson at Monticello in 1811 and recounted contemporary stories of Jefferson fathering children by Sally Hemings, whom Fletcher called "Black Sal." Historians now believe Jefferson had multiple children with her, based on DNA testing in 1998. Jefferson kept his sons with Hemings enslaved, did not acknowledge them as his own, and put them to work as skilled carpenters helping build Poplar Forest. An idealistic Vermonter who came to Virginia to teach, young Fletcher was disturbed by slavery but yielded to his desire for prosperity and social acceptance, inheriting through his wife many enslaved as well as the plantation where Sweet Briar College would be founded in 1901.[17]

Jefferson spent Christmas Day, 1810, at Poplar Forest, where he received a hand-delivered letter from John Lynch concerning colonization. Lynch knew Jefferson and wrote on behalf of Anne Mifflin, a Quaker missionary who had recently visited Lynchburg. While most of the letter relays Mifflin's thoughts, a postscript adds Lynch's own beliefs. He claimed that not only would many slaveholders be willing to give up their slaves, but that many enslaved people had already been emancipated in Virginia. Mifflin and Lynch also endorsed proposals to establish a colony for free Black Americans on the coast of Africa. Jefferson, who at times seemed to favor gradual emancipation, replied to Lynch in a lengthy letter from Monticello a few weeks later. Always cautious with his words, especially about slavery, he said that as a private citizen he could not be effective in establishing colonization. Nevertheless, his reply to Lynch would become one of the founding documents of the movement and was reprinted in the first annual report of the ACS in 1818. Colonization was "the most desirable measure which could be adopted for gradually drawing off this part of our population most advantageously for themselves as well [as] for us," he told Lynch. "But for this," Jefferson continued, "the national mind is not yet prepared." He doubted whether Black people themselves would agree to emigrate. This turned out to be true as only a tiny fraction of the Black population ever chose to leave America, and of that number, many were enslaved who went as a condition of gaining their freedom. Jefferson also felt that Black people in the US were incapable of governing themselves. He concluded that despite the hindrances, the idea was worth a trial run: His letter to Lynch expressed both support and doubt, and he was not inclined to do anything to further it.[18]

Responding to a similar proposal from a Lynchburg medical man to move every Black person in the country to Africa, Jefferson would express more doubts. This was in 1817, a year after the formation of the ACS, but before an organized colonization movement developed in Lynchburg. A native of Scotland, Dr. Thomas Humphreys was a slaveholder, a physician, a druggist, and a peculiar local character. He was popular but also the target of some mockery: "The doctor possessed a colored man, named Bob, who was also an incomparable mimic; and so perfectly could he imitate the voice of Dr. Humphreys, that frequently he would cause a great tumult among the young men, by coming to the door suddenly and beginning to scold and grumble like his master," wrote Margaret Cabell, a contemporary. The Humphreys lived on Main Street in a house "shaded by Catalpa trees" that he had purchased from Quakers who moved to Ohio. Humphreys's enslaved workers and servants illustrated the complicated nature of race and servitude in these years, and the relationships of the white elite. Humphreys owned another Black man married to an enslaved woman of mixed race and their two children. He also had an indentured servant, Nancy Jones, married to a free man of mixed race.

Humphrey's wife inherited other enslaved persons, who were apparently passed along to her son-in-law, John Lynch's grandson, who in turn sent nearly twenty people to Liberia in 1842.[19]

In Humphrey's proposal to Jefferson, he decried slavery as a curse on white people and the enslaved, referring to Black men as good farmers, planters and mechanics, and Black women as tasteful with genteel backgrounds, calling them all "brethren" of white people. He predicted that if Black Americans were allowed to form their own republic that within fifty years they would be "in as high a state of advancement as many of the nations of the Earth have arrived at in the space of 200 years." Many colonizationists believed that separating the races would result in the immediate elevation of Black Americans, highlighting the racial animus that held them back in the United States. Humphrey went on to blast Virginia and the other Southern states as degraded by slavery, saying it was in direct contrast to the US Bill of Rights and the fundamental principles of the US government, and that enslavers were "political hypocrites." Humphreys's letter is the most pro-Black writing from a Lynchburg white that I found while researching this book and he likely would have been run out of town if it had been written a few years later. Jefferson must have been stung by some of his assertions.[20]

Humphreys's arguments turned on the benefits of freeing the South from slavery, not the benefits to the enslaved themselves. His unrealistic plan called for a gradual emancipation, with a tenth of the African American population each year "disposed of." The reality was that for plantation masters like Jefferson, debt alone prevented them from freeing their enslaved. Their human possessions and land were their chief assets. Humphreys did not explain why free Black people needed to be banished along with the enslaved, but perhaps the widespread white belief that they were a bad influence was so obvious it didn't need re-stating. Humphreys proposed that the federal government pay for his colonization scheme and wildly underestimated the cost, which would have included buying all of the more than one million enslaved in the US.[21]

Jefferson turned 74 in 1817 and did not foresee an end to Southern slavery in his lifetime. He told Humphreys that Northern states would never support the federal government paying slaveholders to free their enslaved, and that the current generation of white people had little desire for gradual emancipation: "Personally I am ready and desirous to make any sacrifice which shall ensure their gradual but complete retirement from the State, and effectually, at the same time, establish them elsewhere in freedom and safety. But I have not perceived the growth of this disposition in the rising generation . . ." By the time Humphreys wrote to Jefferson, influential officials of the newly formed colonization society were hoping Congress might finance the exodus of free Black people. Jefferson closed by telling Humphreys that he hoped that "the proposition now on the carpet at Washington to provide an establishment on the coast of Africa for voluntary emigrations of people of color, may be the corner stone of this future edifice." Jefferson himself would free only a few enslaved people during his lifetime. [22]

Although spreading Christianity in Africa was a stated goal of the ACS—most of its agents were clergy—neither Jefferson nor Humphreys mentioned religion in their mutual correspondence. However, the new evangelical faith was a driving force for a few free Black Virginians themselves who had begun to believe they would be better off in West Africa than Virginia. Among them were Lott Cary and Colin Teague of Richmond. Cary, born enslaved, worked in a Richmond tobacco warehouse, rose to a position of responsibility, and purchased his freedom and that of his wife and children in 1815. That same year, he and Teague, a saddle maker who had earned enough money to purchase freedom for himself and his family, founded the Richmond African Baptist Missionary Society. Cary's Sunday sermons in Richmond were heard by hundreds of African Americans. Understandably, his listeners trusted his words more than they did those of white colonizers. Cary and Teague also preached in Lynchburg and Norfolk prior to their emigration, and future Lynchburg emigrants like Joseph Turner may have heard them. The two Richmond men were named missionaries to Africa by their Baptist group, which was cooperating with the ACS, and left for West Africa and the Liberian colony in the early 1820s.[23]

Some free people in Richmond asked to be sent to free territories in the western part of the American continent; other Black people, if they wanted to emigrate, would have preferred Haiti, governed by Black people following their 1804 revolution. Some white people maintained that removing free Black people from North America, not just Virginia, would lessen the chances of a Black revolution in the states. This thinking had evolved following Gabriel Prosser's 1800 conspiracy which resulted in the execution of Prosser and twenty-five others. The letters Jefferson wrote to the state legislature concerning gradual emancipation and colonization after Prosser's revolt were kept secret until they were publicized in 1816 by colonization advocate Charles Fenton Mercer, a member of the Virginia House of Delegates. He won approval from the legislature for colonization to proceed in Virginia, and later that month Congress approved a draft constitution for the "American Colonization Society for Colonizing the Free People of Color."[24]

Sierra Leone, a colony established in 1787 by the British government for Black loyalists from the American Revolution and poor Black people from London, was just north of the future Liberian colony. Paul Cuffee, a free Quaker and ship captain from Massachusetts, took 38 Black Americans to Sierra Leone in 1816, and in 1820, the first voyage involving the ACS brought 88 free Black people from Northern states to Sierra Leone and its Sherbro Island. But the swampy island proved inhospitable, and the first ACS emigrants moved farther down the coast in 1822. Their new colony was named "Liberia," echoing liberation and freedom. Its first settlement, called Monrovia for US President James Monroe, was established at a natural harbor near where the St. Paul's and Mesurado rivers enter the Atlantic Ocean. Known to Europeans as the Pepper Coast and later the Grain Coast, this region of West Africa was easily accessible by sea. It included several slave "factories" where captured and kidnapped Africans were imprisoned and sold to Europeans.[25]

Exactly what happened when the ACS representatives and colonists arrived at Cape Mesurado, site of today's Monrovia, has been told and retold in various histories of Liberia which don't always agree. But one thing is sure: Cultures and people of the Atlantic world had been influencing each other in the region for centuries and this melding pot boiled over when the first American settlers barged into the multiple ethnic/cultural, geographic, and religious polities already in place. ACS representative Jehudi Ashmun was the agent in charge of the settlement in 1821–23, and the following account is taken from his book written a few years later.[26]

On the scene were white Americans; Black Americans whose ancestors had come from Africa; multiple, distinct West African groups including the Dei, the Vai, the Kru, the Manding, the Queah, and the Gola; a confederation of some but not all of these groups; recaptive Africans; a large group of other Africans from the interior who had been captured then abandoned after their owner returned to Europe (they had their own settlement on a small island separate from the local ethnic groups); a British navy crew; and a mixed-race property owner and trader who lived on another small island nearby. In addition to multiple African languages, some West Africans also spoke English, French, Spanish, or Dutch thanks to trade with Europe, and religious practices included traditional West African beliefs as well as Islam. Two small islands at the mouth of the Mesurado River were occupied when the 1822 settlers arrived: One was "nearly covered with houses built in the native style," and "occupied by a family of several hundred domestic slaves, formerly the property of an English factor . . ." The English "factor" was a slave trader, and the occupants of the island had been kidnapped and brought there before he returned to Europe. Ashmun said they were strangers to the coastal people. The other island had already been purchased by the colonization society from mixed-race trader John S. Mill, the "occupant and proprietor" who was African by birth but educated in England. He allowed the settlers to land without opposition.[27]

All the other groups made clear they wanted the settlers to go away. The subsequent negotiations involved African leaders with westernized titles. One was King Peter, a Dei leader who was threatened at gunpoint in the initial colonization society efforts to seize land. His town, Gawalun, was on a larger island nearby which the ACS renamed Bushrod Island after George Washington's nephew, one of the society's founders. Most of the Africans living nearby were also Dei, but the more powerful Vai and Gola groups controlled the region. For several weeks, the colonists worked to build houses in what would become Monrovia. But cultures collided again as a slave ship captured by the British navy with thirty "liberated Africans" on board arrived to refresh its water supply on the way to Sierra Leone. The ship's anchor line broke and it was smashed in the surf. The shipwreck was immediately claimed by the leader of another local town, King George, also a Dei. His armed followers tried to board the wreck but were repelled by the British prize master, who fired on them, killing two and wounding others. The settlers sided with the British, brought forward a small brass cannon, and began firing it at the Dei, who were armed with muskets. King George's soldiers were at a disadvantage because they only fired one volley at a time before withdrawing into the safety of the forest to reload. (Ashmun seems to have considered this unsporting.)[28]

This first skirmishing ended with the arrival and intervention of Sao Boso, Manding leader and the head of the powerful Condo Confederation of Indigenous groups. King George soon moved his town several miles away and began a more organized effort to throw out the Americans. The future of the colony was in doubt as young Africans recruited by the colonists to man their small cannons began to desert, the colonists began to get sick, and the original ACS agents fled. Still, the leader of another Indigenous group, Tom Bassa, "a prince of some distinction," pledged his friendship and fifty-five more colonists arrived in June. But shortly thereafter, King George convinced other leaders and some of the recaptive Africans to join him in another effort to expel the colonists. The West Africans mounted a well-organized assault on the settlement in November 1822, beginning with musket fire and followed by a charge with spears. The colonists led by Lott Cary from Richmond blasted the shoulder-to-shoulder West Africans with cannonballs and grapeshot. "Every shot literally spent its force in a solid mass of living human flesh," reported Ashmun. The colonists kept a list of their own casualties, a few dead and several wounded, and estimated that hundreds of West Africans were slain. The Americans finally prevailed after yet another bloody battle involving settler cannons and West Africans firing large-caliber muskets loaded with copper and iron slugs. Such violence often characterized American attempts to take over the lands of other people, subjugate them, and destroy their culture, mixing expansionism with imperialism and racism.[29]

Ashmun quotes King George with a perceptive statement in the midst of all this: "The Americans were strangers who had forgot their attachment to the land of their fathers; for if not, why had they not renounced their connexion with white men altogether, and placed themselves under the protection of the kings of the country?" The colonists who had been distinguished by their race back in Virginia were regarded by West Africans primarily as American, not Black. The American settlers' purpose was to take over the region, not unite with the people who already lived there. Ashmun himself wanted to establish an American community in Africa, and to seize African territory toward that purpose, which proved difficult because of ongoing opposition from the West Africans, who were experienced negotiators and not easily duped. The settlers eventually prevailed and gained control of the Liberian coast but not the interior.[30]

Fewer than 400 people had emigrated from the United States to Liberia by the time the Lynchburg Colonization Society was formed in 1825. An idealistic young Lynchburg newspaper editor, Richard Toler, helped found the local group. A native of Hanover County, Toler, 26, was not an enslaver, unlike most of the other local colonizationists. He'd come to town in the early 1820s to work for the newspaper.[31]

Toler shared some attitudes with Northern supporters of the movement, believing that colonization would benefit and uplift free Black Americans themselves, not just the Southern economy. He acknowledged in the 1825 announcement of the first meeting of the Lynchburg Colonization Society that the Black predicament was based on race, editorializing that free Black people were "cut off by a line of distinction, drawn by nature and stamped upon them." Toler wrote that granting equal rights to free Black people in Virginia was out of the question, but said they couldn't continue as they were, "always in a state of degradation far below their natures." He wrote that moving to Liberia could bring them rights and privileges they had no chance of ever gaining in Virginia. Toler acknowledged that "we virtually contradict what we do affirm" by practicing slavery while espousing that "all men are free and equal."[32]

His concerns weren't all altruistic and he feared rebellion, writing on July 4, 1825, about the revolution of the enslaved in Haiti who overthrew their French masters. "It is impossible to view the subject of slavery . . . without the most appalling fears. When considered in relation to themselves, their influence upon our manners, & the danger which is continually suspended over our heads, the hours of St. Domingo rush upon us with all their dreadful scenes of massacre, and blood and spoilation." That same day, he spoke about liberty during a July 4 celebration in Lynchburg that included a reading of the Declaration of Independence, a 13-gun cannonade salute, a parade, a barbecue at the Republican Springs, and a dinner on Diamond Hill featuring thirteen toasts to honor the colonies that rebelled against Great Britain. It was a lavish celebration of liberty in a place that denied it to nearly half its people but couldn't stop them from seeking it.[33]

Meanwhile, the growing town was developing close commercial ties with Northern cities, especially Baltimore. Provided it did not endanger their prosperity, Toler wrote a couple months later, Southern people were ready to embrace emancipation. He was expressing his own take on things, a contrarian position, much like commentators of today. But he also said Southern enslavement was no worse than what poor white people experienced, with a life to be preferred over that of an English working man. This, Northerners did not understand, Toler wrote, because they preferred to believe that slaveholders kept people in bondage for economic reasons. Wrong, Toler said, because "the few advantages to [slave] labor are more than counterbalanced by the host of evils they engender. Wherever they are, they . . . demoralize the character of the people." He was a white Virginian moving slowly toward an antislavery philosophy but never getting there, preferring the Southern notion that Black people held all the cards, unconcerned with where their next meal was coming from, well-clothed, working a moderate schedule with lots of free time to corrupt free Black people.[34]

Another young Lynchburg writer, Jesse Burton Harrison, also believed that slavery was bad for the South economically, and that colonization of Black Americans was worthy of consideration as a means of separating them from white people. The son of Jefferson's Lynchburg agent, he was a Zelig-like prodigy born in 1804 who spent summers at Monticello with Jefferson's nieces, attended Harvard Law School on Jefferson's recommendation, was a first cousin of ACS stalwart Henry Clay, interviewed James Madison at Montpelier, met Daniel Webster and Lafayette at Monticello, and interviewed Goethe in Germany. In 1826, he was the chief financial contributor to the Lynchburg Emigration Society, giving $138 of the $148 raised that year. His notes from his conversation with Madison at Montpelier in 1827 report that Madison "has often formed the plan of emancipating the slaves by a law setting free the new born children, the Gov't paying valuation for them the first year of their birth, the masters then to have their labor till 25 being bound to give them a little education. Thinks the national lands a proper fund for this purpose." That same year, Harrison delivered a long speech to the annual meeting of the Lynchburg Colonization Society, which was reprinted as the lead article in the September 1827 *African Repository.* He said Black people had been degraded by slavery and were better off in chains than they were as free men in Virginia, summing up a white conundrum. "Whether, then, we fear or loathe them—whether we feel compassion towards them, as a common feeling of humanity, or compunction [to those] we have cruelly injured, we must all desire to get rid of them and if possible make better their condition thereby." He gave another long speech at the annual meeting of the national society in Washington in 1828. Harrison said separation of the races would allow the United States to become "one homogenous nation." An intellectual, Harrison was likely familiar with the concept of one-race nationhood. In America, this meant that Black people would never become real Americans in the minds of white people. Burton Harrison, as his friends called him, gained a measure of national renown in 1832 when he wrote a widely circulated response to a defense of slavery. But after spending many months in Europe including a stint as a scholar at the University of Gottingen, he decided to leave Lynchburg, which he said was "overrun with a fanatical religious spirit" that foretold an "age of barbarism" and "holy Vandals." Around that time, Clay advised him to move to New Orleans which promised greater opportunity for a young lawyer. He edited a newspaper there before dying of yellow fever in 1841, and his son later became Jefferson Davis's private secretary.[35]

Virginia newspapers occasionally published boosterish reports of goings-on within the colonization movement and in Liberia. Toler's *Daily Virginian* inaccurately informed readers that relations between some of the early Virginia emigrants and neighboring tribes were peaceful, and that they suffered little from disease. He told the Lynchburg Colonization Society that he was "proud that the Free citizens of this Republic are about to . . . offer a 'doomed' people, a country." Of course, he meant they were doomed if they stayed in the US.[36]

Toler became the secretary of the Lynchburg Colonization Society when it was organized on Monday afternoon, Aug. 29, 1825, at the Reverend John Early's Methodist Church on Third Street (today's Court Street) near the courthouse. Lynchburg's economy had suffered in the financial Panic of 1819 but was recovering nicely. The city had grown beyond its original 45 acres, expanding to 12 numbered streets crossed by multiple smaller streets or alleys, encompassing nearly 140 blocks. Property owners along Second Street, today's Main, were required to build sidewalks, and the town had two theaters. Slavery had enabled this growth, but organizers now feared the enslaved and free people threatened the town's future. Lynchburg had already made a feeble attempt to forbid the buying and selling of slaves within the town limits, an ordinance that was repealed after city council learned it could regulate, but not ban, the sales.

Old John Lynch had died at age 80 in 1820. Toler and other members of the group that founded the Lynchburg Colonization Society were the town's second generation of leaders, with several in their 20s and 30s. They were a who's who of 1820's white Lynchburg. Several were ministers and teachers. Some had homes in town and plantations in the country, and their preoccupations of money, religion, tobacco and slavery set the tone for life in Lynchburg for the next century. Assessing their personal motivations is difficult. At best, they thought that their Black neighbors would be better off in a country that did not discriminate against them but did not consider abolishing slavery a viable alternative. Personal motivation aside, the effort to remove Black people from America was the primary driver for the emigration movement's support among white people. It was the reason, the heart of the whole movement, the cornerstone of the whole building. Everything else was based on this, regardless of what happened to these people after they were effectively banished from their own country. Concern for the enslaved people themselves, while not totally absent, was low on the list of Southern white motivations.

John Early, 39, had become Lynchburg's most prominent citizen by now, serving in various public and private offices. As his wealth and status increased, he came to support slavery, advocating a patronizing attitude toward the enslaved. He built a large house on the same street as his church and the courthouse and by 1820 owned a dozen people himself. His portrait depicts a stern, vigorous man in a stiff frock coat and wide clerical collar. In a commentary after he died, a Methodist memorialist wrote, "He felt that he was born to command, and that others were bound to obey." It's little wonder he was president of the new group, which functioned like the board of a non-profit today, with board members called "managers." Early was a local, but most others who gathered that day in 1825 had moved to Lynchburg from elsewhere in Virginia or the North, reflecting the town's rapid growth. Regardless of where they came from, almost all were enslavers yet progressive by the standards of the day, involved in efforts to improve the community, pushing for public schools and the creation of a public water system. They included five past, current, and future mayors, and, like Early, the two vice presidents were ministers. All were born during the Revolutionary era, and their words belied the impossible plan they were espousing. Did they really believe colonization could make even the slightest dent in the free Black population without forced expulsion? Their stated objective was straightforward: ". . . the Colonization of the Coast of Africa, with their own consent, of the free people of color of the United States." Their real goal was to help foster a movement that would remove all of the free Black people from the United States, in order to create a purer racial atmosphere, a homogenous one where no African Americans were free.[37]

Only a few Lynchburg white people freed any enslaved people and sent them to Liberia. One who did was William J. Holcombe, a 27-year-old Virginia native who had studied medicine in Philadelphia, where antislavery sentiment was strong. A manager of the local colonization group, he was often referred to as "the Rev. Dr. Holcombe." This honorific was literal. Practicing in Powhatan County, he was converted to Methodism at a camp meeting in the woods he happened upon on his medical rounds. Other family members were already in rapidly growing Lynchburg, where he met his wife at the ball given for Andrew Jackson. Holcombe moved to town and began preaching himself. He and other family members had brought slaves with them to Lynchburg, but gradually emancipated them, sending some to Liberia and Ohio over the next several decades. By the 1840s, Rev. Dr. Holcombe had evolved into an outright emancipationist, moving from Lynchburg to Indiana so that a large group of enslaved people he inherited could gain their freedom there.[38]

More typical of Southern colonization supporters were managers Elijah Fletcher and Dr. John J. Cabell, who came to rely more and more on slavery for their prosperity. Fletcher, 36, who had visited Jefferson on his way from Vermont to New Glasgow to teach school, once referred to slavery as "a curse on any country." But like the Southern masters from the North described by abolitionist George Bourne who was briefly his neighbor, Fletcher would go on to become one of the largest enslavers in the region. He married one of his students, inherited his father-in-law William Crawford's New Glasgow plantation and enslaved people, and moved to Lynchburg, where he became co-owner of the *Daily Virginian* with Toler in 1825. Although his portrait depicts an austere New Englander, he was mayor of Lynchburg twice in the 1830s, and by 1850, he and his son claimed as property 115 people, mostly on their Amherst County tobacco plantations.[39]

Cabell, son of a wealthy Buckingham County plantation owner, was said to be a polite, cultivated, determined man, interested in politics and an ardent supporter of President Jackson. He studied medicine in Philadelphia and was practicing in Lynchburg by 1801. In 1809 he built "the most imposing house in the city" atop a bluff on a lot purchased from John and Mary Lynch, near the corner of today's Fifth and Main streets. According to one story, he had French wallpaper hung there for Jackson's visit to the city. He also owned a farm outside town, and a salt manufacturing operation on the Kanawha River in today's West Virginia. The number of people he enslaved increased sharply during the 1820s, from six in 1820 to 50 in 1830.

James Newhall had moved to Virginia in 1814 from Lynn, Mass., and was another manager of the local colonization group. His Lynchburg shoe store was known for a life-sized sign of a Black youth pulling off a white man's shoes. In 1817, Thomas Jefferson bought what was likely his first pair of non-custom-made shoes from Newhall but returned them the next day because they didn't fit. By 1826, the Lynchburg Colonization Society had grown to 119 members, paying $1 each, and one lifetime member, paying $20. For the next few years, the Lynchburg colonizationists raised money—not much—made speeches, and wrote occasional newspaper articles. No one, free or enslaved, went to Liberia. That would change in 1829.[40]

3

The First to Leave

1829–1830

> I am going to a new country to settle my family and myself as agriculturalists; to a country where we shall at least be on a level with our fellow citizens; where the complexion shall be no barrier to fulfilling our most exalted station.
>
> —The Reverend George Erskine, aboard the *Liberia*, 1830

For two free men, the Reverend Joseph Turner of Virginia and the Reverend George Erskine of Tennessee, 1829 held the promise of a new epoch away from slavery.

Turner, from Bedford County, emigrated to Liberia on his own with his family, not as a recruit of the Lynchburg Colonization Society. He gained his freedom as young child in the Revolutionary era, when the Quakers banned members from owning slaves. As an adult, he was inspired by Lott Cary, the free Richmond man and early emigrant who once preached in Lynchburg. The enthusiastic Turner, already a licensed Presbyterian minister, was formally ordained on the deck of the *Harriet* in the Norfolk harbor in 1829, "to preach and administer the sacraments among his brethren in Africa." At the same time, his wife, Lucinda, along with three other emigrants, were recognized as a new Liberian Presbyterian church. The Turners' two young daughters accompanied them. The family was the first from the Lynchburg area and among only 205 people from the United States who emigrated in 1829. "We consider Joe a good man & and excellent Bible preacher & possessing ample powers of discriminating between what is and what is not true religion," Lynchburg's Thomas A. Holcombe wrote on behalf of three "Friends of Joseph Turner," who donated $90 to help the family. He didn't mention the local colonization group although his younger brother William was one of its managers. Had Turner remained near Lynchburg, his religious practice might have been curtailed when Virginia passed a law forbidding Black people from preaching or even holding church meetings absent white supervision.[1]

Another free minister, the Reverend George Erskine, bought his family out of slavery in eastern Tennessee and intended to leave for Liberia on the same 1829 voyage as the Turners. The ACS didn't give him enough time to get to Norfolk, so the family, including his mother who was born in Africa, was marooned in Lynchburg and stayed nearby for a year. He spent the time working for hire and preaching, writing vivid letters about life in a slave society as an outsider and free man of color.

Turner and Erskine would leave behind a city that was attracting national attention for its booming tobacco business and general prosperity. Diarist and gossip writer Anne Royall gushed: "The banks of the river are lined with towering trees; the enormous Sycamores, with their outstretched branches: to this we may add, freight boats, the skimming wild ducks, farms and pleasure grounds, falling gardens, rolling carts, rattling stages, thundering wagons, and a busy multitude; the long warehouses, the gay shops and elegant buildings . . ." Her report was an exaggeration, but Lynchburg had indeed become a trade and commercial destination for western Virginia. With roads in all directions, the James River, and mountain gaps, it attracted not only escaped slaves but also emigrants who could then travel to Richmond via wagon or bateau and down the James to the Norfolk docks.[2]

Ralph Gurley, a Yale graduate and Presbyterian cleric in Washington, DC, ran the ACS day-to-day in its early years. Erskine wrote him a letter from Lynchburg in the spring of 1829 as the family settled in for a long stay in Piedmont Virginia. Confident that God would provide, Erskine admitted he did not know by what means. He and his family were willing to work but the local white people didn't want to compensate them. That very day, he had been offered $2.50—a month—for farm labor. Even that meager amount was in doubt. "In this place, those of the family that can labour can get little or almost nothing for it. . . . It is not uncommon in these parts for white men to hire a free man of colour and a few days before the time is out fall out with them and drive them off without paying them." Erskine wanted to go to Africa to spread the gospel, but he also wanted to live as a citizen, something he could not achieve in the United States, no matter his ability and standing. Few of the local enslaved shared his dreams of Liberia: "We suffer most abuse from slaves [here] than we even did from white people where we came from. Which is indeed extremely disagreeable."[3]

Despite Black Americans' general opposition to colonization and its official goal of pushing only free Black people out, colonizers soon turned to coercion by including enslaved people freed on condition they emigrate. Some well-meaning Northerners believed this was the only way enslaved people could ever be free, but it also fueled Southern white fears that the colonization movement was an abolitionist ploy. The ACS required paperwork documenting the emigrants' status, and Erskine questioned Gurley about the convoluted legalisms. He wanted to know if the ACS would accept formerly enslaved emigrants as free citizens of Liberia with only a certificate or letter from their former masters allowing them to go, not a legal emancipation. The answer was unclear.

The 1830s marked the end of most Southern white male ambivalence about slavery, furthering the divide between North and South. The 1831 Nat Turner rebellion, along with the increasing value of the enslaved sold to cotton plantations in the Deep South, bolstered anti-freedom sentiment in white Virginia. A proposal for gradual emancipation failed several months later in the Virginia legislature and a legislator in Buckingham County east of Lynchburg attributed its narrow defeat to "The power of deep-rooted prejudice over the mind of man." Southern white religious denominations like Methodism which previously opposed slavery had already switched sides to support it. In Lynchburg, most of the Quakers had moved away. The Rev. George Bourne who once lived near Lynchburg had returned to the North and redoubled his antislavery activities, publishing an even more controversial version of his observations of Virginia slavery and helping found the American Anti-slavery Society. Northern Black leaders like Richard Allen and James Forten kept pushing abolition and opposing colonization.[4]

Some educated white women in Virginia would continue to support colonization and gradual emancipation for humanitarian reasons and because they saw slavery as morally wrong, something that corrupted not only their husbands and sons but also domestic life in general. Women of the Female Auxiliary Society of Fredericksburg had contributed $200 to the ACS in March 1829, nearly 30 percent of the total $698 the ACS received nationwide that month. Virginia women, many born during the Revolutionary period of 1780 to 1800, had to acknowledge, deal with, or ignore the licentiousness of husbands and sons who sexually assaulted enslaved women and then enslaved their own mixed-race children. Marie Tyler-McGraw wrote of these women, "In its degradation of master and slave in its inefficiency and recalcitrance, in its thwarting of moral and intellectual improvement, [they believed] slavery in Virginia was an evil that had to be ended by voluntary and gradual emancipation." Southern women did more than contribute money. Memoirs from the enslaved mention how white women and girls secretly taught them to read against the wishes of male masters. Born on Maryland's Eastern Shore on the Chesapeake Bay not far from Virginia, nine-year-old Frederick Douglass was taught to read in the 1820s by a white woman. Her husband forbade further instruction a couple years later, but by then seeds of independence within Douglass had been well-watered. "The more I read the more I was led to abhor and detest slavery, and my enslavers."[5]

In this era, Virginia had the most enslaved of any Southern state as well as the most emigrants to Liberia, free or enslaved. One of the early free emigrants, Jane Rose Waring, emigrated with her family as a child in 1824 from Petersburg, which had a large free Black population, and married another free emigrant, Joseph Jenkins Roberts from Norfolk, who went on to become Liberia's first president. Nearly 80 people from the Lynchburg

Jane Rose Roberts emigrated to Liberia from Petersburg, Virginia, and married Joseph Jenkins Roberts, a free merchant who would become the first president of Liberia. She was a close friend of Martha Erskine Harris Ricks, who spent part of her childhood in Lynchburg. (Daguerreotype collection, American Colonization Society, Library of Congress Prints and Photographs Division, Washington, DC, LC-DIG-ppmsca-18522)

area went to Liberia in 1829–30, including the Turners, the Erskines, and more than 50 free people from two families from Franklin County, recruited by the Lynchburg Colonization Society. Seven others were freed to emigrate by members of the local society. The influx from the Lynchburg area equaled 17 percent of the total 464 emigrants from the US for those two years. The colony in West Africa had been home to only about 1,000 Americo-Liberians the year before, infinitesimal compared to an estimated 250,000 West Africans. Nearly 800 emigrants were sent to Liberia from the US in 1832, a total never equaled in later years, although colonization would pick up some momentum in the 1850s.[6]

The early Americo-Liberians soon ventured beyond Monrovia, traveling up the broad, clear St. Paul's River into the tropical rainforest. They established small settlements including Caldwell, and Millsburg, which was about twenty miles upstream where rocks and rapids blocked farther passage. Most of the 1830 Lynchburg emigrants were assigned to Caldwell and future Lynchburg emigrants would also settle near the St. Paul's. West Africans used the river for trade and to bring inland captives to the coast. Dense foliage and tall trees draped with vines and colorful parasitic plants lined the high, broken banks, along with villages of thatched-roof houses set amid broad-leafed, pea-green plantain trees. Fish hawks flew over the river, and monkeys clattered in the trees. At night, the anopheles mosquitoes, nearly invisible, flitted everywhere, seeking their meals of human blood. Another bloodsucker, the tik-tik or tsetse fly, carried a disease that killed domestic cattle, oxen and horses. Wild cattle trod paths into the forest, and the locals used short cutlasses like machetes to hack their way through the undergrowth. Elephants sometimes tracked the muddy banks upstream, and the rainy season stretched from May to November. Timber was abundant, but the colonization society didn't consider sawmills along the river's tributaries a priority, meaning emigrants had to saw logs for their houses by hand.[7]

Monrovia was laid out only a few years before the Turners arrived, but Europeans had operated slaving stations in the region for hundreds of years. The year after the Turners came, a Spanish trader opened a slave factory forty-five miles north of Monrovia where he kept Africans kidnapped or captured in the interior for sale to European ship captains. Just coming into contact with Westerners raised the possibility of enslavement for Africans. In 1829, three Kru men were blown out to sea in a gale and picked up by an Argentine vessel, transferred to a British ship, and dropped off in Mobile, Ala., where they were apparently enslaved and sold by the port collector. By the time the ACS tried to send them back home, they had run away.[8]

Historians Marie Tyler-McGraw, Claude Clegg, and others have documented the mix of cultures, beliefs, trading practices and polities that Black Americans found in West Africa, "unaware and perhaps unconcerned that their presence was disruptive." As the Americans became more established over the years, they worked to disrupt some African cultural ways, including slave trading and religion. Simultaneously, they adapted to other West African cultures themselves, intermarrying, taking African children into their homes to raise, and depending on West Africans for rice and trade goods like palm oil, salt, and kola nuts. But the slave trade had grown dramatically for two centuries and by the nineteenth century was the foundation of Indigenous wealth. The Americo-Liberians eventually suppressed much of it within the borders of Libera, disrupting the economy of the region.[9]

When the Americans arrived, the Manding controlled the region's trade between the interior of Africa and the Atlantic coast, had a sizable army, and had formed their confederation with other Indigenous groups. The Manding had come into West Africa from the northeast in the late seventeenth and early eighteenth centuries, preceded by Muslim traders from the old Sahara kingdoms seeking coastal access. They mostly settled in the "hinterland," away from the coast, but by the early 1800s were living throughout the region. They impressed the American settlers with their tall, dignified appearance and commercial skills.[10]

It wasn't unheard of for a European ship captain to take a young African to Europe to learn the ropes of coastal commerce from another perspective, and Africans served aboard slave ships and other trading vessels. Sao Boso, who understood English, was known to the colonists as King Boatswain because it is likely he had filled that role on a British vessel. His Condo Confederation was headquartered at Bopolu, a trade nexus about fifty miles northeast of Monrovia. The early colonial traders marveled at its hundreds of clay-plastered circular houses topped by thatched roofs with overhangs to provide shade, a large mosque, a market, and clean, hard-packed streets as well as the hundreds of soldiers serving Sao Boso. In 1831, the colonial secretary mixed European and frontier imagery to call him "the Napoleon; of these wilds." Sao Boso and the Mandings sometimes helped the colonists, seeing them as allies against the often-hostile Dei, who would eventually be decimated by slaving. Sao Boso himself was a Manding, born in the Loma region of Guinea which overlapped Liberia, and raised by a Bandi. Some Manding spoke multiple languages and could read and write in Arabic. Their sophistication belied the colonization society's ethnocentric view of the region as one that needed to be "saved" by white civilization and Christianity.[11]

Generally friendly toward the colonists, Sao Boso held sway over much of the hinterland and was the most influential Indigenous slaver in the region. One story says Sao Boso had settled the original argument between the Dei and the Americans over the sale of land by telling the Dei that they had sold the land, received payment, and now must suffer the consequences. Still, Sao Boso's men attacked African towns throughout the colony and beyond, selling captives into slavery. His soldiers burned a Dei village on the St. Paul's not far from Monrovia a few months after the Turners arrived from Lynchburg in 1829.[12]

By then, the ACS had seized about 140 miles of African coastline, with eight settlements including those along the St. Paul's. The ACS grasp on the country was tenuous: A Richmond ACS agent insisted in 1829 that all future emigrants be sent immediately up the river to Millsburg to avoid the feverous coast, but the settlement lacked buildings suitable to accommodate emigrants. Some Virginians refused to locate there and instead were sent to Caldwell, where the Erskines settled. The American and African cultures along the St. Paul's were always blending, but a war broke out in 1832 after some Dei captives escaped just as they were about to be sold to Spanish slavers. They fled to the safety of a village of recaptive Africans under the protection of the colonists. In retaliation, Dei chiefs threatened to burn Caldwell and Millsburg, with soldiers coming out of the woods across the river, blowing war horns and firing muskets. The ACS agent dispatched a couple hundred recaptive Africans and Americo-Liberians, who attacked a Dei fort with much shooting but minimal loss of life and the Dei surrendered. Victories in skirmishes like these enabled continued trading by the emigrants who found buying, selling and bartering easier and more profitable than the agriculture promoted by the ACS, although they often had to employ Dei brokers to deal with Sao Boso and the Manding.[13]

In Monrovia, Lott Cary established a commercial trading business after he emigrated from Richmond. He was motivated by a desire for personal success, security, and wealth as much as he was by humanitarian concern for the enslaved, writes Tyler-McGraw in *An African Republic: Black and*

White Virginians in the Making of Liberia, although he saw Liberia as a better alternative than America for already-free Black people. Cary must have been an extraordinary person with a magnetic personality. *Encyclopedia Virginia* calls him a folk hero, one of the most famous Black men of the day, and he became the de facto leader of the Liberia colony in 1828 after a white ACS agent left. "He possessed an energy of thought, and a firmness of purpose, combined with the most inflexible integrity, which . . . could not fail to command the respect of all around him," wrote a white Richmond colonization supporter who also mentioned the multi-talented Cary's work as the colony's medic.[14]

When they sailed, the Turners did not know that Cary had just been killed in a gunpowder explosion as the colonists prepared to attack a French ship cruising off Monrovia in search of slaves. Richmond colonization advocate David Burr was relieved that the news of Cary's death wasn't received prior to the emigrants leaving, fearing it might have dissuaded them. Joseph Turner was associated with another free Black minister from Richmond, Joseph Shiphard, and they were among the leaders of their 1829 emigration. The national society agreed not to charge the *Harriet* emigrants for the passage itself, but Black people acting on their own like this troubled Burr, who urged Gurley to appoint a white committee to oversee who could go to Liberia.[15]

Before he died, Cary wrote frequently to friends and associates, "who have at last made up their minds to go and join him," reported a Williamsburg man who watched the Turners and many others leave Rocketts Landing on the James River near Richmond on January 18, 1829. The scene at Rocketts was emotional, a precursor of the 1865 mass departure from Lynchburg. It included speeches, prayers, preaching and hymn singing, with thousands watching the steamboats depart for Norfolk. Another eyewitness described the leave-taking later that day: "They were all hustle and bustle and movement, shaking hands, embracing and bidding farewell . . . to the numerous friends and acquaintances they were about to leave behind."[16]

The departure was a scramble. The ACS wanted to pack emigrant ships with as many people as possible but was often unable to coordinate sailing dates with emigrants' arrivals, so the *Harriet* sailed with room to spare. Still, the ship left Hampton Roads on Feb. 9, 1829, with 152 emigrants, many of whom, like Turner, could read and write. "Many . . . had long been free and had acquired considerable property, and took with them a very liberal supply of provisions, household furniture, tools, and agricultural implements, and articles for trade," claimed the *African Repository,* the ACS journal. Actually, almost a third of the emigrants had been freed only if they agreed to go to Liberia. All were allowed the equivalent of two barrels of baggage each and had to pay an additional fee for any excess. In Norfolk, the *Harriet* was loaded with forty-two barrels of beef and pork, twelve barrels of flour, thirteen barrels of corn meal, two hogsheads of molasses from the West Indies, one box of cotton, one box of hardware, one box of crockery, seeds, Bibles and sewing materials, along with the emigrants' mattresses, which they used as berths. The ACS also shipped a sawmill but packed the blade between two boards and it was never unloaded in Liberia.[17]

Histories of the colonization movement stress how ill-equipped the colonists were. While they could trade for food or grow it themselves, they generally lacked even the simplest of manufactured items: nails, tools, cloth. For this voyage, one of two in 1829, the ACS provided ten hoes and thirteen axes, hardly sufficient for even a few families trying to clear raw bush and forest, and only one cask of nails. Nonetheless, an ACS agent bragged that the ship carried a large variety of tools and possessions, claiming they had been paid for by the emigrants themselves. Statements like this reassured Southern enslavers that the Black people weren't receiving an excess of charity. The ACS took full credit for the emigration even though it was mostly organized, except for chartering the ship, by the free community of Richmond.[18]

Among the onlookers dockside in Norfolk, the dangers of emigrating to Liberia were well-known. One white man commented that anyone seeing the emigrants boarding the *Harriet* without knowledge of the facts would think, "There goes another boat load for Georgia." But the 1829–30 *Harriet* emigration was an important one in Liberian history. It included two future presidents of Liberia: Joseph Jenkins Roberts, then twenty-one, who became the country's first president; and James S. Payne, ten, who was president twice, in the 1860s and 1870s. Both were freemen. Also aboard was Abdul Rahman Ibrahima, a nineteenth-century celebrity. He was an African emir and soldier in what is now Guinea when he was captured and sold into slavery in the late eighteenth century. He labored in the American South for forty years until he became somewhat of a cause célèbre after managing to contact relatives back home. He was known as "the Moorish Prince" because he wrote in Arabic, and his plight was covered extensively in the newspapers, with abolitionist financier Arthur Tappan of New York convincing the ACS to get involved.[19]

The *Harriet* arrived in Liberia in March 1829. They found colonists who were "a comely and well-formed race of [American] negroes, neat and clean in their persons, modest and civil in their manners, and regular and comfortable in their dwellings," according to a boosterish 1831 history by William Innes, a minister who based his work on pamphlets sent to him by an unnamed Virginian, letters, the diary of an early colonial agent, and ACS reports. He acknowledged that newcomers generally fell ill, and some died, but nonetheless declared the colony a complete success. The second edition of his book, published in 1832, included upbeat letters from George Erskine and Joseph Shiphard, Turner's Richmond associate.[20]

Shiphard wrote a more realistic account of life and death in Liberia in 1829, noting that the situation there was not as advertised, although he remained hopeful. He said that some of the emigrants who had arrived the previous year had been put out of their house by the society's agents to make room for more recent arrivals and refused rations from the public store. Shiphard listed recent deaths, touched on colonial politics, and apologized for the disjointed nature of his letter, blaming it on the fever, before detailing his need for a seine, twine, and corks for fishing. Beef and pork were very expensive, and the rivers were full of fish, but the colonists had no fishing tackle. Shiphard wanted a debt he said the ACS owed him paid in nails and requested that a nail-cutting machine be sent to the colony to help the colonists support themselves. He wrote that his wife was initially "disgusted on coming here," but became more content after he acquired a small house. "If gentlemen would build houses and furnish houses and one year's subsistence for the emancipated sent here, our population would increase three times as fast as hitherto . . . new comers suffer ten times as much at the Cape as at St. Paul's or they would higher up the river [near] the fresh water and high vegetable lands." A schoolteacher back in Richmond, Shiphard also requested a spelling book, a reading book, quills, ink, slates, and lead pencils.[21]

Public image, not pencils, was paramount with the ACS's leadership. This involved satisfying conflicting desires from slaveholders in the South and abolitionists in the North, an impossible task. The society did not regard the lives of the individual Black people as particularly important, so their needs took a backseat to the politics of emigration. It exaggerated successes to its white sponsors and blamed all shortcomings on the

Black people themselves. The ACS often quoted emigrant ship captains as authorities, although they were part of the apparatus of colonization and had a vested interest in promoting the colony.

Turner and Shiphard arrived in a Monrovia that looked like a rural American town, with brick and stone public buildings and frame houses set along grassy streets. Monrovians were trading for rice with the West Africans when not skirmishing with them, making Shiphard worry about the town's lack of fortification. Fortunately, he wrote, the local West Africans, probably the Dei, were themselves on the run from another ethnic group, probably the Vai or Manding. The colony was also under occasional threat from Spanish, French, and even illegal American slavers. These slavers set sail for West Africa with the stated purpose of trading supplies to the Liberians but were actually buying enslaved captives at the nearby factory. They made port at Monrovia, where they could extort high prices for their goods from needy settlers. A Richmond agent detailed the slaver activity to ACS leader Ralph Gurley, cautioning that it was not to be made public. Among Virginians promoting missionary work in Liberia, the situation was no secret. "The papers have filled me with the most painful apprehensions . . . of our poor emigrants. . . . Truly the malediction of Heaven seems to be upon their devoted hearts," wrote one.[22]

A 1731 woodcut published in Amsterdam showing a small African settlement at Cape Mesurado, near today's Monrovia, including a kitchen, a residence, a small clay hut, a public square, and a covered meeting place. Indigenous groups traded with Europeans for centuries before Liberia was colonized. (Maisons des Negres du Cap Mezurado, K. De Putter, engraver; The Library Company of Philadelphia, 1691.D)

This malediction did not spare the *Harriet* emigrants. Joseph Turner, the first Lynchburg-area emigrant, was also the first from Lynchburg to die. Fever hit the *Harriet* emigrants hard, and immediately. A total of twenty-six were dead less than a month after landing, primarily from malaria contracted from the abundant *anopheles* mosquitoes. Never short on flowery language, the Lynchburg Colonization Society memorialized Turner at its Aug. 1, 1829 annual meeting: ". . . the Rev. Joseph Turner, a man of colour, late of the county of Bedford, hath departed this life since his arrival at the colony of Liberia; Resolved, that this society bearing in mind his worth, high respectability and distinguished virtue while living, do deeply deplore the loss of the deceased, and sincerely sympathize with his surviving relatives, and also with the Colonists at Liberia, for the loss they have sustained in his death." Turner's older daughter, Harriet, died of a "diseased brain" when she was 19, in 1836. But his wife and youngest daughter survived: The first Liberian census in 1843 lists Lucinda Turner as remarried and working as a washerwoman in Monrovia. Living with her and her second husband was the Turners' daughter Elizabeth, now a teenager who had learned to read.[23]

The ACS blamed the mortality on the colonists themselves, saying they did not take enough time to recover from the fever, and ate too much fruit, especially pineapple, which upset their stomachs. Prince Abdul Rahman Ibrahima died on July 6, his children still enslaved in Mississippi, his brother now a king in central Africa. The ACS mourned him but criticized him for waiting too long to seek medical assistance after he was stricken with diarrhea. The *African Repository* claimed that deaths in Liberia were simply the price of exploration of a "barbarous shore" and, in one of its boldest falsehoods, said the colonists regarded the deaths as "nothingness, compared with the surpassing object of Africa's redemption." The *Harriet* brought the news of the deaths of Joseph Turner and many others on its return to Norfolk. The ship's skipper pronounced himself optimistic, maintaining the colonists were "steadily advancing to higher destinies." Perhaps he meant in Heaven, not on earth, for Liberia had proven itself no paradise.[24]

Richmond emigrant Gilbert Hunt, who emigrated with the Turners, was so dissatisfied that he returned home about a year later. Hunt said the state of agriculture in the colony was poor and that Monrovia was unhealthy for old and new emigrants. His accurate reports helped curb the colonization movement among Richmond's free Black people. Even the local ACS agent advised new emigrants not to spend a single night in Monrovia, but instead to go immediately up the St. Paul's to Millsburg, which was even less prepared to receive them than Monrovia. Hunt, a 45-year-old blacksmith, couldn't find work in Monrovia: The ACS had touted iron as abundant, but it was rarely mined, and he proceeded to advise other African Americans not to emigrate. "A complete croaker," commented Burr, a Richmond Colonization Society manager. "He has done his utmost to prejudice the mind of the colored free among us."[25]

But Hunt's eyewitness report helped convinced Burr that what the ACS was doing for the Virginia emigrants was inadequate. He wrote that if enslavers wanted to send people to Africa, they needed to have houses built and ready for emigrants in Millsburg, and to provide clothing for one year. Burr, who owned a Richmond foundry, also advocated supplying them with agricultural implements, and enough money to buy a year's worth of rice. He didn't push very hard for this because most Virginia enslavers were unwilling to contribute anything, considering the loss of their human property sacrifice enough.[26]

A few ACS officials in routine contact with the emigrants were not so cynical and wished them well. But any seeming sincerity from the white people paled in comparison with that of Black emigration proponents like Turner and the Reverend George Erskine who were willing to stake the lives of their families on their future liberty. Erskine was well-known in eastern Tennessee, where antislavery sentiment was stronger than in Virginia. The mountainous region also had fewer enslaved people than Virginia, and more tolerance for free Black people thanks to the influence of local Quakers and Presbyterians. Erskine was purchased out of slavery in 1815 by the Union Presbytery of East Tennessee for $450. Although he was a grown man who could read and write, his owner described him in the bill of sale as a "negro boy." Trained for the ministry by the founder of what later became Marysville College, Erskine was licensed to preach in 1818. He traveled and preached to mixed audiences in Tennessee and other states in the 1820s and was able to earn and raise enough money to buy his wife, Hagar, and children out of slavery. He once had a white congregation and was formally ordained as a Presbyterian minister the year before he emigrated. A white minister who heard Erskine preach in Tennessee wrote: "He was received by Presbyterians with the consideration due to a gospel minister, ate at the table with the families where he lodged, and slept in the best bed. . . . I remember his lofty bearing in the pulpit; and how white people hung upon his oratory, as he proclaimed the everlasting gospel. He preached with great fervor and fine command of language; often with tears streaming down his black cheeks, as he dwelt on the love of Jesus in dying to redeem the lost."[27]

Most records mentioning Erskine say he was "sent" to Liberia as a missionary by Union Presbytery, implying that the Presbyterians somehow helped him get there. Actually, Erskine decided to emigrate with his family and made the arrangements himself. The church contributed little to his efforts to get to Africa other than authorizing him to work as a missionary once he arrived. His family sailed on the *Liberia*, chartered by the Pennsylvania Colonization Society, the nation's most active. The ACS touted his determination in its journal, referring to his purchase as a "ransom" payment, a term often used by abolitionists: "Mr. Erskine is a highly respected and intelligent and Coloured Minister of the Presbyterian Church, who, a few years ago, was, with his entire family, in slavery. His correct and exemplary character, recommended him to the benevolent notice of the Rev. Dr. [Isaac] Anderson, of Maryville; who assisted by several other individuals, obtained his ransom, and for three years supported him and gave him instruction in the doctrines and duties of our holy religion. . . . [he] has resolved to emigrate to Liberia, in the hope he may there do something to rescue his unenlightened brethren from their superstitions, crimes and miseries, and to conduct them to the knowledge of the true God . . ."[28]

Erskine chided ACS chief Ralph Gurley for not notifying him in time to get to the coast from Tennessee: "You knew I was at a distance of five hundred miles from the port." Erskine had hired a wagon to take his family to Norfolk only to arrive in Lynchburg too late to complete the journey. "I made considerable sacrifice . . . we suffered a great deal . . . on our way to this place . . . we are in a land of strangers." Marooned in Lynchburg, Erskine made clear to Gurley that he wanted a place on the next ship for himself and his family, including his mother, Martha, who was born on the Gold Coast southeast of Liberia; his wife; seven children, and two young men. He acknowledged that despite all the disappointment, his family was well and signed his letter, "Yours in friendship."[29]

From Lynchburg, Erskine soon developed a network of white friends in the Virginia ministry. Pleading his case, he corresponded with a northern Virginia colonization agent who was also a Presbyterian minister and missionary, telling him: "White people are dispose[d] to give very small or low wages to free people of Color, which makes our passage here the more difficult." Erskine said it was all his family could do to support itself in Bedford County while awaiting the next ship, let alone purchase necessities for their eventual emigration. "For aid of this kind we are . . . dependent on a generous public." But the local public wasn't generous. By now not only the Black population of Virginia but many of the white people, who did not want to lose their enslaved and feared that the ACS was abolitionist, were ill-disposed toward colonization. Erskine said colonization had become so unpopular around Lynchburg that he was exposing himself to abuse even to speak of it. When Lynchburg colonizationists distributed 200 pamphlets written by a women's colonization group in Fredericksburg, they reported that people were either unaware of colonization or that it sparked violent prejudice. The white people wanted to keep the enslaved in place, knowing the Southern economy depended on them, and Black Americans had little desire to leave where they had lived for generations.[30]

Nevertheless, Richard Toler, the Lynchburg editor and colonizationist, claimed in December 1829 that as many as 100 local free people of color were interested in emigrating. Several local masters had mentioned freeing their enslaved if the colonization society would immediately pay to send them to Liberia, and colonization was discussed at the first Virginia Conference of Methodists, held in Lynchburg that year. The denomination had not yet fully segregated, so Erskine attended and reported that several of his brethren were anxious to emigrate. Inspired by the *Harriet* emigration, a free man from Petersburg was convinced that Liberia "was the only asylum offered us at present."[31]

Ralph Gurley tried to arrange for the Erskines to emigrate in the summer of 1829 but again could not manage to notify them in time. Erskine had just received a job offer, two months' work as a missionary about fifty miles east of Lynchburg in Prince Edward County, at the "handsome compensation" of $50 per month, quite a contrast with the paltry wages he was offered for farm labor in Bedford. "But my dear sir, understand me," Erskine wrote, "I do not mean to let any consideration prevent us from going in the [next] vessel . . ." He asked for reassurance that moving to Prince Edward would not interfere: "It would make very much against us to remain in this Country through the winter." Erskine continued traveling to preach, speaking in Richmond where his audience included influential Petersburg colonization agent William Atkinson, who afterwards urged the ACS to pay for the Erskines' emigration. At the same time, the energetic Erskine was also corresponding with someone in Boston to procure Bibles for distribution in Africa. He also wanted 25 or 30 spelling books for his son, Hopkins, and daughter, Martha, to use to teach English. "They both spell and read well," he wrote, and would be able to instruct others in grammar, geography, and arithmetic. He suggested that Gurley might write him in care of Hampden-Sydney College or the Prince Edward courthouse with word of "your next outfit" for Liberia and asked for at least twenty days' notice.[32]

Erskine was not dissuaded by the deaths of the recent emigrants, which he likely heard about in August 1829 when the Lynchburg paper published its brief report on Joseph Turner. He went to Richmond again in October to press his case, spoke at the First Presbyterian Church, and called on the treasurer of the Richmond colonization group. In November, Lynchburg colonizationist, newspaper publisher and enslaver Elijah Fletcher weighed in on Erskine's behalf with Gurley, saying that the family now had enough money to defray its own expenses. The Erskines had moved again, this time to the New London area of Campbell County near Lynchburg. Always courteous, Erskine apologized for pestering Gurley but wrote that his desire to emigrate had grown even stronger, involving an "anxiety . . . to preach a crucified savior." He had learned that a Presbyterian minister was needed in Liberia, where current Baptist and Methodist clergy were "ignorant, uninformed, selfish, worldly minded men."[33]

By now, the ACS was planning the January 1830 voyage of a leased ship renamed *Liberia* that would take the Erskines, finally, to West Africa. Petersburg's Atkinson, one of the most active colonization agents in Virginia, urged the parent society to make sure the family had a place on the upcoming voyage. Atkinson believed helping the Erskines might convince doubters that the society was concerned with promoting Christianity, not just deporting Black people. He said that while the Lynchburg society had been a strong supporter, few emigrants had come from Lynchburg and locals felt they were owed the passage of Erskine and family at the parent society's expense. Finally, the ACS agreed. The departure date left the Erskines barely enough time to sail before Liberia's rainy season, meaning that carving out an existence would be even more difficult.[34]

Despite months of planning, the departure of the Erskines' ship was a hurried, last-minute affair. By the Jan. 10, 1830, date set for sailing, only about thirty passengers had reached Norfolk, including one Tidewater man and his wife who had just managed to purchase themselves and their three daughters, and were still trying to purchase their son. Along with three other Lynchburg people, the Erskines finally reached Norfolk and boarded the *Liberia* on Jan. 14. It sailed two days later with only fifty-eight emigrants. Also aboard was the colony's new physician and assistant colonial agent, who mentioned that the Erskines had arrived and that all the emigrants had been warmly welcomed in Norfolk. How warm the welcome was is questionable: Lynchburg bricklayer Robert Fields, a free man of color, changed his mind about emigrating at the last minute and found work with some Norfolk masons but had problems with his free papers. When the ACS agent in charge of the voyage found out, he arranged for Fields to be jailed until the next departure. Likely saying what he knew the agent wanted to hear, Fields told him he was now willing to go. Did he? He's not listed in the next ship's records.[35]

The first 10 days of the Erskines' voyage were rainy. The emigrants saw a whale, sharks, and flying fish, but many became seasick on a ration of mostly biscuit and dried beef. The captain suggested that future emigrants receive a better diet including corn meal, fish, molasses, plenty of potatoes—and no whiskey. During the voyage, Erskine preached each Sunday, "sermons that would have been listened to with pleasure by any Christian audience," wrote the ship's captain. He queried Erskine about his views on emigration, to which he replied, "I am going to a new country to settle my family and myself as agriculturalists; to a country where we shall at least be on a level with our fellow citizens; where the complexion shall be no barrier to fulfilling our most exalted station. I shall cultivate the land assigned me by the colonization society, and if [it] please God to spare my life, shall be always ready to do good as opportunity offers."[36]

After a few weeks in Monrovia, the *Liberia* emigrants were sent upriver to Caldwell where they were to receive their land on the banks of St. Paul's. Property around Caldwell, mostly forest and bush country, was reputed to be especially fertile. But more than a few emigrants viewed their new liberty in part as freedom from the field labor of American slavery. Dr. John Anderson, arriving with the Erskines, described a lack of energy among Americo-Liberians in general, and said most who could get items to trade with the Africans, such as tobacco, cloth, or rum, depended on that instead of farming. Trade was tempting and Erskine himself wrote, "Was I at Virginia, and had five hundred dollars to lay out at Richmond I could, in a short time, convert it into a fortune here." Still, once he had cleared his land, farming should be good, Erskine reported, and Caldwell seemed healthy with a sea breeze from two directions.[37]

"Never did I feel so much like a freeman as I have since I came here," Erskine wrote. "I would heartily recommend to every freeman of colour, to leave the United States for Liberia—and any one that wishes to do well; particularly those who have a little property." He was also looking forward to the prospects of preaching, with a "large field for the labours of a gospel minister." Still, the key to Liberia's eventual nationhood, Erskine believed, was not religion or business or agriculture, but education, something the enslaved were denied in the US. The Presbyterian Synod of Richmond was collecting money to build a small school and chapel in Caldwell for Erskine, who wrote, "The thing most to be deplored in this colony, is the want of a good school, and an enlightened teacher for poor children, whose parents cannot school them; for, in this tropical country, where there is an abundance of Gold, Ivory . . . Coffee, and Sugar, Indigo, and many other lucrative fruits, we could have an enlightened Christian community." He reported that only seventeen of his shipmates could read their Bibles.[38]

Erskine himself was immediately regarded as a very important Americo-Liberian, and the ACS urged him to confine himself to preaching and teaching and withstand the temptation to make money from trade. For his part, Erskine hoped that Liberia would grow into a country where emigrants from America could establish plantations employing West Africans and recaptives, grow crops that could be marketed, and trade goods on the international market.

One of Erskine's letters was so positive that it was published almost immediately by the ACS in a pamphlet touting the virtues of colonization. The Lynchburg colonization society helped pay for 3,000 copies, which were distributed around the country for use by ministers in their July 4, 1830, sermons. The pamphlet also reprinted a boosterish letter from Shiphard, the former Petersburg school teacher who had come over with the Turners and said privately Liberia was not as advertised. He survived his bout with fever and had just returned from an expedition exploring the countryside. He said that with "a trifling sacrifice for liberty," his brethren back home would become "lords of this fertile land, and masters of this majestic stream," and went on to extol the virtues of his 18-inch cabbage plants, "as sweet as the best I ever saw in the Richmond market." This pamphlet and the sermons it spawned turned out to be mildly successful in increasing contributions, if not emigrants, and small donations flowed from ministers around the country in the months following July 4.[39]

One donation from a church in Candor, NY, was accompanied by a horrific suggestion to speed the elimination of slavery in the US: castration of the enslaved. This would put a definite end to the "natural increase" which was producing more Black Americans as the years passed, wrote William Bacon. He suggested that the practice begin in Virginia, with the emasculation of all male Black youngsters. Then, other states could follow Virginia's lead while the colonization society deported all the free Black people, and "America would be well rid of her black population." This letter was so grotesque that I first wondered if its intent was sarcasm, but Bacon was serious and said he did not expect "high-minded philanthropists" to solve the problem, urging Gurley to forward the idea to the ACS board. Suggesting that the cruelty suffered by the enslaved every day was worse than that which would be suffered by the emasculated youngsters, he also claimed no "individual" would be harmed, meaning no white enslavers would lose any money by giving up their current slaves.[40]

Solutions like this were one reason Erskine was glad to be out of the United States. But despite his cheery letters from Liberia, he also acknowledged that everything in this new land was contingent on simply staying alive. This was often impossible in Caldwell, which was revealing itself to be a malarial nightmare, as bad as Monrovia. Malaria causes protracted suffering via debilitating fevers, where the victim seems to improve every other day, but eventually is weakened to the point of death. Even without the deadly mosquitoes, day-to-day living was hard. "Carved from mangrove swamps and dense woodlands, life in Caldwell was overwhelmingly rural, arduous and monotonous," writes Claude A. Clegg III in *The Price of Liberty—African Americans and the Making of Liberia.*[41]

Reality, and the fever, might take months to settle in. Surviving the arduous voyage, and the prospect of freedom and liberty, cast a temporary glow over some emigrants' first letters home. Arriving in Caldwell with the Erskines were Mars and Jesse Lucas, brothers from Loudoun County in Northern Virginia. By June, Mars Lucas was thoroughly disillusioned. Recovering from the fever which had already killed his brother's wife, he wrote to their former master that everything he'd been told about the country was a lie. Some Caldwell residents were making no effort to clear land or build houses, preferring to trade with the Africans and live day to day. Jesse Lucas pleaded with his former master not to send any of his relatives to Liberia. He was homesick, wanted to know the latest goings-on with his loved ones in Virginia, "white and colored," and offered to send a young white friend a pet monkey.[42]

Erskine remained hopeful in the spring of 1830, despite facts that were becoming apparent. He cited a lack of sickness, at the same time noting that 13 or 14 of his fellow emigrants had climate fever and that he hoped God would spare his own life. But later that month his wife, Hagar, and a daughter died of the fever, which also killed the colonial physician. More than half of the emigrants from the *Liberia* would die within a year. In the summer of 1830, Erskine himself had only partially recovered from his own bout with fever when he visited Millsburg, suffered a relapse, and died. The colony desperately needed educated, vigorous emigrants like Erskine, and the colonial agent noted that his death was great calamity.[43]

In the official ACS record, Erskine is listed not as a fever victim but as a casualty of prescribing to himself. Never missing a chance to blame the emigrants for their own demise, the ACS described Erskine's last days: "The season has been uncommonly unhealthy . . . we have lost a considerable number . . . many of these have fallen victim to their own imprudence. Mr. Erskine, after partially recovering from the fever, contrary to all the advice of his friends, [took] a jaunt to Millsburg; on his return, he got wet, which threw him into a relapse, from which he never recovered." Despite Erskine's importance to the colony, the ACS was not interested in dwelling on Liberian misfortunes when it was trying to raise money from white Americans and convince Black Americans to emigrate there.[44]

By the end of the year, the rest of his group had also died, except for three young people: Martha Erskine, 13, her brother Hopkins W. Erskine, 10, and a Tennessee friend of the family, Sion Harris, 19, who emigrated with them and later married Martha. They would all go on to become prominent citizens of Liberia. The Reverend George Erskine's mother was 71 in 1830 and only survived long enough to return to her native continent. Three other family members died from fever, one drowned, and another was listed as a casualty of "going into the country." Lynchburg's Jane Holcombe, 25, who also traveled aboard the *Liberia,* died of fever. Plymouth, 29, and Francis Reid, 25, of Lynchburg lived. Francis died of a "wound" in 1840 but nothing more is known about the couple. They were the lucky ones, unlike members of the free Mars and Crockett families from Franklin County west of Lynchburg. They had just begun to arrive in Caldwell when George Erskine died.[45]

4

The Graveyards Always Look Fresh

1829–1839

> Go back to Lynchburg, pay back the 300 dollars, the price of blood, and set the woman free . . . and then you may talk of the love of God.
>
> —The *Liberator,* 1832

THE LIMITED support for colonization and emigration from Piedmont Virginia withered among both races in the 1830s as slavery became more entrenched. The rise of abolitionism infuriated many white Virginians, and the fear of Black revolt, accelerated by the 1831 Nat Turner rebellion, frightened them. Virginia's legislature flirted with the idea of gradually outlawing slavery, but the measure failed, and colonization was increasingly seen by former Southern supporters as a scheme to free the enslaved and support abolition, not just to expel them from the country and Christianize Africa. Enjoying the rising value of the Lynchburg enslaved who could be sold South, many white people dug in their heels to preserve enslavement as a core value of their society. Inflamed by abolitionist pamphlets arriving at the city post office in 1835, they held a public meeting to double down on the authoritarianism and racial prejudice that kept free and enslaved Black people under their control. By now, the white churches in Lynchburg all supported slavery, which was practiced by white Baptists, Presbyterians, Episcopalians and Methodists alike. Slavery had pushed Quakers out of the faith or to Ohio.

But as the decade began, the Methodists and Presbyterians who led the Lynchburg Colonization Society were still optimistic and pushed the large emigration of more than 50 free people of color from Franklin County. Mosquitos and the harsh Liberian environment soon killed nearly all of them, leaving only two little boys and an elderly woman alive a year later. The ACS tried to suppress this tragic news, only to be outwitted by a Black businessman in Philadelphia and a white abolitionist from Boston. The deaths of the free Mars and Crockett families were particularly poignant because many of them were descended from a Black Revolutionary War soldier who had owned a 100-acre farm in Franklin County. Another grandfather, Hercules Mars, had been free since at least 1788. They were among about 47,000 free Black people living in Virginia in 1830. Emigrating with the more than forty members of the Mars family were fourteen Crocketts, also free, led by their mother, Polly Crockett, a weaver. After learning that the families might be interested in Liberia, the Lynchburg Colonization Society roused itself to hold a special meeting, send three envoys to Franklin County, and act as go-between with Ralph Gurley, manager of the ACS in Washington.[1]

The Mars and Crockett families lived and farmed in the Blue Ridge Mountains near the headwaters of the Blackwater River, about sixty miles southwest of Lynchburg, not far from today's Blue Ridge Parkway. Named for Benjamin Franklin, it had been a starting point for eighteenth-century "long hunters" seeking game and furs in western lands still controlled by Indians. About 30 percent of the nearly 15,000 residents were enslaved. Brothers Benjamin and George Mars, and Polly Crockett, were among twenty-two free Black people, eight of them women, listed in the census as heads of a household there.[2]

Franklin County residents, Black and white, knew Lynchburg well. The well-off sold their tobacco and produce there, shopped, and traveled the James River to Richmond. The less-well-off were bought, sold, and separated from their families at downtown slave stands, one near the Franklin Hotel. Commerce like this had helped Lynchburg rebound after the national financial panic hit the town's over-extended wealthy people hard in 1819. By 1829, the city boasted an astounding four grocery stores, as well as eleven hardware stores, eighteen dry goods stores, a brass foundry, three shoe stores, and five saddle shops. Shoppers could patronize five milliners, two booksellers and six tailors, fifteen lawyers and eighteen physicians. A large fleet of bateaux "employed" hundreds of hands, mostly enslaved Black people but some free, to haul tobacco, flour and other cargo to Richmond via the James River. The crews gambled and visited prostitutes dockside in what became Lynchburg's notorious Buzzard's Roost neighborhood. The reality of slavery contrasted with the harmony of the landscape—mountains, fields, forests, rivers—that pleased visitors. "In point of scenery, [Lynchburg] is far beyond Richmond, and very little behind it in business," wrote Anne Royall. But her white sensibilities were offended as she headed south out of town: "The little huts, crammed with shabby dressed negroes, is a great drawback to the pleasure of the traveler." A visiting Quaker minister from Ohio commented in 1830 that the town was probably at its most prosperous, predicting that trade would inevitably decline as more and more fields gave up their nutrients and could no longer nurture the golden leaf.[3]

Word that a large free family from Franklin County wanted to emigrate reached the Lynchburg colonizationists in late 1829. Richard Toler, the Lynchburg *Daily Virginian* editor and secretary of the Lynchburg Colonization Society, alerted Ralph Gurley in Washington, adding that other people from Lynchburg also wanted to go. Boasting that "many warm and efficient (white) friends have put their hand to the plough and will not look back," he also told Gurley that "almost violent and unfounded prejudice" against colonization prevailed in some neighborhoods. The Mars and Crockett emigrations, on two separate voyages, were financed by the national group and donations from Philadelphia, not Lynchburg.[4]

Records are scanty on the Crocketts, but the Mars brothers and their wives left behind deep roots in Virginia. They had been paying taxes in Franklin County for decades. Benjamin Mars, 49, and his wife, Margaret Saunders Mars, 46, had been married for 26 years. George Mars, 46, a shoemaker, had been married for 22 years to Elizabeth Beverly Mars, 44, the daughter of Sylvester "Sill" Beverly. Beverly was a free man of mixed race who owned 126 acres of land in Franklin County in 1822 when he petitioned for a pension for his service in the American Revolution. What convinced a stable family that had been in place for generations, owned property, and was not enslaved, to leave Virginia for the unknown via the colonization society? Pioneering Black historian Luther Porter Jackson wrote in 1939, "Ranking above all the others in condemnation of the free Negro was the American Colonization Society." But anticolonization sentiment was weaker among rural Black people because of their limited access to accurate information, particularly from returnees. They did not receive as much word-of-mouth news as people living in Lynchburg or Richmond, although the Great Wagon Road, called the Carolina Road in Virginia, passed through Franklin County. It brought Americans pushing south and west along the Valley of Virginia, among them the Dunkards, a small religious sect that did not support slavery. Several hundred Dunkards settled in Franklin and founded churches there. Perhaps the Franklin County families heard about the promise of freedom in Liberia from the Dunkards, or other travelers on the Carolina Road, or from the Lynchburg or Richmond newspapers.[5]

Abraham Mars, 50, who led the first group of emigrants, was a farmer with some education and was quite intelligent, wrote Toler. He may have intended that comment to elevate Mars above other Black people, but what did the word "intelligent" mean to free Black people? Scholar Molefi Kete Asante explored this in an essay that illuminates what Abraham Mars may have been thinking as he sought his own identity not centered on life in a racist society. "There are several laws of intelligence. One is to have a clear sense of one's situation—psychological, social, economic, cultural, and spiritual. The second law of intelligence is to have a healthy sense of self," Asante wrote.[6]

Targeted at idealistic free Black Americans, ACS marketing materials echoed sermons about Christian salvation that justified suffering and danger on earth in hopes of eventual glory in heaven: "The inhabitants of Liberia will trace the history of the American Colonization Society, down to their own greatness, as we trace the history of our own country from the settlers of Jamestown and the pilgrims of Plymouth."[7] Discerning the Franklin County families' motivation is difficult because they left no letters or accounts that survived in ACS records. In 1830s Virginia, the fact that Abraham Mars was smart, free, and owned property paled in comparison to the prejudice he faced as the state put more restrictions on Black people. The desire for citizenship and the chance for a better life, especially for their children, had an overwhelming appeal to some free emigrants. Nearly 30 of the Mars and Crocketts were children or teenagers, and emigrants often mentioned wanting their children to grow up in a free country.

The departure of the first Mars ship, the *Montgomery*, involved much dithering by the ACS bureaucracy, and the first group of Mars emigrants initially had to turn around on their way to Lynchburg and go back home. Their ship finally sailed from Philadelphia to Norfolk in late April 1830. Signing a contract to lease the ship at the last minute, the ACS had little time to procure supplies for emigrants, who were always ill-equipped. The Philadelphia agent managed to ship four boxes of wine for missionaries aboard, but only eleven plows, a bundle of seeds, some clothes, and a few other farming implements, along with three boxes of smoking pipes. The ACS paid for some pork and tobacco at the last minute in Norfolk but often justified not equipping emigrants with basic tools by saying they needed to learn to fend for themselves. In addition to the dilemma of how to support themselves for the days and weeks in Norfolk while they waited, emigrants faced abuse from opponents of colonization who spread "all sorts of malicious falsehoods," wrote a colonization agent who had just been in Lynchburg. The top Maryland colonizationist, Baltimore's John Latrobe, later the longtime president of the ACS, lamented confusion over the departure date, but remained patronizingly optimistic: "The negroes are a slow moving lot; but give them time to think, make up their minds, and ample time to prepare when they have decided, and there will be, I think, no want of immigrants." Who wouldn't want time to think and make an informed decision about moving to another country? How momentous a decision this was for the Black families never seems to have occurred to the white officials. While they sometimes praised individual emigrants as "intelligent," "industrious," "pious" or "sober," they kept their primary emphasis on sending as many Black people as possible to Liberia.[8]

Lynchburg residents Lucinda Holcombe, 21, and her three sons were freed to emigrate with the Mars and Crocketts. The Lynchburg Colonization Society paid for their emigration, probably because their owner, physician, and minister William Holcombe, was a member. The first Mars group, with the Holcombes, left in April and arrived in Liberia around June 1. The larger second group, with the Crocketts, left in the fall on the *Carolinian* and arrived in Liberia in early December 1830. This trip included Abraham's two brothers who each appear to have owned one enslaved person themselves, although this is difficult to decipher from old records. If true, it would make them among about 950 Black slaveholders in Virginia in 1830. About 12 percent of free Black heads of household in Virginia had slaves, although some owned family members as a legal maneuver to keep them from being separated. The ship records listed no former slaves among the emigrants. When the Mars and Crocketts reached Norfolk in October 1830, their ship was already crowded with water casks and cargo from Philadelphia. The Mars and Crocketts and the other emigrants were sent almost as cargo themselves, packed into the crowded hold. Sounding frantic, ACS agent John McPhail wrote from Norfolk that 141 emigrants were on hand, there wasn't room for all their baggage, and emigrants were still arriving. He feared many would be left behind. The ship sailed on Oct. 30, with room for only 107 emigrants, many of them the Franklin County families. Traveling as cabin passengers were two white ACS representatives.[9]

To finally sail across the mouth of the beautiful Chesapeake Bay into the vast Atlantic must have been a relief and a wonder for the emigrants until many became seasick. Worse, measles broke out a few days after the ship left Norfolk and killed twenty emigrants, mostly children. The survivors landed in Liberia in early December 1830, expecting to go up the St. Paul's River to join the rest of the Mars family. But they soon learned all but one of their relatives had already died. And that wasn't all: The colonization society didn't have the resources to maintain the building in Caldwell where the Virginia emigrants were to wait out their acclimation and it wasn't fit for habitation, so the December arrivals remained in pestilent Monrovia, which was hard-pressed to accommodate them. Fever killed Polly Crockett and her adult son within a month. All the remaining Mars were dead within a year, although the oldest member of the group, seventy-year-old Catherine Saunders (Benjamin Mars's mother-in-law), lived until 1833. Some of the Crockett children survived another year or so, but only one, John Crockett, would live longer than a few years.[10]

While high mortality was the norm for Liberia, the deaths were normally spread over months and years. For so many people to die so quickly was a disaster for the cause of colonization, and the ACS tried to hide or deny it. Normally, the colonization society controlled public information from the colony back to the US through the *African Repository*, which brushed over the deaths the following year. Colonial Agent Joseph Mechlin, whose position was similar to a royal governor in colonial Virginia, dismissed the initial 1830 fatalities, only saying they were more numerous than he anticipated, "chiefly in those families from the mountainous parts of Virginia." In a July 1831 report, "Health of Liberia," the *African Repository* mentioned a larger than usual number of deaths, blaming the fact that doomed emigrants were often from mountainous areas, accustomed to clean, clear air, and were more susceptible to fever than those from Tidewater or states farther south. Mechlin wrote that the colony was generally healthy "except for the heavy affliction it has pleased Providence" to inflict on the emigrants from the *Carolinian*. These reports didn't mention the Mars or Crocketts by name, what state they came from, or the total number of deaths. The Lynchburg Colonization Society ignored the deaths in its annual report the next year. The ACS's initial cover-up was assisted by the colony's boosterish newspaper, the *Liberia Herald*. Its editor, John B. Russwurm, part of the colonial power structure, claimed that only two of the Mars had died. The colonization journal devoted more space in these years to an orangutan purchased by Mechlin than it did to the Franklin County deaths.[11]

James Forten, a Revolutionary War veteran and businessman in Philadelphia, soon learned the truth. Forten was a fourth-generation American and an abolitionist. His great-grandfather was brought to America as an enslaved African; his grandfather was born into slavery in America but gained his own freedom; his father was a free man who also served in the Revolution. After attending a Quaker school, young James became a colonial army drummer, was captured by the British, and turned down an offer to switch sides. He later went into the sailmaking business and in 1813 published *Letters from a Man of Colour,* advocating more civil rights for Black people in Pennsylvania. He was an early supporter of colonization but had long since come to believe he had been deceived. In 1817, soon after the national colonization group was founded, Forten chaired a meeting at Mother Bethel in Philadelphia. It was attended by hundreds of African Americans, free and enslaved, and "resoundingly concluded that colonization was an attempt to solidify slavery's grasp by removing free Blacks from American Soil." Read one resolution, "We will never separate ourselves voluntarily from the slave population of this country." By 1830, Forten was in his 60s, one of the wealthiest businessmen in one of the biggest cities in the country. A profile portrait shows a deliberative man with sideburns and carefully knotted white neck sash emerging from a thick-collared black coat. Forten objected to white people referring to Africa as his native country and believed that the ACS's chief purpose was to remove Black people from the United States, not to help them gain freedom and prosper in another land. Instead, he urged free Black people to remain in the US and work to end slavery. Because of his thriving business in the Philadelphia port, Forten had contacts with ship captains, friends and acquaintances who sent him information outside ACS channels. In fact, Forten "had a seemingly inexhaustible fund of information, all of it negative, on Liberia and the ACS," writes his biographer, Julie Winch, in *A Gentleman of Color: The Life of James Forten.*[12]

Philadelphia was a Quaker city with a large free Black population and the Mars and Crockett emigrations had been mostly paid for through public donations there. Forten soon learned many had died. His initial details, published in a Philadelphia newspaper, came in a letter from another friend in Liberia and included mistaken information about the number of deaths, and said those who died came from Ohio on an earlier voyage. Because of these errors, colonization supporters dismissed the whole story as false. Forten then consulted another source who told

Abolitionist James Forten, who helped expose the deaths of more than forty emigrants from Franklin County, Virginia, was a wealthy Philadelphia free sailmaker and businessman. The first meeting of the American Anti-slavery Society was held at his home in 1833. (Leon Gardiner collection of American Negro Historical Society records [ID151], Collection of the Historical Society of Pennsylvania)

him that the Mars family was actually from western Virginia, most came over on the *Carolinian,* and almost all died. He sent this new information to his Boston friend, abolitionist William Lloyd Garrison, who published the correct information in the *Liberator.* The ACS journal finally acknowledged in January 1832 that the number of deaths was high but said it could not be blamed on the Liberian climate, that the Black man's natural place was Africa, and that he should aspire to live there. That was all nonsense to Garrison who believed that colonization was a deception concocted to avoid freeing the enslaved and granting them equal rights. Blasting Southern enslavers in general and Virginians in particular, he would single out Lynchburg and its newspapers over the coming years in the *Liberator.* He published a sarcastic response to an 1832 editorial from the *Virginian* which said that enslavers would consent to give up their enslaved as long as everyone else did and that they could be removed immediately. Replied the *Liberator:* "Wonderful! So conscientious are many of these men-stealers, that they are willing to cease from robbery and oppression as soon as such a measure shall be universal—*not before!*—and as soon as their victims can be *at once removed*—that is, as soon as upwards of two millions of human beings can be coercively and unitedly hurled from one continent to another . . ."[13]

Garrison, Forten and the American Anti-slavery Society continued to counter misleading information from colonization proponents. In 1834, Forten paid the expenses for a Liberian returnee in Philadelphia to testify at a public hearing in New York that included cross-examinations. Conducted by a joint committee of colonizationists and abolitionists, the contentious proceedings lasted two days and featured frequent interruptions and complaints from colonization supporters as returnee Thomas C. Brown detailed all that was wrong with the colony. Two of his children and his brother and sister died there, and he had not been well himself for more than three days in a row during the fourteen months he spent in West Africa. A freeman from South Carolina, Brown was a master carpenter, builder and property owner. Like Forten, he was a fourth-generation American and said he "by no means" considered himself an African. He said he went to Liberia to better his condition but returned because of his health and the lack of work. He described a poor land without resources, where the few people associated with the government lived well and many others were reduced to begging. The ACS had hoped to impeach Brown and cast doubt on his account, but the attempt was a spectacular failure. Ralph Gurley, one of the questioners, was unable to counter the damning descriptions or Brown's accurate statement that about half the people who came to Liberia died. Colonization supporters frequently shouted at Brown from the audience, and another question about slave traders coming to the colony provoked such a disruption that the proceedings were adjourned until the next day. By then, the damage to colonization efforts had been done. Said Brown, "The grave-yards always look fresh."[14]

The deaths didn't dissuade the colonizers, but Piedmont Virginia whites who could sell their enslaved to cotton planters of the Deep South had little interest in sending such valuable assets to Liberia. Lynchburg's roads, canal, and later railroads made it a nexus for slave sales, assisted by advertisements from buyers in the Deep South. The demand for cotton was high, especially in England with its mills sending manufactured cloth all over the world, including to West Africa: Far from ameliorating slavery, the white elites had discovered another way to make it profitable. That trumped lingering humanitarian impulses and turned Black Americans into even more of a commodity to be bought and sold like livestock. Floyd Whitehead, Nelson County's sheriff, sold 73 enslaved people to the Mississippi cotton fields in the 1830s. These were mostly people he had purchased to re-sell, using one of his enslaved men to seek out local bargains. In 1830, his rural county, one of three between Lynchburg and Charlottesville, was home to nearly 6,000 enslaved people, more than half of its population. In urban areas, industrial growth fueled the need for enslaved labor and the number of tobacco factories in Lynchburg jumped from 15 in 1830 to 45 in 1860.[15]

The economic benefits for the white people went hand-in-hand with their deep fear of Black insurrection. Nat Turner's rebellion in August 1831 brought that to life via the death of fifty-some white people followed by the hanging of Turner and his fellow revolutionaries. Lynchburg residents learned about the Southampton County rebellion in a bulletin published the next day and then in a lengthy report two days after the rampage. The *Virginian* tried to tamp down fears, claiming, "Everything is quiet here; and no uneasiness is felt, as indeed there is no occasion for any." Actually, local white people were on edge. In a massive overreaction, they prepared to send a mounted artillery company and volunteers, likely a mob, to Brookneal in southern Campbell County to quell an insurrection that turned out to be a half-dozen supposedly intoxicated Black men who were not rebelling. White Virginians long regarded Nat Turner as evil and demented, but in 2002 Molefi Kete Asante ranked him, along with abolitionists James Forten, Martin Delany, and Jefferson critic David Walker, as among the 100 greatest African Americans who ever lived.[16]

About a week before the Nat Turner rebellion, Lynchburg attorney and enslaver Charles L. Mosby, 23, spoke with the confidence of youth and the overstatement of nineteenth-century oratory in a lengthy address to the Lynchburg Colonization Society. He described any suggestion that colonization would interfere with "the rights of the slave-holding community" as "an extremity of madness and folly, wholly unprecedented in the history of the world." He claimed that the Liberian colony was a "smiling region . . . enlivened by the voice of freemen, and bears the impress of civilization and even of comparative refinement." He was one of the few Lynchburg white people who would continue to boost Liberia over the decades and encouraged the 1865 emigrants from Lynchburg. In the wake of the Turner rebellion, and narrow defeat of the legislative measure that would have allowed for the gradual ending of slavery in Virginia, the ACS shifted its focus even further toward sending enslaved people coerced and freed to emigrate. Lynchburg's free Black people were well aware of the situation: "The free negroes generally seem to have an unconquerable prejudice against the whole scheme, regarding it as a plot of the white people, whom they look upon as hereditary enemies, to [send] them to a barren soil and sickly climate, anxious only for their departure from among them, and indifferent whether they afterwards prosper, or fall a victim to their credulity," Richard Toler wrote in 1833.[17]

A few Black people remained curious. Two young free men from Lynchburg looked into emigration in 1833 and concluded that it was worthy of further investigation. Toler said they had decided to travel to Liberia with the assistance of the colonization society to explore the country, then return to Lynchburg with their findings, but claimed he was confident that if the two men were transported to Liberia, they would like it so much they would never return. (The pair apparently reconsidered their plan and never made the journey.) About fifteen other local Black people were willing to emigrate, Toler said, but again, the American Colonization Society could not pull its efforts together in time to give them adequate notice to get to Norfolk. They were fortunate. Their prospective ship, the *Jupiter*, turned out to be overloaded with cargo, the deck piled with planks and casks. Its 50 emigrants, many from Petersburg and mistakenly listed as from Lynchburg in old records, were jammed into a 20 x 20-foot space for themselves and their bedding, with only a 4-foot square hatch for fresh air.

Trying to convince his superiors to provide more support for emigrants, temporary Colonial Agent J. B. Pinney described Liberia's situation around this time. Things were in disarray. Emigrants often spent their six months of society-provided assistance trying to live out the fever, arriving at the wrong time to plant crops. Then, once the six months were up, at best they could expect to be was "a pennyless stranger, without house or food." Some had to rent or borrow a saw, find a companion, and wade into the swamps to cut wood. Without oxen, the wood had to be hewn on the spot, which often took days, then somehow hauled back to Monrovia, another two days' work, where it could be sold. After a couple years, a man might earn enough to build a plain frame house for his family. Pinney pleaded with Gurley to do more for the colonists. Some colonization officials blamed the six month's aid, mostly food, for the problems, believing that the freed people became lazy when they received assistance. This, despite the fact that some were already knee-deep in the swamps trying to support their families. The colonization society claimed that emigrants to the Western frontier of America—who were mostly white and had always been free—did not receive any public assistance and prospered without it.[18]

The frigate USS *John Adams* called in Liberia on its way back from the Mediterranean in December 1833. Reporting to the Secretary of the Navy, Cmdr. Phillip F. Voorhees wrote that the colonists needed to procure a supply of rice from the Kru to avoid starvation and that he left them some sails so they could repair their small schooner to fetch it themselves. The neatness and comfort of the houses in Monrovia surprised the skipper and he said the town itself was thriving. Out in the country, things weren't going so well. Those settlers needed more than six months' support, Voorhees wrote, and needed to work harder. Fever wasn't the only danger in the tropical land. Emigrants were often sick for their first six months and then too weak and demoralized to take on the arduous tasks necessary to make a go of it. Franklin County's Joseph Mars Jr. drowned. George Mars, one of the three brothers, died from "exposure to the sun" within weeks of arrival. In some cases, becoming "seasoned" to the country could take up to a year, with the old and the very young particularly susceptible to death from fever. With a year's support from the colonization society, the naval officer said, the settlers should be able to survive and even thrive. "The country is fertile and productive of every variety of sustenance necessary to man, and no settler, however poor, with industry and frugality, after a year's support, need to be in want. An old settler, in comfortable circumstances, assured me, he had done all for himself by the sweat of his own brow; and that, too, under the disadvantage of having an axe in one hand to clear his land, and his gun in the other for self-protection, against the occasional attacks of the natives."[19]

The Americo-Liberians who managed to survive and succeed were justifiably proud but tended to overstate in their letters to the colonization society. A free man from Norfolk, Beverly Wilson, wrote back home in 1834, describing a paradise, "fruit in abundance," "horses, cattle, hogs, sheep, goats, jacks [mules] and all kinds of poultry we have at home . . . The fish are fine . . . I have seen them weigh 186 pounds . . . the land is as good as any in America . . . sugar cane and the coffee tree, both very thriving." Wilson had apparently arrived with enough money to buy land on the Junk River, "abounding with excellent fish and oysters." He acknowledged that people sent to the country unprepared for farming "or anything else" were in need of help. Just clearing raw land to get started was hard, although many of the colonists were used to that type of work in

Virginia. Survival also required adapting to different seasons and crops. Solomon Bayley, who'd been in Liberia for several years, offered this seasonal description of farming in Liberia: "To secure a crop, the land must be cleared in the dry season and made ready for planting. In clearing, we cut down the trees and brushwood, and burn them. The dry season is one fall month, the three winter months and part of two spring months. It will do to plant cassavas soon after Christmas, and continue to plant them until spring. The rice and corn should be planted in the second spring month. You [will] be very busy the last spring month to prepare your gardens for the rainy season."[20]

Survival in Liberia required luck, determination, and purpose. Cmdr. Voorhees talked with an "intelligent old man" who told him about the essence of Liberia's appeal to formerly enslaved emigrants. "He had not yet the luxuries nor the accommodations which he had been accustomed to in America, but the want of these were not to be brought into competition with his rights and privileges, as a man, in Liberia; for here only, in the consciousness of having no superior, did he feel himself a man, or had he ever known what it was to be truly happy."[21]

Rights and privileges for Black Americans were out of the question in Lynchburg, which responded bitterly to the rise of the abolition movement in the 1830s. Abolitionists demanded an immediate end to slavery in the United States, something even the most liberal Southerners could not imagine, partly because they feared it would lead to further mixing of white blood with black. Black leaders like Forten and Allen had been pushing abolition for years, and Garrison crystalized their opinion of the ACS with his 1832 book, *Thoughts on African Colonization.* He believed that colonization was at its heart an effort to support slavery and wrote that if Southerners lacked the moral gumption to stop it, the enslaved should do it themselves by physical force; that slaveholders should be expelled from their churches; and that colonization was sinful. He had researched the reports of the ACS itself in the *African Repository,* and described what he read as "sinful palpitations, fatal concessions, vain expectations, exaggerated statement, unfriendly representations, glaring contradictions, naked terrors, deceptive assurances, and unchristian denunciations."[22]

The reaction to Garrison's book illustrated the nature of white attitudes toward colonization. His denunciations diminished Northern support, especially among clergy. But many Southerners focused on his pro-abolition argument instead. They no longer believed that colonization would help prop up slavery. Colonization involved freeing their racial inferiors, not to mention shipping part of their labor force overseas, so they believed it was actually part of the abolition movement, regardless of any evidence to the contrary. Supporters of gradual emancipation received no quarter from the abolitionists. Garrison targeted Lynchburg in 1834, when he reprinted a letter from Thomas A. Holcombe, the white supporter of the first Lynchburg emigrant family, to the *New York Evangelist.* The *Evangelist* favored immediate abolition, and Holcombe could not stomach that. "We are all friends of gradual emancipation and the colonization scheme; and some of us have liberated a part of our slaves, and are ready to emancipate more, when we can better their condition; but the plan of amalgamating the black and white population is visionary, and never will be accomplished." In Lynchburg, "visionary" was not a positive attribute where slavery was concerned. Holcombe's letter canceling his subscription was apologetic, but Garrison didn't care, referring with sarcasm to the Lynchburg subscribers as "a gang of religious man stealers whose consciences were wounded by . . . attacks upon the benevolent system of oppression."[23]

Garrison also reprinted one of former New Glasgow resident and early abolitionist George Bourne's sermons. It told of "another man-stealer, who was a preacher" who sold a woman in Lynchburg for $300 and was rebuked by a parishioner who jumped to his feet and told the preacher, "Go back to Lynchburg, pay back the 300 dollars, the price of blood, and set the woman free . . . and then you may talk of the love of God." The *Virginian* provided more copy for Garrison in September 1834, when he reprinted a lengthy account of the trial of the enslaved man Nelson, who belonged to Richard Chilton of Campbell County, for the murder of Edward Jones, another enslaver. Nelson ran away, went to Jones's kitchen where he hoped to roast a few ears of corn to eat, but was spotted and chased by Jones. They got into a fight over an axe Nelson was carrying, each striking the other with it, before Nelson finally hit Jones in the head, killing him. Nelson was convicted and sentenced to hang. Garrison offered this item without comment to illustrate the depravity of enslavement in general.[24]

Monetary contributions to the Colonization Society of Virginia dwindled in 1834–35. The Lynchburg Colonization Society's annual report noted, "The greatest cause which weakens the claims of Colonization is the infatuated and misguided efforts of . . . abolitionists." A few opponents of slavery still held out hope for colonization. Around this time, a North Carolina Quaker wrote to a Friend in England, summing up the situation in the South: "The roots of the tree of slavery are too deep and too widely extended here to be torn up by the strong wind of northern satire and eloquence; and perhaps too deep and broad to be torn up at all: but support and aid the Colonization scheme, and the tree of slavery, large as it is, may be gradually cut down, and every chip and sprig of it be removed from this continent . . ."[25]

But the roots of enslavement would grow even deeper in the Blue Ridge foothills as slaveholders reacted violently to the threat of losing their human property. As social media has the power to enflame hostile feelings almost instantaneously today, so did the mail in 1835. The American Antislavery Society knew that and began to bombard the South with pamphlets delivered via the US Post Office. The society had developed a mailing list with 20,000 names and printed 175,000 copies of four antislavery periodicals, sent out in late July from New York. When some arrived in Lynchburg, they set off a frenzy and helped dissolve any lingering support for gradual emancipation. Lynchburg editor Richard Toler immediately called for Congress to ban abolitionists from using the mail, saying only madmen believed that the two races could live together if Black people were free. A local colonization supporter, "Virginius," cited one of the pamphlets, "*Human Rights*," at length. Money, not human rights, was his concern and one of the pamphlet's stipulations particularly enraged him: "We maintain that no compensation should be given to the planters emancipating their slaves." This had "Virginius" frothing with apprehension, particularly considering that a contract to build a canal from Richmond through Lynchburg to the Ohio River was in the offing, something locals hoped would tie Lynchburg to the West and reduce its dependence on Northern commerce. "Virginius" concluded by predicting the dissolution of the Union.[26]

The fervor peaked in Lynchburg with a public meeting called by the mayor in late August 1835. Toler was the meeting's secretary and helped prepare a resolution adopted by the participants. It was similar to others around the state. Abolitionism, not slavery, should be abolished across the country. Like "Virginius," one resolution backed future disunion, arguing that holding slaves was a natural right, that ending it would deny white people their rights under the Constitution to life, liberty, and property, and that they therefore had a right to dissolve the Union, which the petition referred to as "this confederacy."[27]

The Lynchburg citizens then turned to local race relations, resolving that it was a high misdemeanor for white people to even associate with Black people, and specifically to sell liquor to them. The Lynchburg resolution demanded increased vigilance to suppress unlawful mixed gatherings, and particularly, to put down the unlicensed brothels "where white men and negroes mingle indiscriminately to plot and hold their midnight revels." The postmaster was also told not to deliver any more abolitionist material. Several white men were appointed to committees of vigilance to keep an eye on certain neighborhoods and report suspicious activity. The city also asked that merchants resolve not to trade with Northern locations which allowed any interference with Southern slavery. Because it involved endangering their income, most Lynchburg businesses appear to have ignored that part. If there were any Quakers left in Lynchburg by the mid-1830s, they left after this 1835 meeting. Hysteria was in full swing across the region. A group of African American miners in nearby Buckingham narrowly avoided execution after some school children saw them with picks and axes and thought they had rebelled. Just over the mountains in Lexington, James F. Otis, a man from Portland, Maine who commented that Southern people were all talk, was nearly lynched. Otis saved his skin by protesting that he was not an abolitionist, but he was exactly that and had signed the Declaration of the National Antislavery Convention in 1833.[28]

The word "lynching" is believed to have originated with Lynchburg founder John Lynch's uncle, said to have hung British sympathizers in Campbell County during the Revolution, or hung them up by their thumbs, or administered some other form of punishment. The act of hanging was often personified in the *Virginian* and other newspapers as "Judge Lynch." Toler wrote that the mob in Lexington decided that "Judge Lynch would take the matter in his own hands." Another local newspaper, the short-lived *Lynchburg Democrat,* attracted Garrison's attention when it reported a sighting of the *Antislavery Record* at the Lynchburg post office. The *Democrat's* editor said that fanatics were trying to instruct Southerners, but that their "pupils will teach them a different lesson, if they will come within the jurisdiction of Judge Lynch." False reports circulated that "Postmaster William Lynch of Lynchburg" had written letters about burning anti-abolition material. William Lynch, the grandson of John Lynch, was in his teens but was not postmaster and did not write the letters. It was all made up. The Virginia mania of 1835 also included a bizarre incident involving mistaken identity, in which contemporary reports indicated that a mob near Lynchburg killed someone named David Robertson, a Scotsman, because they thought he was David Robinson, believed to be an abolitionist who distributed an antislavery newspaper in Richmond. Later, it turned out "David Robinson" was actually the name of an Englishman who had been stripped and scourged for saying in private that Black people deserved freedom shortly after the Nat Turner rebellion in 1831.[29]

Arthur Tappan, president of the American Anti-slavery Society, was almost as reviled as Garrison after the abolition pamphlets hit Lynchburg. A Lynchburg writer, "Sigma," addressed Tappan in a long September 1835 letter to the editor. He pulled together much of the thinking in vogue among Southern white elites: acknowledging that slavery was a problem, but blaming it on the North, claiming that it had turned Black people into an inferior race if they weren't already, and asserting that the solution of emancipation was far worse than the problem itself. He said slavery was merely the "misfortune" of the South, not its fault, and that current Southerners had only inherited the problem, which was actually caused by Northern support for the overseas slave trade. Delving further into justifications for white supremacy, "Sigma" asserted that immediate emancipation would result in the extermination of the Black race at the hands of the white people. Framing the whole thing as a matter of survival for the white people, Sigma referred to the abolitionists as a "brood of scorpions who are endeavoring to sting us to death."[30]

Lynchburg editor Richard Toler's support for colonization hinged on his belief that Black people were inherently the equal of white people but had been degraded into inferiority by slavery, which was too big a hurdle for the country to ever leap. Only getting rid of all Black people, free and enslaved, could make emancipation work. He thought the alternative was a race war that would make slavery seem like a blessing, so he and the Reverend John Early, first president of the Lynchburg Colonization Society, continued to look for any opportunity to move Black people out of Virginia. Thomas Higginbotham of Amherst had freed 50 enslaved people in his will who were working for hire to pay their expenses to go to Africa, Early said, adding that it was important they be sent as soon as possible, before they were corrupted by freedom. Early then inadvertently revealed something of the nature of the relationship between white masters and female slaves in the South, treating it as a matter of course: Another recently deceased Amherst enslaver had lived for many years with an enslaved woman with whom he had several children. He freed the enslaved woman and their four children in his will and left them money to move to a free state, but Early hoped they could be convinced to go to Liberia instead.[31]

Neither Amherst family actually emigrated. The 1835 hysteria cooled, leaving most white Virginians even more mistrustful of any attempt to free the enslaved, although some, especially women, continued to support colonization for religious and humanitarian reasons. By 1838, the American Colonization Society was near collapse, and the Lynchburg Colonization Society had withered away. The national group "devolved into an emigration society relying on the private philanthropy of slaveholders," writes historian Manisha Sinha. The society's 1838 receipts totaled less than $11,000, the lowest since 1825. The following year, it could only muster enough resources for two voyages, carrying a total of forty-seven emigrants, the fewest since 1820. An 1839 pamphlet endorsed by the ACS noted that as part of its reorganization the society was trying "to wean the colonists from too much dependence, and to throw them upon their own resources and powers." In an unusually blatant expression of American imperialism at the expense of Indigenous people, the pamphlet also declared, "The commonwealth is ours, having been planted and established by us . . ." not acknowledging the role of the colonists themselves, let alone the West Africans. In Lynchburg, this era marked the end of any organized effort by white elites to support colonization. The ACS continued to operate in a realm of wishful thinking and propaganda, speculating that some immigrants could find employment with the West African leaders in Liberia, and that those leaders would give up the ongoing slave trade once they were exposed to the Bible.[32]

Congressman James P. Garland of Nelson County, who would soon move to Lynchburg where he became commonwealth's attorney and a longtime judge, addressed the 1837 annual meeting of the American Colonization Society in Washington, DC, noting that he and the society's president, Henry Clay, were the only Southerners participating. Garland came from a well-known family of Piedmont Virginia enslavers. His brother, a lawyer, was the namesake of Garland Hill in Lynchburg; his nephew, Confederate Gen. Samuel Garland Jr., was killed in battle in 1862, and his sister married Confederate Gen. James Longstreet.[33]

Rep. Garland said he had turned against colonization. He said that neither the federal nor state governments had the power to abolish "the right of property by slaves," adding this could only be done by the people, "in their primary sovereign capacity." On the other hand, he said, speakers at the annual meeting had convinced him that the society was not an abolitionist group and only wanted to deport free Black people. (Between 1820 and 1843 less than half of the more than 1,600 people sent to Liberia from

Virginia were free prior to emigration.) Repeating the old white arguments about the free people of color, he said that in the North and South they were "riotous, disorderly and debased," and that in the South free Black people disquieted the enslaved and incited them to rebellion. "It is in the interest of all to get rid of this population," he concluded.[34]

In Liberia, a Mars child who survived the fever died in 1842 at age 15. Lucinda Holcombe and her son Powhatan Holcombe from Lynchburg survived their 1830 voyage and subsequent fever. Powhatan's brothers Robert and Thomas did not. Only one member of the Mars and Crockett family lived long enough to be enumerated in the first Liberian census in 1843: John Crockett, 23, was working as a laborer in Caldwell, where a few farmers persevered. A rural river village in a huge tropical forest, it remained isolated, and although long-term survivors gained some immunity to malaria, the mosquitoes continued to infect new arrivals. At a crucial time when the colony should have been growing and developing its own resources, emigration from Virginia and the other states had diminished. Northern Black people, the abolitionists, and the *anopheles* had prevailed and no one from Lynchburg emigrated between 1830 and 1842. Toler, one of the founders of the Whig party in Virginia, was elected to the House of Delegates in 1839. In 1846, he moved to Richmond where he edited the *Richmond Whig*, succeeding his old boss at the *Daily Virginian* who was killed in a duel. John Early continued his rise to national prominence in the white Methodist Episcopal Church, which he later helped split into separate Northern and Southern branches. Control of the ACS shifted to Northern states, with its constitution rewritten and positions on its board of managers assigned according to the amount of each state's financial aid to the national group. Most of the Lynchburg white people involved in colonization had moved on, and many of the Black emigrants had died, but not all. One would return to Lynchburg in the early 1840s on behalf of his new homeland, about a year before the grandson of the city's founder freed 20 people he inherited, the Black Lynch family.[35]

5

Holding On Against the Odds

1840–1849

> We have been oppressed long enough. We [mean] to stand our ground & contend for our rights until we die.
>
> —Sion Harris, Liberia, 1849

THE SURVIVING American emigrants of the Liberian colony established a tenuous foothold in West Africa but numbered only a few thousand by 1840. Conflicts could be violent as cultures continued to clash, not unlike the American West. In the face of such odds, every surviving emigrant was important, and Sion and Martha Erskine Harris, who left Lynchburg in 1830, were among them. With Martha's brother, Hopkins W. Erskine, they were determined to survive, and lucky. So were some members of the large Lynch family who arrived in 1843, freed by the grandson of Lynchburg's founder. The Lynches were encouraged to emigrate by an enslaved but semi-independent local man who was developing a lifelong interest in Liberian liberty, and who had a hand in the emigration of several multiple family groups in the later 1840s and 1850s. Perhaps they were also inspired by Sion Harris, who returned to Lynchburg in 1841 and met with enslaved people during a recruiting trip to Tennessee.

Like the Harrises, colonists who prospered in Liberia generally made their way via multiple livelihoods. Some had craft skills like carpentry or sewing or shoemaking, others became teachers and preachers. The surest way to success was through trade, but money was scarce, so trading often involved swapping items like manufactured cloth or metal cookware with the West Africans in exchange for commodities brought from farther inland. Commerce like this was discouraged by colonization officials, who wanted the Americo-Liberians to follow the hardest path, farming, but only a few thousand acres were under cultivation in the 1830s, the equivalent of a large plantation or two in Virginia. Sion and Martha Erskine Harris lived on a farm on the St. Paul's River, where Sion was also a carpenter and hunter and Martha, a teacher and seamstress. Within a few years, Sion added trading to his résumé. As the emigrants' place in the new society improved, Sion Harris was elected to the legislature. Hopkins Erskine, Martha's brother, studied, preached and taught, and later served as Liberia's attorney general. William H. Lynch, one of the 1843 Lynchburg youngsters, would later become a Monrovia tobacco trader, a member of the city council, and Liberia's secretary of the treasury. His brother, John, also rose into the Liberian elite.[1]

The chance for self-fulfillment and financial security like this helped motivate emigrants in the first place. It's hard to fault colonists like the Lynches or the Erskine-Harris family or Liberian founding father Lott Cary of Richmond for turning to trade. A Maryland colonization official who spent years in Liberia wrote, "The whole coast-line is a market," with a canoe landing or trade village every ten miles or so. African goods once included pepper, gum, wax, hides, gold, and ivory, all brought to the coast from the interior. By 1840, British merchants who first gained influence because of their role in the slave trade wanted camwood and palm oil for the English textile mills. The shrubby camwood tree's fiber was ground to produce red dye. Oil from the nuts of the tropical palm trees was used in wool manufacturing, for cooking, and to make soap. These resources were in demand on the world market, but the colonists had to depend on the same European merchants for both buying and selling. To purchase manufactured goods from British merchants, colonists had to get those same merchants to take their palm oil or camwood as payment, putting them at a competitive disadvantage and hampering economic growth. Despite its popularity, colonial trading never amounted to enough to benefit the society at large. But it was often necessary to make ends meet for individuals.[2]

Once colonists survived the fever and began to establish themselves, another constant concern was stamping out the slave trade in their new land. "African American descendants of slaves, some of them free people themselves, had not come to Liberia to tolerate the slave trade," writes historian Lisa A. Lindsay, who describes a determined, resolute effort by the colonists, lasting decades. Although the United States and Great Britain had outlawed the trade in 1807–8, slavers continued to ply the Liberian coast, purchasing Africans for transport to Cuba and South America. Wars among the West African groups vying to dominate this trade ravaged the St. Paul's River region following the death of the powerful Manding ruler, Sao Boso. Control of the countryside around Clay-Ashland where Martha and Sion Harris lived in a brick house on a 110-acre farm, about 12 miles up the river from Monrovia, was still disputed only a few years before the Americo-Liberians declared the colony an independent nation in 1847.[3]

Under Sao Boso's hegemony, the Africans had tolerated the American settlements because they provided additional markets for trade. Sao Boso himself had been generally friendly. His successors were not and opposed Americo-Liberian efforts to disrupt the local economy and stop the slaving. After Sao Boso died in 1837, fighting broke out between rival African groups, with a Bopolu chief, Getumbe, leading the Condo confederacy. His soldiers defeated the local Dei, sold some into slavery, and attacked Millsburg upriver from Caldwell. A Baptist missionary reported, "The Deis once numbered 6,000 to 8,000. Several pleasant villages belonging to the Deis formerly greeted the eye of the traveler in passing down the St. Paul's River, but through the desolating influence of the slave trade, they have mostly disappeared."[4]

Previously, the Colonial Agent had been the top official on the ground in Liberia. But as the American Colonization Society's financial condition worsened, it allowed the colonists to elect delegates to an 1837 constitutional convention which endorsed the creation of the "Commonwealth of Liberia." The society named Thomas Buchanan, the ex-governor of the Bassa Cove settlement, governor of the commonwealth, which united most settlements with Monrovia, and took on some of the powers to make treaties and war that had been under the purview of the society. A step toward formal nationhood, it set up three branches of Liberian government, executive, legislative, and judicial, as in the United States. Virginia also called itself a "commonwealth," and former Virginians played a key role, with Baptist missionary Colin Teague chairing the Constitutional Convention which named Joseph Jenkins Roberts lieutenant governor. Both were from Virginia: Teague was one of the original Sierra Leone emigrants and once spoke in Lynchburg with Lott Cary; Roberts emigrated with the Turners from Bedford County aboard the *Harriet* in 1829.

The fighting in the St. Paul's region distressed Buchanan, a white man from Philadelphia. "At this moment the whole country along the northern bank of the St. Paul's river is involved in bloody wars. Whole districts are laid waste; towns are burned. The old and the young who are unfit for the market are butchered, and hundreds and thousands are driven in chains to the coast, or compelled to fly the country . . . Fire, famine, blood and chains are the necessary elements of the slave trade, and every conceivable combination of these elements are daily produced in this wretched land." As in Virginia, slavery was the flashpoint between two cultures, and Buchanan blamed the United States. "Oh, my country! how enormous is thy guilt in this matter—how deep thy debt to poor Africa!"[5]

Most colonial agents had been slow to take the offensive against European slavers and their African suppliers, but Buchanan was different. When the British Navy seized a slave ship and turned it over to the colonists, he used it to attack a slave depot south of Monrovia. This was another example of multiple cultures and nations of the Atlantic world coming together in West Africa, involving enslaved people bound for Cuba, other West Africans trying to sell them, American settlers, French and English slavers, and the British Navy. Buchanan led a volunteer force, including recaptive Africans, which attacked and destroyed a slaving operation run by a Frenchman and Englishman and manned by local Africans. Only a few months before, Buchanan said, some colonists themselves had been assisting the slavers due to the depressed state of the colony's economy: "The slavers offered them plenty of work, high wages, and good Spanish doubloons for pay." These colonists were likely desperate laborers: Some who helped slavers were paid with wheat.[6]

That Martha Erskine, her younger brother Hopkins, and Sion Harris had survived their emigration to what she called "this dark world" was a miracle. Soon after arriving from Lynchburg in 1830, Martha and Hopkins's father, mother, grandmother, brothers and sisters died. That loss was almost unimaginable, but she wrote that life got even worse when "we were left to wander in a strange land" after friends took their food. Unlike many colonists from the South, they could read and write. Who they were likely gave them a leg up as well—despite his early death, their father, the Reverend George Erskine, was well-known in Liberia. By 1839 Sion and Martha were married and living on their St. Paul's River farm, with pork from their own hogs, dozens of chickens, and wild game. Sion operated his trading business from two frame buildings and Hopkins was teaching and studying religion. They'd adapted to West Africa: In 1839, Martha wrote that Liberia was a "very good country for wild meat," praised her husband's hunting prowess, and offered to send the ACS a selection of animal skins.[7]

But West Africa had not adapted to the Americans, and relations were confounded by the different cultures. Getumbe's chief warlord, Goterah, a Loma ruler, was wearing a leopard-skin cap with a long tail and a long sleeveless gown decorated with cowrie shells and animal hair when he and his retinue visited Gov. Buchanan for two days of negotiations in 1839, involving an interpreter on each side. Buchanan, the white Philadelphian, probably wore a dark frock coat with a vest, and spoke English. Goterah spoke a Loma dialect, which his interpreter translated into the Vai tongue. Then, Buchanan's interpreter translated the Vai into English. Goterah brought a drummer with him and began the proceedings with what the colonists perceived as a threatening dance involving spears. Buchanan had invited a reporter to observe Goterah's visit, and the "grand palaver" conducted in the parlor of Buchanan's house caused a commotion in Monrovia. The negotiations over stolen property involved misunderstandings, and two women whom Goterah said belonged to him via war and inheritance. Buchanan decided that both women were now "American," under protection of the colony, and would not be returned to Goterah. The *African Luminary* writer who reported this encounter was probably John Seys, a Methodist missionary and explorer who edited the newspaper. He was allied with the colonization society and wrote that Goterah accepted this decision but "looked as if he ruminated future revenge, and seemed pondering how to execute it."[8]

The West African and the American negotiated from opposite world views. Goterah viewed his actions, ransacking and burning Dei villages and taking the women, as standard procedure for a man in his position. He offered to force the Dei to compensate two Liberian citizens who lost property in his raids, provided Buchanan would allow him to continue to make war on the Dei. The *African Luminary* portrayed him as a savage but also praised his "shrewdness and logic." He said his only means of recovering the unspecified property was bloodshed, but the Americo-Liberians forbade that while still insisting he compensate them. In substance, he said, "Tell me, who makes English men of war pay back for property they destroy when they break up a slave factory belonging to Spaniards on the coast? If Africans or Americans have goods there at the time, and in the war they are plundered, from whom is redress sought? . . ."[9]

Earlier in the negotiations, after saying he didn't want to fight the Americans, the account claims Goterah had declared himself "a very bad man; it is my fashion to take and burn a town, kill and eat the people." Rumors of cannibalism weren't unusual in this part of Africa. In fact, Sion Harris claimed Goterah brought a cooking pot with him several months later in 1840 when he raided the remote Heddington mission, where Sion was building an addition and Martha Harris was teaching. With a missionary, an assistant carpenter, and a few African workers, they were attacked at dawn by a large force of West Africans led by Goterah.[10]

The Americo-Liberians were outnumbered, but they'd anticipated the attack and were better armed, with at least twenty muskets, six pounds of buckshot, gunpowder, lead slugs, and axes. Some of the West Africans who had been helping them switched sides at the last minute, taking muskets to join the attackers. Harris, the other carpenter, and the missionary poured buckshot down their musket barrels and blasted away while Martha helped reload. All were nearly hit themselves and expected to die when Goterah, wielding a large knife, charged Sion who shot and killed him at point-blank range, ending the attack. Harris wrote a minute-by-minute after-action report to the ACS a month later, full of details like the number of buckshot per round (50–60), his gun (English musket), his defensive positions (picket fence then large stump), and wounds suffered by the attackers ("his bowels were out.")[11]

Harris didn't discuss his motivation for what happened after he killed Goterah, but he described it in a letter, revealing savagery which rivaled anything the West Africans themselves had been accused of: First, he cut off Goterah's genitals. Possibly he wanted to complete the humiliation of an enemy to impress the other Africans who believed their leaders possessed supernatural powers. Goterah's warriors retrieved his mutilated body and tried to hide it but were followed by a rival group who insisted that a "head-man" was needed to decapitate the body. Harris accompanied this rival group and sent ahead a recaptive African leader who handled the beheading and returned with the gruesome trophy, which Harris saved for the governor. Buchanan, who died of malaria the following year, confirmed he received it, and Goterah's skull and the musket Harris used to kill him eventually made their way to the ACS offices in Washington.[12]

Harris didn't mention cannibalism in this first account but added it to speeches in America later, saying he had met Goterah previously and seen strips of human flesh stewing with rice in a kettle. The ACS censored Harris's letter prior to publication in the *African Repository* to remove references to the beheading and the mutilation, casting Sion, Martha and the others as Christian heroes. Martha wrote from Caldwell, ". . . I have been surrounded by war and death. Indeed, I thought my end was nigh; but God has saved my life . . . God fought the battle, and delivered us out of the hands of our enemies." She returned to her riverfront farm about twenty miles away for the duration of the war. Meanwhile, the settler militia and volunteers recruited by Buchanan went on the offensive against the warring Africans, eventually defeating Getumbe, and leaving him "to wander the wilderness without followers or family," according to several sources which read like wrath-of-God Old Testament stories.[13]

Violence like this was characteristic of nineteenth-century expansionism involving the US government or surrogates like the colonization society. Military accoutrements including uniforms, flags, forts, and cannons were an important part of the colony's self-image. The martial airs were "designed to elevate the settlers into the roles of masculine tamers of the African wilderness," writes scholar Robert Murray in *Atlantic Passages: Race, Mobility, and Liberian Colonization.* Murray's book also illuminates the lasting impact of Americo-Liberian violence: Goterah's was among five African skulls from the Heddington battle preserved and studied years later, helping spark the nineteenth-century "scientific racism" theory involving brain size of white people compared to everyone else. [14]

The defeat of Getumbe and his warriors ended much of the raiding of the American settlements, turned Sion Harris into a folk hero, and freed him to fulfill a deathbed promise to Martha's father to bring more family to Liberia. He sailed back to the states in 1841, stopping in Lynchburg for several days on his way to Tennessee, speaking to mixed audiences, boosting the visibility of colonization. He met with a group of about thirty enslaved people in nearby Bedford whose master had just died, but the majority remained "unquestioning in their opposition" to colonization, reported an ACS agent traveling with him. "They have their heads full of the horrors of Africa," the agent said, and Harris, a convincing speaker, didn't help himself if he told the story about the attack. He and the agent, Levi Walker, raised enough money from Lynchburg churches to buy a horse and carriage to continue their journey to Tennessee. They were careful not to offend enslavers, only meeting with the enslaved provided "request is made from proper authorities," as was the case with the Bedford families. Harris and Walker attracted the attention of the rector of St. Paul's Episcopal Church in Lynchburg, who decided to send his enslaved servant, Ansley Walker, 27, and her daughter, Mary, 2, to Liberia, with her husband, Henry Walker, 35, a free stone mason. (The ACS may have given them the same last name as the agent.)[15]

Harris's new status as a foreigner and his white companion likely helped shield him from some of the scorn heaped on free Black Americans in the

South. In Tennessee, he dined with white people, stayed at their homes and spoke to mixed audiences, but his visit apparently provoked some white people to increase their harassment of Black churches there. Harris wrote a few years later that he was not treated like a "man" during his trip to America: ". . . it was all the time, boy, where are you going . . . I wanted to be a man again; but never found it until I hit the coast of Africa."[16] He was in America nearly a year, preaching to 1,000 people at a Presbyterian camp meeting in Tennessee. He returned to Liberia in 1842 with multiple family members and relations and more than 50 other people, free and enslaved, including the Walker family from Lynchburg. On the return trip, Harris left the emigrants under the care of the ACS agent while he told his story in Boston, New York and Philadelphia and raised money with Ralph Gurley, the chief spokesman and most forceful advocate for Liberian colonization.

In Lynchburg, the Harris emigrants from Tennessee sold some horses and wagons and completed the trip via canal boat to Richmond, then steamer to Norfolk. But as usual, lack of money and planning complicated the departure from Norfolk, which was delayed for months. First, the ACS sent the ship to New Orleans to pick up a large group of freed slaves, meaning the Harris group arrived in Norfolk months early. In Norfolk, they needed to find some type of employment to provide for themselves, and colonization agents fretted they would come under the influence of the local free Black community. They had to wait so long that at least three died and barrels of pork and beans, procured for their use in Liberia, were opened to feed them. With the New Orleans group, the Tennessee people, 17 from Virginia, and multiple emigrants from other states, more than 220 people finally sailed aboard the *Mariposa* in mid-July 1842. The ACS touted the emigration as a high-water mark for colonization after years of decline.[17]

One of the multiple ACS agents in Virginia who assisted the *Mariposa* group was working out of Lynchburg a few months after the Liberia-bound Harris group passed through. Samuel Cornelius, a Baptist minister born in 1794 in England, was an itinerant agent who traveled the state. Before coming to Lynchburg, he helped arrange supplies for the *Mariposa* emigrants in Richmond but reported a lack of enthusiasm bordering on hostility among many Black people there. He asked the ACS to reassign him to the North, but instead, he was sent to Lynchburg, where in late October 1842, he was approached by the wealthy young grandson of founder

Daguerreotype view of the James River waterfront in Lynchburg, ca. 1848–53, looking east toward Richmond. The James River and Kanawha canal is visible between the buildings and the river on the left. Most Lynchburg emigrants began their journeys in this area. (The Valentine, Richmond, Virginia)

John Lynch. That meeting set in motion a rapid series of events which resulted in the December emigration of three related Lynchburg families, nineteen people in all, led by Nancy Lynch and including ten young men encouraged to emigrate by enslaved Lynchburg carpenter Washington Copeland. Copeland received no written acknowledgment from the ACS or Lynch, nor was the Harris recruiting visit credited. At this point, Copeland's influence was either unknown by the white people or considered so insignificant that it was not worthy of mention, or maybe they just didn't want to acknowledge that a semi-independent man like Copeland or a free Black man like Harris had more influence than the enslavers.[18]

William B. "Will" Lynch Jr. met with Cornelius and handed him a statement which landed like a message from the Almighty at the ACS offices on Pennsylvania Avenue in Washington. Lynch he said owned three families, wanted to send to them Liberia, and was willing to pay for a voyage to take them there and to provide for them after they arrived. Further, Lynch wanted to free the families because he didn't believe in slavery—thus appealing to the antislavery faction of the ACS. Will Lynch was "very anxious to be rid of his slaves . . . not from any fault in them generally, but from principle," Cornelius wrote. Lynch, in his early 20s, was a "youth of sterling reputation," which was dubious since he'd already been kicked out of the University of Virginia, disappeared for a couple of years, then returned to town claiming to have been kidnapped in the South Pacific.[19]

Following Quaker dictate, Will's grandfather John Lynch had freed his enslaved more than fifty years before. Will Lynch's father and mother died of consumption (tuberculosis) when Will was a child, and the enslaved she had inherited passed to him, along with one-sixth of his grandfather's real estate. Like Lynchburg itself, the 1826 appraisal of Will Lynch's parents' property reflected a mix of high culture, farming, and barbarity. It began with a library that included works of philosophy, the Federalist papers, and novels like *Don Quixote* and *Gulliver's Travels.* Between a pair of iron wedges and more books, it listed nine African Americans, including Nancy Lynch and other future emigrants. By 1842, the natural increase white people feared meant these Black Lynch families had nearly doubled in size.[20]

The 1842 emigrants included 18 enslaved family members, and one free man, Morris Johnson. All the enslaved had been under the control of Will Lynch's guardian, Micajah Davis, another Quaker descendant, until Will turned 21 around 1840. Like their mother, Nancy Lynch's daughters Lucy and Sarah were seamstresses, as was Eliza Lynch, who may have been Nancy's sister. Provided they or their customers could acquire cloth, it was a skill that would help them in Liberia. James Lynch was a carpenter and wrote back to Lynchburg the year after he arrived, praising life in the colony. With a shared occupation, James Lynch was an acquaintance of Copeland, who mentioned him in a letter, and the same age as Will Lynch.[21]

But Will's life was very different from that of an enslaved young Black man. After his parents died, he grew up in the grand, two-story brick Davis home and enrolled at the University of Virginia in 1837. The university, about fifty miles north of Lynchburg in Charlottesville, had been open for only twelve years and was a wild place with a few hundred students. The often-criminal misbehavior of "the young gentlemen" reduced founder Jefferson to tears in its first year. No records exist of how Lynch treated African Americans in these years. The culture at UVA did not foretell that a few years later he would free his own enslaved and help them toward what he hoped would be a better life in Liberia. Students "bullied, beat and abused slaves who had little protection by law and custom. They pummeled overworked slaves who failed to promptly light the morning fire in their dorm rooms. They kicked slaves who failed to respond quickly to orders. And they had no qualms about clubbing those who showed insolence," wrote Carlos Santos and Rex Bowman in *Rot, Riot and Rebellion: Mr. Jefferson's Struggle to Save the University That Changed America.*[22]

Early records of the university detail Will's undistinguished academic career and his violation of rules the professors enacted to get the students under control. Soon after his arrival in Charlottesville, he was hauled before the faculty for purchasing his student uniform from a merchant who sold liquor. In October 1838, he was suspended for two weeks for violating an early-rising requirement. He was summoned to explain himself and said that he first made an effort to comply with the rule but now had "abandoned all effort" to do so. In December 1838, the professors of ancient languages, modern languages, and mathematics reported to a faculty meeting that Lynch was "inattentive and not making due proficiency." The faculty voted to tell Lynch's guardian that unless the young man showed quick improvement, he would be dismissed. On New Year's Day 1839, Lynch's continuing transgressions were detailed. He was again summoned to appear before the faculty, said he had no excuses, and was kicked out.[23]

What became of Will Lynch between early 1839, when he was dismissed from UVA, and 1842, when he freed the enslaved families? Margaret Anthony Cabell, the city's first historian and his contemporary, picked up the story. The daughter of a local Quaker who wrote John Lynch's obituary, she related a tale of Will's missing years that, if true, is astounding. Her book lists no sources other than personal knowledge, but her other details about the life of Will Lynch are accurate.[24]

By the time he was dismissed from UVA, Will had begun to fear that the disease which killed his parents would also strike him. His friends were "ignorant of his plans and intentions," Cabell writes. Her book contains a frustrating omission at this point. "For a long time, his fate was involved in doubt; his friends fearing that with all the ship's crew he had gone down to a watery grave." Ship? What ship? She doesn't say, reporting next that young Lynch was seen and recognized by an officer aboard an American vessel "touching at one of the South Sea Islands." (The US Exploring Expedition and the US Navy's Pacific Fleet had ships in the Pacific in this era.) The officer "brought tidings of him to his friends in America." The story gets more implausible at this point but could shed light on why

Will wanted to free his enslaved only a few years later. He was more or less enslaved himself: "He was a captive in the Islands, condemned by his master to strike in a Blacksmith's shop." The hard work in the Pacific smithy's shop exercised his lungs and chest muscles to the point where he believed he was free of consumption. How did he get back to Virginia? Again, Cabell doesn't say, but Will had quite a story to tell when he returned: "He mingled in society, admired for the graces of his mind and person and invested with romance from the circumstances attending his voyage."[25]

Further, she wrote in a footnote, "This gifted and generous young man inherited, from his mother, more than twenty valuable servants. On Christmas morning after his return, they all went to him to ask for a Christmas gift; he told them, he gave them themselves; and he not only liberated them, but provided the means for sending them to Liberia." Lynch didn't need income from renting out the enslaved families or working them himself, which put him in a position to act on any humane, possibly Quaker, impulse to treat them as human beings. As freed slaves, they knew they would have to leave Virginia, and Lynch initially agreed to send them to a free state. The Black Lynches were no doubt aware of their owner's family connections to southwest Ohio. The Miami Valley area was already home to hundreds of former Lynchburg Quakers including Will's uncle Edward. Will himself owned two houses in the village of Springborough. Ohio was adjacent to Virginia prior to the Civil War, and the terrain was similar but flatter—rolling hills, rivers and streams, good farmland. It was a free state, but not sympathetic to free Black people themselves. Lynch wrote, "I offered them their freedom and agreed to allow them to go to the northwestern states . . . but on going out to those states and seeing the wretched condition of the free Blacks there, I have persuaded them to go to Liberia . . . believing that they will be much more comfortable there." The colonization society, always eager to tout Liberia as a better option for Black people than their own country, reported that the enslaved Lynches "coincided" with this opinion. Maybe so. But with emigration to a free state ruled out, their only choices were Liberia or continued enslavement.[26]

The colonization society scrambled to accommodate Lynch and because he was willing to contribute $500 (about $15,000 today), found a place for the Lynches aboard the next voyage. The *Globe* had already been chartered by the Maryland Colonization Society to take some emigrants to Cape Palmas, its own settlement south of ACS territory.[27]

The *Globe* was due to sail from Baltimore in mid-December, and the Marylanders agreed to drop the Lynches off in Monrovia. Usually, enslavers who sent people to Liberia handed off all responsibility for getting them there to the ACS, but Lynch went with them to Baltimore. Once they arrived things moved quickly. Although no previous notice had been given, "a vast crowd assembled on the wharf," reported the *African Repository*. A white minister invoked God's blessing as Nancy Lynch and her family kneeled and prayed with more than 100 emigrating Marylanders. The Maryland journal deployed dramatic imagery to describe the 1 p.m. Dec. 15, 1842 departure: "The emigrants arose from their knees—the sails were sheeted home—the hawser cast loose—and the majestic bark moved slowly down the wharf, favored by a slight northwester, and cheered by three rounds from the admiring spectators; and never did three cheers receive a more hearty response than arose from the joyous mass of emigrants on board . . ."[28]

They were landed in Monrovia, which had about 1,000 residents in the early 1840s, mostly colonists, along with recaptives and West Africans. Only about half of the previous 4,571 emigrants to Liberia were still alive. One of the surviving colonists in Monrovia was Plymouth Reid, forced to leave Lynchburg after he was freed in 1830 and now a carpenter. His wife had died a few years before, but he kept in touch with Lynchburg, had remarried, and had a new baby. Reid and his family were all well but the new emigrants from Lynchburg were immediately stricken with the acclimating fever. Five of Eliza Lynch's children, all 7 or under, died. Governor Joseph J. Roberts mentioned Morris Johnson, the free man from Lynchburg who had also died, in a letter to the ACS in which he described the others in the Lynch group as continuing in poor health. Roberts said the colonial doctor blamed the deaths and ill health on imprudence, but it's hard to understand how small children could be blamed for imprudence. Most of the remaining Lynches appear to have survived, although several were still listed as feeble months later. The ACS touted the Lynch family as a counter to critics who said it only sent elderly people—less valuable to enslavers than healthy young men and women—to Liberia.[29]

By the time the Lynches arrived in the early 1840s, Martha Erskine Harris was teaching settler and African students at the Methodist mission school in now-calm Heddington. In addition to reading, writing, and arithmetic, children and adults learned Christianity. The settlers had established twenty churches around the colony, many colonization officials were ministers themselves, and they claimed hundreds of Africans had been converted. One, a Dei named "Simon Peter" by missionaries, had previously been taken prisoner by Sao Boso, kidnapped by "Arabs" who cut his feet to prevent him from running away, rescued by another group of Africans, and finally returned to the Dei. He became a trader and slaver himself, eventually ending up at Heddington, where he converted to Christianity and began to convert others until he died of exhaustion after helping round up friends who had fled after the Harris-Goterah battle. A few years later, Hopkins Erskine wrote that the Heddington mission, one of two principal Methodist missionary outposts in Liberia, was in decline, with converts alienated from Christianity and Indigenous leaders returning to their traditional ways.[30]

As the Lynches adjusted to West Africa amid the pervasive fever, their former owner was fighting health problems of his own. Will Lynch had contracted tuberculosis, the disease he feared for years. Seeking a better climate, he went to New Orleans where his health continued to decline, then returned to Lynchburg where he died in 1845. Unmarried, he was around twenty-five years old. Among many bequests, Lynch's will directed that an engraved set of silver plate be crafted for his old guardian at a cost of $500, the same amount he spent to send the families to Liberia. "He only returned to Lynchburg to breathe his last, and to be laid quietly to rest in the old Quaker burying ground," wrote Margaret Cabell.[31]

More typical of the modest revival of colonization was the next Lynchburg family, the Murrells, who emigrated in 1847. Jack, 60, Patience, 48, and their son Cabell, 11, were freed to emigrate by young physician Dr. Edward Henry Murrell of Lynchburg, whose family was enmeshed in slavery and colonization. Murrell's father was a charter member of the Lynchburg Colonization Society. His brother was a wealthy tobacco merchant who subscribed to the *African Repository.* Their uncle bought the Tally-Ho sugar plantation and enslaved labor camp in Louisiana along with sixty-nine African Americans the year after the Black Murrells emigrated.[32]

The Murrell emigrants sailed aboard the *Liberia Packet,* a ship recently acquired by the ACS to make regular trips to Liberia. When they arrived in Monrovia, the packet's emigrants refused to leave for agricultural Millsburg, preferring to stay in town, even though Jack Murrell had been a farmer in Virginia. The emigrants were apparently impressed by Monrovia's resemblance to the towns they had left behind. Even Gov. Roberts was unable to convince them to leave the capital, where successful emigrants had begun to build homes with stone above-ground basements for storage and livestock, with frame second stories and wrap-around porches to catch the breeze.

Fever soon killed Jack Murrell, but his wife and son survived. Sion Harris mentioned the family briefly in a letter written one day after the first session of the newly formed Liberian legislature. Liberia had become the Republic of Liberia about a month before the Murrells sailed in 1847 and was the first colony on the African continent to declare independence, partly because the ACS could not afford to support it. By then, Sion Harris was exasperated with the ACS and the United States: "I can say that I thank God I am at home in Africa. . . . I never expect to conten[d] with the 'colored' man in America no more. If they come, well; if not [it is] well with me. I expect to die in Africa where the free air blows, for here [is] liberty. We have been oppressed long enough. We [mean] to stand our ground & contend for our rights until we die." Harris's letters radiate self-confidence and pride in his new country. In 1851, he mentioned his service in the Liberian legislature and said, "Did you ever hear of such a thing in America? No, no—nor never will." He was killed by a bolt of lightning in 1854.[33]

Attaining personal fulfillment like what Harris experienced was becoming more and more unlikely for Black people in Virginia as the sectional divide in the United States increased and white attitudes hardened. Virginia was more strictly enforcing the law that freed slaves had to leave the state, and the ACS took advantage. The Virginia Colonization Society, reconstituted in 1849, mentioned colonizing the enslaved along with free Black people in its goals, and two more enslaved families from the Lynchburg area emigrated aboard the *Liberia Packet* that year. Nina Davis, 30, and her three children were freed to go to Liberia by the will of their Campbell County owner. Like the Lynches, this family's freedom may have had Quaker roots. Nina Davis had been enslaved by both the grandson and great-grandson of a South River Quaker. Also aboard the 1849 packet was a friend of Washington Copeland, William Helms, 41, a millwright. With his wife, Esther Helms, 45, and their two children, Octavia, 6, and Caroline, 4, he was freed on the condition he emigrate. Each emigrant on the packet was allowed to take two barrels of possessions, as well as mattresses and bedding to use as berths on the ship. Most of these emigrants did not get the option of staying in Monrovia—they were almost immediately sent up the St. Paul's to wait out the fever.[34]

Liberia and the ACS continued to struggle even as emigration increased. A Piedmont Virginia minister who preached to Black congregations and worked as an ACS agent, G.W. Leyburn of Liberty (today's Bedford), was discouraged not by fever and death in Liberia but by the lack of interest among white Virginians, writing, "The greatest obstacle has been the state of ignorance and indifference . . . into which the public mind has fallen of late years though the want of proper efforts on behalf of the cause." The national society acknowledged in its 1848 annual report that a large number of emigrants "were slaves, whose freedom depends on their removal to Liberia," reflecting its shift toward emancipation. But for every emigrant like Sion Harris who evangelized for Liberia, there were many more who criticized it. Several 1848 emigrants, some from North Carolina, returned to the United States, describing both the soil and the people of Liberia as poor. One even claimed that President Roberts was engaged in the slave trade, a persistent Liberian rumor. Emigration of freed slaves would continue to rise in the 1850s but still represented only a minuscule fraction of the African American population. If they weren't hostile to colonization, most Virginians were indifferent. Lynchburg's enslaved carpenter Washington Copeland would spend the rest of his life fighting that indifference.[35]

6

The Era of Washington Copeland

1842–1859

> When Mr. Miller first owned me he was much opposed to the cause and said he would give five hundred dollars more for me if he could get [Liberia] out of my head—but he could not.
>
> —Washington Copeland, Lynchburg, 1859

MULTIPLE FACTORS influenced the mild revival of colonization which saw more than 100 residents of the Lynchburg area emigrate between 1842 and 1859, many of them people freed and coerced to go to Liberia after their enslavers died. Slavery was more entrenched and even more important to the Southern economy than before, but many remarkable Black people worked to rise above their circumstances, and Washington Copeland of Lynchburg was such a man. An enslaved carpenter, he was one of Virginia's most enthusiastic advocates of Liberia and wrote often that Black people would be better off out of Virginia. He had a hand in the emigrations of nearly 50 people, including eight he convinced his wealthy owner, Samuel Miller, to free and send to Liberia. He managed to buy his own freedom just before the Civil War.

Liberia had become a sovereign nation in 1847, and Lynchburg-area people emigrated almost every year thereafter until 1860. A few Black abolitionists even began to support colonization as part of a nascent Black nationalism movement, writes Manisha Sinha in *The Slaves' Cause: A History of Abolition,* and moved to Liberia themselves. Nationwide, about 5,800 people emigrated to Liberia between 1848 and 1860, more than had been sent since the colonization society was founded, as the ACS moved further toward convincing the enslaved to emigrate. Reducing the ever-increasing Black population was still its primary motivation and states like Virginia in the upper South slightly increased their financial contributions to colonization around 1850.[1]

Some white people imagined colonization functioning as a safety valve, releasing the pressure on the slavery dispute that was tearing the country apart. After helping send the Erskines, Mars and Crocketts in 1830, the Lynchburg Colonization Society continued its annual meetings for a few years but sponsored no further emigrations. A few local white people continued to back the national group, corresponded with the ACS, and bought Liberian coffee, syrup and sugar for resale. The ACS used its slightly improved financial status to publish multiple pamphlets which were often sent to Lynchburg. Liberia itself had a distinct flavor of Virginia, which provided many of the emigrants who had risen to the top of the Liberian social strata, including the first president, Joseph Jenkins Roberts.

Surviving emigrants from the Lynchburg area sometimes wrote letters home, and Washington Copeland stayed in contact with "his" emigrants into the 1860s. He was a self-confident man and seems to have known almost everyone in Lynchburg. His body may have been enslaved, but not his spirit. "I am 55 years old, a carpenter by trade—can do almost anything—can read write & cipher very well." He worked as a semi-independent contractor, owning carpentry tools and a lathe, and shared an attitude with writer and abolitionist Martin Delany, who "escaped the prison of inferiority that was created by the practice of white supremacy and found his strength in the acceptance of his innate capabilities as a man," wrote scholar Molefi Kete Asante.[2]

Copeland, born around 1804, was a family man with a wife, two daughters, and two sons. How he got his education is unknown. He had subscribed to the colonization journal since 1834 and was well-informed about the activities of the ACS. The contradictions inherent in the colonization movement were exemplified by Copeland, who fit no stereotype. Most Black Virginians still didn't want to leave their home state, despite their worsening situation in Lynchburg. Copeland did want to leave, and believed that all Black Americans would be better off if they left the US. He happened to be enslaved but considered himself every bit the equal of the white people he dealt with. He must have known that many hundreds of people had already died in Liberia but never mentioned it in his letters. With limited documentation, understanding his full motivation and the contradictions of his life is impossible. Still, his letters and those of the emigrants reveal far more than was recorded for most of Lynchburg's Black population. As David Brion Davis writes in *The Problem of Slavery in the Age of Emancipation,* "Few exiles and expatriates have cared to address their former oppressors and describe their achievements and hardships, their hopes and grievances."[3]

Copeland wrote that the young men who emigrated in 1842 with the Nancy Lynch group freed by the grandson of Lynchburg's founder "went through my influence." A letter from one was read at an 1843 meeting in Lynchburg, part of several held around the state to drum up financial support for the ACS. The news that an enslaved man was helping other enslaved people leave the country would not have helped the cause of colonization among white people, and the ACS did not correspond directly with Copeland until after he bought his freedom from the eccentric Samuel Miller in 1859 for $500.[4]

Copeland was comfortable in the white, Black, free, and enslaved communities, mentioning multiple enslaved and free people by name in his letters, and noting that he'd convinced local white philanthropist Thomas Holcombe, who had endorsed the first emigration from Lynchburg in 1829, to pay for Copeland's subscription to the colonization journal. Copeland's work skills were valuable in rapidly growing Lynchburg and allowed him to keep in touch with enslaved people throughout the area. After helping convince the Helms family to go to Liberia, he talked the Davis family from Amherst County into emigrating instead of choosing a new master when freed by their owner's will. He kept a precise count of his emigrants, 48, accounting for nearly half of all Central Virginia emigrants between 1840 and 1860. A local white minister confirmed in 1859 Copeland had been instrumental in persuading many to emigrate. In fact, Copeland claimed, it was he who convinced his master that colonization was a good idea, a reverse of the normal Black-white dynamic. "When Mr. Miller first owned me he was much opposed to the cause and said he would give five hundred dollars more for me if he could get it out of my head—but he could not and finally through my influence he has sent 8 persons to Liberia."[5]

COPELAND'S OWNER was Lynchburg's wealthiest citizen and one of its strangest. He enslaved more than 30 people in 1840. Local historians have called Samuel Miller generous and foresighted, but also enigmatic and misogynistic. Born in 1792, Miller died in 1869, and his bequests founded both the Miller Home, today a girl's home in Lynchburg, and the Miller School, today a boarding school near Charlottesville. A self-taught investor, he was reputed to be one of the richest men in the South by the time of the Civil War.[6]

Miller fathered at least one child, a girl, with a woman he enslaved. He freed the child, Sarah Lee, sometime prior to 1850 and she moved to Ohio. Miller left Sarah's daughter, his grandchild, a house and lot in his will, as well as $12,500 in stock. While Miller did not mention the relationship in his will, he did acknowledge it to his friend and former business partner, colonization supporter Ambrose Rucker, a Main Street merchant and another Copeland acquaintance. Miller also freed Rose Gregory, 27, and two children, in 1839, sent them to Ohio, and left her an annual bequest in his will. Whether the children were his is not known. Miller never married, but he had six other children with a white woman, Mary Davidson, who lived in a cottage on his property. Her mother had signed a contract for Mary "to live with him in that way" as a business arrangement, according to a witness in the court case over his will. His first child with Mary Davidson was born around 1850, when Miller was 58, and the last when he was past 70. She and the children received bequests in his will.[7]

Miller was born into harsh poverty in Albemarle County about sixty miles north of Lynchburg, but his mother somehow paid a tutor so he could learn to read. He soon moved to Lynchburg to join his older brother who had opened a grocery store in the growing town. Possessed of innate business sense, he owned a Lynchburg tobacco warehouse in his twenties and by the 1840s was dealing tobacco with brokers in Richmond, New York, London and Amsterdam while investing his profits in Kentucky and Illinois. Miller also made money speculating in hemp and silver, but his financial success did not bring happiness. In 1829, as his health began to decline, he bought a farm a few miles west of the city, not far from the old Quaker meeting house. The reclusive Miller was a hypochondriac, nearly always ill, nervous, his stomach upset, abstemious with food and drink. Still, he managed to live to age seventy-six and a posthumous portrait painted from his disinterred corpse shows a tall, silver-haired, neatly dressed man. He once told Rucker that he attributed his long life to never using tobacco, the original source of his fortune.[8]

Copeland's advocacy of Liberia was well-timed, because Miller was among the Virginia enslavers who had too many slaves. He had owned Copeland since at least 1850 but needed fewer enslaved as his wealth increased and he diversified from tobacco and farming. By 1850, he reduced his estate to 18 enslaved persons, and in 1860, to 6 enslaved persons. He gave away one enslaved man to cover a debt. A few were freed and sent to Ohio; some, presumably, were sold, and others were sent to Liberia at Copeland's urging. Another, Willie Ann Kelso, remained at his home outside Lynchburg until he died in 1869, nursing him through his lengthy final illness. His will, written ten years before, directed that on his death she be freed and sent to a free state. But she was freed by war, not by his will, and successfully sued Miller's estate for nearly $2,000 owed for his care. According to testimony in another suit over his will, "She continued to tend him, to be in vigilance his friend, in absolute devotion his slave, to the last hour of his life. He shattered her health by the incessant watching and laborious service which his condition and his preference for her ministrations imposed upon her." The judge blasted Miller following lengthy testimonies: "None of the ordinary relations and associations of life, suggesting familiarity with home and fireside are alluded to," concluding that Miller's was a life "unilluminated by even one ray of affection."[9]

The sporadic manumission and emigration of the enslaved Millers reflects the way their owner bought and sold stocks and bonds a few lots at a time, carefully judging the success of each venture before proceeding to another one. His brief letters to the ACS were cordial, to the point, and businesslike. He paid the fees for each emigration, and also donated small amounts to the ACS after Copeland convinced him it was a worthy cause. But Miller did not include Copeland in his will. Maybe Miller resented Copeland's persistence and independent spirit, his self-described hard-headedness. Nonetheless, Miller first acquiesced to Copeland on colonization around 1850 when he freed Louisa Miller, 25, and a namesake, Samuel Miller, 18, and sent them to Liberia.

Miller's wealth was exceptional, but he was not the only person getting rich in booming Lynchburg during the twenty years before the Civil War. By 1840, the former ferry landing had grown to become Virginia's largest town west of Richmond (excluding today's Wheeling, West Virginia) and was among the 100 largest cities in the mostly rural United States. Rapid changes in transportation and communication modernized Lynchburg and the country as manufacturing began to replace agriculture. State support for railroads produced "almost magical results" and Lynchburg soon had a factory manufacturing railroad cars on the already-busy riverfront. The Virginia and Tennessee railroad (first called the Lynchburg and Tennessee) yards there included machine shops, an engine house, a roundhouse and by the early 1850s a handsome passenger depot with twin spires rising alongside the James River and Kanawha

Canal. Freight came into Lynchburg from the western regions of the state where it was off-loaded and shipped to Richmond.[10]

"The transportation revolution expanded markets, spread commercial agriculture, fostered manufacturing, extended mining, and not least important, reinvigorated slavery's economic position," wrote historian William A. Link. To build, maintain, and operate their new factories and old farms, owners preferred enslaved labor to that of white workers. Former Lynchburg publisher, mayor and colonization advocate Elijah Fletcher had retired to his Sweet Briar plantation north of the city and anticipated construction of a new railroad from Charlottesville to Lynchburg through his land: "None of the Contractors on the public work will employ White Labor if they can procure Black." For enslavers with increasingly worn-out tobacco lands, this was profitable, earning them $100-$120 per year per adult laborer, while costing as little as $25 per year to feed and clothe them. Other Virginia enslaved like Copeland became self-hiring, contracting themselves to white people for work with minimal interference from their owners. In the process, they tasted a bit of the independence that the white people feared, and helped erode "Virginia's traditionally paternalistic system of controlling its slaves," wrote Link. "Paternalistic" certainly did not describe Copeland's relationship with Miller. Copeland's written comments about his owner were something less than respectful, veering into mockery, more like that of a wary acquaintance.[11]

These were years when the leadership of the 1865 emigration from Lynchburg began to think about emigration. Mac Nuckles, who would change his name to John McNuckles after the war, became a skilled brick mason working to build the growing city. He dreamed of moving to Liberia where he could own his own land, vote, and participate in civic life. So did his brother, Woodson, a carpenter like Copeland. Levi Norvell, who shared their hopes, was working in a Lynchburg tobacco factory and preaching. Another planner, Jack Averitt, would come to criticize the continued exploitation of Black labor after slavery was outlawed. Men like these made poor white people jealous, and elites nervous about revolt, so they attempted to further limit Black life. Lynchburg established a night watch in 1850. No matter how talented Lynchburg Black people were, free or enslaved, they were required to get off the streets every night when the courthouse bell rang at 9 p.m. or face punishment. White citizens also organized the Lynchburg Southern Rights Association "to further protect themselves." The rights of Southern slaveholders—not the rights of the enslaved—had come to dominate the national debate. Congress passed the Fugitive Slave Act in 1850 as part of a compromise that allowed Southern masters to apprehend slaves who had escaped or had been brought to a free state. Virginia governor Henry A. Wise supported the position that any white Virginian had a right to chase down a runaway slave anywhere in the country, and that every Black American was presumed to be enslaved unless proven otherwise. Receiving national attention from abolitionists, the *Lynchburg Republican* opined in 1855, "We demand for Slavery not merely protection from Abolition attacks, but we demand that its existence shall be more palpably recognized and more certainly secured. We wish to see the right of a Southerner to travel with his slave anywhere in the Union fully secured. The Union is worthless, unless Slavery is placed upon a footing which will secure to its advocates every right enjoyed by its opponents . . ."[12]

The sectional crisis splitting North and South coincided with the mild revival of colonization and illustrated how the movement was rooted in a visceral and contradictory racial bias. Most white Virginians, including colonizationists, still considered Black people inherently inferior, a subspecies. White people might praise individual Black people, and like them personally, but at the same time cultivate the stereotype of Black people in general as lazy, incapable of looking after themselves, and needing to be enslaved for their own good. The *Daily Virginian* expressed white Lynchburg's prevailing view, editorializing, "[slavery] is terrible only in name . . . it diffuses among the laboring classes . . . more of the comforts of life, than freemen (as they are called, though they be every way as dependent as slaves) . . . ever enjoyed." As sectional tensions mounted, colonization was seen by some Southern white people as a middle path, a way to reduce excess Black population while keeping enough people enslaved to do the labor required for economic growth. The colonizationists' goal of diminishing Black numbers remained absurd, especially in Virginia, which had more people enslaved than any other state. Multiple counties east of the Blue Ridge were majority Black. Adjacent to Lynchburg, Campbell and Bedford were among the largest slaveholding counties in Virginia by 1860, with more than 10,000 enslaved residents each despite the thousands sold South.[13]

As the momentum for disunion grew, some white leaders began to view colonization as a necessity, terming the removal of free Black Americans from their homes in Virginia an "amputation" that needed to happen.

Changes by the Virginia legislature in 1850 strengthened the law expelling the newly freed from Virginia, while half-heartedly encouraging freedmen to emigrate, and taxed all free Black men to pay for it. In 1853, the Colonization Board of Virginia was created, ostensibly to aid colonization. Although it had little power or money, and was disbanded in 1858, it did help pay Miller's expenses for a couple of people and "authorized" the emigration of a large Bedford family in the 1850s. But Black men like Washington Copeland had far more influence in their community than a state colonization board, and he wasn't the only one.[14]

A Lynchburg freeman, William T. Valentine, wrote the colonization society for information on emigrating in 1850, mentioning that a group of more than twenty men and women viewed the prospect favorably. "We have appointed committees to atten[d] to getting on all is very much excited . . . they all have agreed to go in the first steamer that sails next fall and want all the information that they can possibly get by that time." The ACS obliged, sending Valentine multiple copies of its *Information About Going to Liberia* pamphlet and the *African Repository*, maps of Liberia, the 1843 Census of Liberia, the *Liberia Herald* newspaper, and two copies of the ACS annual report.[15]

James Winn was another Lynchburg freeman considering emigration in 1850. He read the pamphlets that the ACS sent to Valentine and helped distribute them. He said that he and his family were thinking of emigrating, but his wife could not make up her mind to go and was afraid of the acclimating fever. Winn said they were mixed-race and had been told by white friends that as such they would not be able to survive it. They had also learned that many emigrants from Lexington who had lately passed through Lynchburg were dead and others sick. Winn had acquired more accurate numbers about emigrant mortality than the colonization society was willing to provide. He had heard that about a third of all emigrants died. Apologizing for his spelling, he wrote that "thar is a great many here wants to go to Liberia this fall," and he requested more information about the fever before deciding.[16]

The ACS financial secretary and treasurer, William McClain, wrote to Valentine with a final encouragement and another booklet about Liberia. McClain was a prolific letter writer and a "whole soul colonization man," as Washington Copeland once described himself. A graduate of Miami University in Ohio, he was involved in an unsuccessful effort to establish "Ohio in Africa" in the late 1840s, and sometimes expressed moral outrage

This fanciful mid-nineteenth-century illustration of Liberian President Joseph J. Roberts's house in Monrovia was used to promote emigration, depicting well-dressed Americans and friendly Indigenous people. (Library of Congress Prints and Photographs Division, Washington, DC, LC-USZ62–107635)

at the way Black people were treated in the US. He encouraged Winn: "If you are ever going, now is the time . . . Cast your lots with that interesting government without delay and you will never regret it. I have given Mr. D. B. Payne [a Lynchburg bookseller] some copies of colonial physician Dr. J. W. Lugenbeel's *Sketches of Liberia,* and told him to keep those until called for and then to give them to any of you who want to see . . ."[17]

Lugenbeel, like other physicians of the day, believed that the fever stemmed from the severe change in climate experienced by the exhausted American emigrants and the dank air of the swamps. He recommended one effective treatment for the symptoms, quinine, along with remedies such as herb tea, a pepper poultice, calomel (a purgative containing mercury), ipecac (used to cause vomiting), and laudanum. He also wrote in his *Sketches of Liberia* that the fever was worse among emigrants who were already weak or in ill health or didn't take care of themselves; and that disease and culture shock contributed to some emigrants losing hope, hastening their deaths. As an employee of the colonization society, he was interested in encouraging colonization but his chapter on the fever was anything but that. Leeches were plentiful in Liberia, and Lugenbeel swore by them, once having nearly 100 applied to himself. It's doubtful a mental image of herself or her children with 100 leeches attached and draining their blood provided the needed assurance for Winn's wife and neither the Winns nor the Valentines emigrated. Undaunted, McClain continued to urge white people like Ambrose Rucker and Samuel Miller to convince the area's free Black people to go, telling Miller "the people in Lynchburg need stirring up." A few months earlier, he told Rucker to do something to rouse the attention of free Black people.[18]

Rucker replied that emigrants could be found if some combination of state money, donations, and ACS contributions paid for their passage. "The mass are distressingly poor," Rucker wrote, describing a free family of four tobacco factory workers—a woman, two young men, and a teenager—who were "sober, industrious, and easily controlled" who wanted to emigrate but could not afford it. Even if the ACS paid for their Atlantic voyage and provided six months' food and shelter, getting to Norfolk or Baltimore cost money that many free Black people did not have. The reality was more complicated than just poverty. McClain told Rucker the ACS could take the four tobacco factory workers, but that the state would pay only if they had been free by March 11, 1850, when the new law took effect. I found no indication the factory workers ever emigrated.[19]

Most free Black people still wanted to stay home in Piedmont Virginia where they had lived for generations. The enslaved lacked even that choice and lived with the fear that they, their spouses, or children could be sold south where the cotton culture and its slave labor camps required constant replenishment. Southern slave buyers were frequent advertisers in the Lynchburg newspapers and so many Lynchburg residents were sold between 1850 and 1860 that the enslaved population dropped by about 20 percent. In 1847, an abolitionist newspaper, *The National Era*, reported, "The whole way from above Lynchburg to Wytheville seemed almost blocked with emigrants from old Virginia and North Carolina, traveling to the West and South. We met on our way out and back, including four days, about fifteen hundred people. About twelve hundred were Blacks."[20]

The contrast between who the ACS urged to emigrate from Lynchburg and who actually went was dramatic. While McClain continued to target free Black people in his rhetoric, behind the scenes he spent much time arranging for enslaved Black people to be freed and sent to Liberia in accordance with the wills of their dead owners. This often involved those who didn't want to emigrate and court fights with the owner's relatives who wanted to keep them enslaved. Anyone freed was forced to choose between continued poverty in a free state like Ohio, re-enslavement in Virginia, or emigration. Large groups freed by wills were not just individuals or families but often whole Black communities which had lived and worked together for generations.

Like the Quakers before them, a few Lynchburg white people could no longer stomach life in a society supported by slavery and one charter member of the Lynchburg Colonization Society, Dr. William J. Holcombe, had evolved into an outright abolitionist. His brother, Thomas, was one of Washington Copeland's early benefactors. William Holcombe inherited about a hundred enslaved around 1840 from a relative and moved with them to Indiana so they could be free, and he could teach physiology and pathology at La Porte University's new school of medicine. Another Lynchburg physician from an old Piedmont Virginia family with many enslaved, Dr. Gustavus Rose, had already moved to Indiana, writing: "I again repeat, that I thank God, I have not only escaped from Slavery itself, but all the insidious evils consequent upon it, to the rising generation in the South . . . You may ask would you have the state of Va. depopulated? I answer, of the wise men."[21]

These "insidious evils" touched all facets of society as the Southern nightmare of Black freedom continued to gain adherents in the North. Even man's best friend, the dog, was a target of racial bias in Virginia. Black people using their dogs to hunt annoyed white people, who also blamed Black people for problems with wild dogs roving across the state. Some counties began taxing dogs in an effort to restrict their ownership, and Chesterfield County near Richmond tried to prohibit Black people from owning any dogs. The canine situation further devolved in 1852 when Lynchburg enacted a dog tax to restrict their ownership to well-off white people, and the tiny police force began shooting and poisoning stray dogs. Lynchburg white people rarely expressed opposition to whipping, torturing, or lynching Black people, but dogs were another matter. They held a funeral procession for a dead dog, culminating with the stoning of a city councilman's home and the resignation of the entire council.[22]

Publisher and abolitionist Frederick Douglass reprinted the story of an unnamed enslaved man in Campbell County who teased a white youth about pigeon hunting. The outraged white youth said he hadn't killed any pigeons but could kill the Black man and proceeded to fatally blast him in the head with a shotgun for his insolence. *Frederick Douglass' Paper* said the incident was an example of the "appalling influence which the system of slavery exerts on the moral sentiment and feeling of the South" and noted it was reported by the *Virginian* "as coolly as any commonplace occurrence." Some abolitionists like Douglass opposed the Liberian colonization movement but expressed lukewarm support for emigration to Haiti, because Haitian emigration had been sparked by the Black nation itself, not American enslavers. White abolitionist Horace Greeley also supported emigration to Liberia. As the publisher of one of the the largest circulation newspapers in the country, *The New York Tribune,* he had reported plans for the 1842 Lynch emigration on its front page.[23]

Lynchburg, by now a prominent tobacco town and a center for slave trading, was also growing its general manufacturing and trade ties to the North. New York and Baltimore papers kept up with everything from Miller's financial wheeling and dealing to a major James River flood in 1857. Harriet Beecher Stowe cited slave ads in Lynchburg newspapers among her factual evidence for the abuse she described in *Uncle Tom's Cabin.* Anecdotes about the horrors of slavery in Central Virginia were often published in Northern newspapers. Articles about a Lynchburg slave catcher who went to Canada to retrieve runaway human property; a local Black baby kidnapped to be sold; and a Nelson County enslaved man whipped to death by an overseer provided lurid reading and nurtured an atmosphere of defensive reaction and opposition to free speech: A railroad man who expressed abolitionist sentiments was arrested in Lynchburg, and an Amherst County man suspected of not being sufficiently proslavery was dunked in a pond. The enslaved sometimes fought back. A Bedford enslaver punished a slave, who retaliated by killing him with a hoe, and an Amherst enslaved man, said to be one of the best farmers in the region, was sentenced to hang for the attempted murder of an overseer. The governor of Virginia commuted the death sentence imposed by a local court on two Black youngsters convicted of burning a Lynchburg factory.

White Virginians continued to regard all this as a necessary evil required to maintain the economy and keep Black people under their control. Like freedom of speech, freedom of the press was restricted. Antislavery commentary had become intolerable in Lynchburg, where postmaster Robert Glass banned distribution of Greeley's *New York Tribune* because of its "incendiary character." Greeley responded to Glass with a defiant letter, refusing to stop mailing the paper to local subscribers and telling Glass: "Go ahead in your own base way: I shall stand steadfast for Human Liberty and the Protection of all natural rights. Yours, stiffly, Horace Greeley." Postmaster Glass, not an enslaver himself, was also a newspaper publisher. His *Lynchburg Republican* depended on the prosperity of the slave city for its livelihood, and Glass passed his belief in racial discrimination to future generations. His son was future US Sen. Carter Glass, who claimed to remember the first US troops riding into Lynchburg after the Civil War and would help rewrite the Virginia constitution in 1902 to disenfranchise Black voters.[24]

When Rep. Preston Brooks of South Carolina beat Sen. Charles Sumner of Massachusetts almost to death on the floor of the Senate in 1856 after taking offense at Sumner's antislavery stance, the citizens of Lynchburg invited Brooks's accomplice, Rep. Laurence M. Keitt, a South Carolina planter, to speak a few months later. His remarks were greeted with cheers and Virginia Gov. John B. Floyd's attendance caused something of a national sensation. The *New York Times* called the meeting "a Disunion festival in Lynchburg." John Early, the first president of the Lynchburg Colonization Society in the 1820s, helped split the Methodist Episcopal Church over slavery in 1845 and by 1862 was arguing that the Southern states had been appointed by God to protect and evangelize the Black race, that disloyalty to the Confederacy was heresy against the church, and that the federal government was committed to preventing the spread of Christianity among Black people. [25]

The Dred Scott decision in 1857 was a major setback to both freemen and enslaved as it further codified racial bias and established a bar to citizenship for Black people in America. The US Supreme Court ruled that the Constitution prevented all Black Americans, enslaved and free, from ever becoming US citizens. The right to citizenship, not just freedom, was frequently cited as a major factor by both enslaved and free people who went to Liberia. The pent-up desire to belong, if not in America but somewhere, was expressed by James P. Skipwith, freed by his Albemarle County owner in 1858 on condition he emigrate. The following year he wrote that he was enjoying the privileges of citizenship in Liberia, including serving on juries and voting, rights that were "sumthing strong to me." On the eve of the Civil War, Washington Copeland summed up the difference between mere freedom from enslavement, and true liberty, writing, "No man is free in any country unless he is a citizen of the country." The following year he would finally get to Liberia, but not as an emigrant.[26]

7

A Freedom Odyssey

1859–1863

> They say abolish slavery and after they get us [free] they will not do anything for us except Rob us of everything.
>
> —Washington Copeland, Ohio, 1860

In 1859, Washington Copeland of Lynchburg had finally saved enough money from his independent carpentry work—$500, the equivalent of about $15,000 today—to buy his freedom and that of his wife, but they went to central Ohio, not West Africa, moving to the small town of Circleville. His two sons were still enslaved in Lynchburg and the rest of the family would not emigrate without them. Virginia freedmen, banished from their home state, had been moving to Ohio towns and rural areas in groups large and small for decades and included several who had been enslaved by Copeland's owner, Samuel Miller, who sent his daughter by an enslaved woman to Circleville and bought her a house there. But Ohio was no paradise for Washington Copeland. His wife died within months of their fall 1859 arrival, and he blamed it on what he called "this cold country."[1]

The family continued to face racism and discrimination in Ohio, but for the first time in their lives, they were counted by name in the 1860 US census. The census shows Washington "Copland" living in the 2nd Ward of Circleville, with Martha, 33, James, 12, Elmina, 8, Virginia, 6, Josephine, 5; and Rosanna, 3, all "Coplands," and two other women, Ophelia Harris, 57, and Mary Napper, 24. Everyone except Napper was born in Virginia. Martha was recently emancipated by Samuel Miller and later would receive a bequest of $1,000 in railroad bonds. Copeland, 55, wrote a poignant sentence about his family to the ACS before he moved to Ohio: "My wife, two daughters and five grandchildren are free and in Ohio but my two sons are slaves and I cannot persuade [my family] to go to Liberia until my boys could go also . . . can you not put me on some plan by which I could obtain their freedom or at least one of them?" He called Ohio an unfriendly place where he received even less respect than in Virginia and still lacked basic rights of citizenship. He wrote that God made Black people suffer slavery and racism in America so they would want to go to Africa and Liberia, "the promised land." No abolitionist—"I hate them"—Copeland said he was a "whole soul colonization man." Was he really opposed to abolition, or did he believe that was what the ACS wanted to hear? A later comment indicates he disliked abolitionists for his own reasons, writing, ". . . they say abolish slavery and after they get us [free] they will not do anything for us except Rob us of everything." Like Northern antislavery writer and abolitionist Martin Delany, he drew a sharp line between simple freedom and true citizenship. Wrote Delany, "No people can be free who themselves do not constitute an essential part of the ruling element of the country in which they live . . . this position in community is necessary for personal safety . . . The liberty of no man is secure, who controls not his own political destiny."[2]

A vigorous writer himself, Copeland was as quick with his words as he was with his carpenter's hammer and always ready to advance the cause of colonization. He frequently returned to his most audacious suggestion, that the ACS send him gratis on a round trip to Liberia to scout the country, return, and become an ACS agent, traveling and lecturing in the states. He said many people of color in Ohio had never heard of Liberia. The colonization society was not enthusiastic, but Copeland and his Lynchburg supporters were persistent. The Reverend Jacob Mitchell, a slaveholder and colonization agent who was pushing the Rogers families [see chapter 8] to emigrate from Bedford around this time, urged the ACS to send Copeland without charge: "He is very anxious to go that he may be useful to his colored brethren in this country . . . He is trustworthy and . . . perfectly reliable." Mitchell confirmed that Copeland had been instrumental in sending about forty people (forty-eight by Copeland's account) who if still alive were now Liberian citizens.[3]

Liberia was never far from Copeland's mind. He said that not even the risen Christ would have been able to convince white Virginians they were wrong about slavery and race and giving Black Americans a fair chance at success and prosperity. "For my life I can not see where a colored man can be free but in Liberia I do not care what his talents what can he do with it in America . . . there is not a [spot] of land in America but the white man wants it . . ." The desire to own their own land for self-sufficiency influenced the large group of Lynchburg emigrants in 1865 and Copeland mentioned several by name in the same letter. He said he would drum up ACS journal subscribers in Ohio and contacted the editor of a Circleville newspaper (briefly suppressed the following year for pro-Southern sympathies) to set up a subscription swap with the editor of the *Liberia Herald*.[4]

October 1860 found Copeland still complaining about the cold weather and unhappy he could not earn fair wages. The *M.C. Stevens* was sailing for Liberia in a few weeks, and he wanted to be aboard. The ACS had finally agreed to pay for his passage, but he was mindful of the group's strained finances and said he would try to have his former master, Miller, pay his expenses "as he is rich." He was still in contact with previous emigrants from Lynchburg and thanked McClain for forwarding letters to him from one of them, John H. Lynch. By now a businessman and trader in Monrovia, Lynch was among the youngsters who emigrated in 1843 at Copeland's urging with their mother from Lynchburg.[5]

Whether Samuel Miller chipped in isn't known, but McClain finally arranged to give Copeland a free passage to Liberia, slipping him aboard the *M.C. Stevens* on Nov. 1, 1860, with some emigrants from Georgia. After each voyage, the ACS noted the running total of people it had sent to Liberia, and this voyage brought the number to 10,545, again documenting the utter futility of the white effort to reduce or even impact Black numbers in the United States. After 40 years, the emigrants equaled a less-than-minuscule sliver of the Black American population of 4.5 million. Still, the surviving emigrants and their descendants had created a more or less functioning, sovereign, Black American nation in Africa, although it was a very small country that still needed ACS support and educated and talented emigrants. Aboard Copeland's ship was Episcopalian missionary Cadwallader Colden Hoffman who declared these *M.C. Stevens* emigrants "of a better class" than his previous trips, presumably because many were free people from states like Ohio, Illinois and Pennsylvania.[6]

Hoffman was a cabin passenger, but Copeland traveled with emigrants in the hold. He soon befriended one of the other cabin passengers, Dr. James Hall of Baltimore, a longtime white colonization official who helped found the Maryland Colony in the 1830s at remote Cape Palmas where he served as its first governor. Hall and Copeland voiced similar themes about Liberia. Hall told Maryland freedmen in 1859, "Go where you can become men—*freemen*—MEN, in the largest sense of the word . . . No where else, but in Liberia, does the man of color live under a free Government of his own organization and administration." Hall compared that with the US, where "You cannot hold any office of trust or profit in the government. You have not the right of trial by a jury of your peers—your jurors are of your masters. Your testimony, where the property or person of a white man is concerned, is not admitted in any court. You are declared not citizens of the United States, or of any State, by a decision of the highest tribunal in the land. You are not allowed to take part in any election or vote for any office. You are not permitted to bear arms in defence of the country in which you live, or for personal protection." Copeland certainly agreed, but no doubt would have challenged Hall on one of his other assertions, that Black Americans did not equal white people in intellectual power and ability.[7]

Also headed for Monrovia on the *M.C. Stevens* were three African youngsters—Tony, 12, Pilo, 13, and Sagado, 12—"intelligent little fellows"—who had endured the Middle Passage on a slaver bound for Cuba with 400 others. The boys hid while the rest of the captives were landed and were later rescued by a US warship which intercepted the slaver on its return voyage. They were among 3,500 Africans rescued from slave ships, whom Liberia absorbed around the time of Copeland's visit. The US Navy referred to them as "recaptive Africans," making them sound like wild animals. Scholar Claude Clegg writes: "The psychological implications of this harrowing odyssey of capture, recapture and colonization, were . . . different for each person who endured it," and involved "unscrambling and reinventing one's notion of self." Today, we might call them refugees.[8]

Moving the recaptives to Liberia was a key part of the ACS's finances in 1860–61, according to political scientist David F. Ericson, although the ACS did little for them other than allowing them to be dropped off in Liberia. The ACS struck a deal with President James Buchanan, with Congressional approval, for the US government to reimburse the colonization society for each recaptive it resettled, a total of more than $400,000. As a result of this arrangement, thousands of recaptives from other parts of the continent arrived in a country that couldn't take care of the people it already had. It added to the mind-scrambling mix of cultures with recaptives from new ethnic groups soon making up a major part of the population. This arrangement also raised questions about who was really in charge of Liberia—the ACS and the US government, or the Americo-Liberians themselves who often objected to this influx of humanity they were not prepared for? Essentially but unofficially, Liberia was the US government's first colony, in a public-private partnership with the colonization society.[9]

Copeland's ship brought $14,000 worth of supplies for the recaptives, but its next voyage was canceled as the Civil War broke out. "The terrible civil war . . . has already begun to affect us here," wrote the Reverend John Seys, recently appointed manager of recaptive matters for the ACS, in June 1861. The war would damage Liberia's already weak economy, curbing trade and the already-meager support from the United States. Chief ACS agent H.W. Dennis wrote, "We expect a pretty rough time for breadstuffs next season, as the rice farms of the natives have not turned out very well, and we have so large a number of recaptures added to our population."[10]

Previous and recent recaptives in Liberia now totaled perhaps 5,000 or more. Where the United States reflected binary divisions, white v. Black, North v. South, the population division in Liberia was tripartite: the emigrants and their descendants, the multiple West African ethnic groups, and the recaptives. The Americo-Liberians were in control but numbered only about 10,000 emigrants and their descendants. The addition of thousands of independent-minded recaptives threatened this dominance. The colonization society wanted to turn the new recaptives into independent settlers in their own communities, while Liberia's second president, Stephen Benson, envisioned molding them into a labor force for the settlers. As traders and the educated elite solidified what would become a century-plus grip on power, the Liberian government asserted its independence and convinced the ACS to yield control of the recaptives in 1860. Copeland's shipmate Hall was there on behalf of the society to approve the necessary documents. Some of these recaptives were eventually placed with Americo-Liberian families, although Benson cut the support the families had been promised for each recaptive they boarded. "Their treatment has been shameful because of our meddling population. . . . much harm has been done," wrote ACS physician Dr. Isaac H. Snowden. Even in death the recaptives were a point of contention between the ACS and the Liberian government and its citizens. In a morbid episode, the City of Monrovia declared the old ACS building there a public nuisance because the corpses of dead recaptives were piled outside its walls. The fate of the youngsters aboard Copeland's ship is not known.[11]

Copeland stayed in Liberia several weeks. His first glimpse of the country was beautiful Grand Cape Mount, northwest of Monrovia on the

Atlantic coast, where about fifty houses dotted a leafy vista. A few miles down the coast, just north of Monrovia, the St. Paul's River flowed into the Atlantic. Nearly three-quarters of a mile wide at the ocean, it was navigable for about twenty miles upstream to Millsburg. The tropical topography was different from the Piedmont Virginia that Copeland knew, flatter, more like coastal Georgia or Florida, with exotic flora and fauna. Copeland's sojourn in Liberia began during one of the most pleasant months in West Africa, December. By March, the heat would become oppressive, with the rainy season beginning in June and lasting until October, reversing the planting seasons emigrants were accustomed to in America. To trade produce, rice and commodities, emigrants and West Africans navigated the St. Paul's River to Monrovia. Relying on the river held back settlements away from the St. Paul's, because the emigrants had built few roads.

The Monrovia Copeland visited was not an isolated little Southern-style town. It was also a port city, a market town, and the capital of a sovereign nation with commercial and military ship traffic as well as a small ship-building industry, surrounded by Indigenous people and Africans from other parts of the continent, all with vibrant cultures. While Copeland was in Liberia, the town saw the arrival of Prince Marmora, a successor of Sao Boso, with a retinue of 100 people including a band with five horn players, drums and cymbals. Marmora, a Muslim who spoke English, met with President Benson on behalf of other chiefs who were interested in keeping Indigenous commerce flowing between the interior and Monrovia. On market Saturdays, as many as sixty canoes from up-river farms brought produce and Indigenous commodities.[12]

The capital city was in a picturesque setting with a lighthouse and a fort atop Cape Mesurado. Like Lynchburg, Monrovia was built on a hill, with stone warehouses and stores at its base. Fruit trees flourished in the quarter-acre lots, but so did weeds as the original structures deteriorated. The Americo-Liberians worshipped at three churches—Methodist, Baptist, and Presbyterian. Two newspapers documented the goings-on, the *Liberia Herald* and *African Luminary.* Many of the emigrant families had Indigenous children living with them, a custom that continued into the twentieth century. Liberia College had been completed (but not opened) in Monrovia, with three professors, two of whom would be appointed in 1862 as commissioners to travel to the United States and urge free people to emigrate. US Navy warships from the Africa Squadron often anchored at Monrovia, with the *Saratoga* in the harbor around this time.[13]

Where did Copeland stay during his visit? It seems likely he boarded with the people he called his "fellow servants" from the Samuel Miller farm. The most recent, Harriet Miller, had arrived in Monrovia a few years before to join her sister and several other Millers who had emigrated one or two at a time throughout the 1850s. The Millers had survived their own initial exposure to the *anopheles* mosquitos and were doing well, with no interest in returning to the US, Copeland wrote. He also claimed he found about 100 people he knew around the country. After arriving in Monrovia, he sent a note to William Helms, who had emigrated from Lynchburg twelve years before at Copeland's encouragement. Helms "immediately came down the river" from where he had been working on a mill wheel in upper Caldwell on the St. Paul's for an emotional reunion with his friend: "You ought to have witnessed the greeting between us," Copeland wrote. Helms had ordered a barrel of flour and two barrels of dried mackerel to be shipped on the same voyage that brought Copeland to Monrovia. Like Copeland, Helms was a talented craftsman who could do a little of everything and was planning to build a boat, as well as a machine to clean coffee beans for processing. For projects like this, he relied on the ACS to ship him tools and materials like nails, sheet iron, brass wire and a grindstone, which he could afford but were not available in Liberia.[14]

Determined to collect as much information about the country as possible, Copeland didn't spend all his time with people he already knew. The Liberian legislature, modeled on the US Congress, was meeting when he arrived. Far from shy, Copeland not only attended four sessions, where he said the legislators were as talented as those in America, he also called on a future president and dined with him. Liberian Sen. Edward J. Roye, an Ohio native, was one of the wealthiest men in the country. (Roye posed for a daguerreotype portrait in 1856 that shows a tall, youngish man with arm raised as if swearing an oath, dressed in a frock coat and vest. The photographer was free emigrant Augustus Washington, talented and successful in this new art form back in the United States, where he photographed abolitionist John Brown glowering at his lens in 1846.) Roye owned a merchant ship and a fine home in Monrovia but Copeland promptly informed the Liberian senator that people back in Ohio thought Roye was dead. The very much alive Roye offered a hearty rejoinder: "He said 'not so Copeland for I am in better health than ever I was in my life.'" Roye would be elected President in 1870 after serving as Speaker of the House and Chief Justice of the Supreme Court, but what impressed

Liberian merchant, senator, and later president, Edward Roye, in 1856. Lynchburg's Washington Copeland introduced himself to Roye and told him people back home thought Roye was dead: "Not so Copeland, for I am in better health than ever I was in my life." (Photograph by Augustus Washington; Library of Congress Prints and Photographs Division, Washington, DC, LC-USZ6-1933)

Copeland the most in 1860 was Roye's material success. He said Roye was worth $300,000 dollars and that his ship cost him $15,000. "I dined with him in Monrovia, he has a large home . . . full of dry goods of all kinds." A barber in America, Roye had accumulated $1,000 in capital to help launch his merchant career. By the time of Copeland's visit, he was advertising that he wanted to buy $50,000 worth of cotton and pay in cash. The Mandings and other ethnic groups grew Liberian cotton from native seed about 100 miles into the interior and wove it into cloth for their own use and to trade in Monrovia. The world demand for cotton was strong but the settlers themselves couldn't grow enough to make export profitable.[15]

The Americo-Liberians relied on trade with the Indigenous people to supply exports like palm oil, camwood, and ivory. The country had not overcome never-ending problems like disease, the insufficient food supply, sporadic Indigenous rebellions, and an economy that lacked a key ingredient—money. President Benson was in office during Copeland's visit. He begged farmers to create other exports of their own, and even the boosterish *Liberia Herald* editor acknowledged "the want of money is great." Still, Copeland arrived during a time of guarded hope along the St. Paul's River. "The farmers all seem to be going ahead in growing cane, making sugar syrup and many planting coffee," wrote Lynchburg emigrant Martha Erskine Harris Ricks, who had remarried after her husband, Sion, died. But processing sugarcane into syrup was laborious, and shipping raw cane was prohibitively expensive. Of the nine sugar mills along the St. Paul's, only two were operated by steam, and one by waterpower. The others were smaller, less productive, and turned by oxen, or men. The mill owners had to make their own barrels for shipping the finished syrup, although there wasn't much of a market for the limited quantities from the smaller mills. For labor, at least one St. Paul's grower depended on recaptives. He wrote that his entire operation, employing seventy-five people in the busy season, was manned by recaptives and a few Golahs. He had a steam mill and employed a Vai youth to run it. He also told the *Liberia Herald* that his cooper and sugar-maker were recaptives who excelled Americo-Liberians at their crafts. A large amount of wood was required to fire the mill and make the barrels, and the farmer bragged that seven recaptives had cut 175 cords (today, one cord is the rough equivalent of two pickup truck loads) in three weeks and earned $25 for their labor.[16]

One of the many Liberian realities was that a few individuals were doing well for themselves, usually with a combination of occupations. Copeland didn't mention meeting them, but the success of the Erskine siblings exemplified the promise that Liberia could hold for people from the United States. Despite losing everything including the rest of their family shortly after arriving in the early 1830s from Lynchburg, Martha and Hopkins Erskine overcame the odds. They were bolstered by faith, determination, and education instilled by their late father, the Reverend George Erskine, who bought their freedom from a Tennessee enslaver. By 1860, Hopkins W. Erskine was a lawyer, preacher, teacher, trader, and sugarcane grower, and, judging from his letters, one of the most learned men in Liberia. His son George, named for Hopkins's and Martha's father, received a scholarship to the University of Edinburgh. Martha Erskine Harris Ricks was friendly with Liberia's first president, Joseph Jenkins Roberts, and his wife, Jane, accompanied them on a trip to the United States in 1848, and may have been with them on a following trip England and Europe. Martha was well-known to colonization officials thanks to her independent spirit, longevity, and chatty letters. She referred to Ralph Gurley, the founder of the ACS, as her best friend and kept up with the health of his family, once apologizing for not sending his wife some oranges. In turn, the colonization society used Martha Erskine Harris Ricks to advance the cause, frequently reprinting her upbeat letters, describing her as "one of the most sensible, pious and benevolent Christian people in Liberia. . . . No person has cherished a livelier interest . . . or more cheerfully and constantly contributed to its welfare."[17]

Despite the piety of many white colonizationists, the chance to spread Christianity and Western culture in Africa remained a secondary goal of the ACS behind moving Black people out of the United States. But for some emigrants, Christianity was paramount. Martha's letters revealed her faith in evangelical terms, once referring to the recaptives: "I often wish I were a man, so I could go out amongst them, crying behold the Lamb of God." Hopkins Erskine focused on the missionary aspects of his Liberian experience, despite the setbacks of the 1840s: "Our hope of building up a nation of independent and industrious civilized and Christian people is not predicated alone on emigrants by any means but we are looking to our untutored brethren of these vast forests debased though they be, not more so however than many of the Serfs in Russia, and many parts of Europe. To teach them Christianity and [civilization] is our aim . . . this faith is in God as a Covenant-keeping Jehovah." He'd established the Presbyterian church in Clay-Ashland, which had fifty-five members, a day school, and three Sabbath schools. The Baptists and Methodists also had brick churches in the same St. Paul's River settlement.[18]

Protestant Christianity was but one of the multiple cultures competing to dominate or at least survive with its traditions intact in Liberia, and church membership was far from universal. Islam had been spreading throughout the Mediterranean and Eastern Africa for a thousand years, brought to West Africa and sub-Saharan regions by Muslim traders centuries before the Americans arrived. Two of the dominant Indigenous groups, the Vai and the Manding, were Muslim, and President Benson had forwarded to America some old letters written in Arabic by travelers in Monrovia. Colonizationists who read the letters noted that Islam was similar to Christianity other than the belief in Jesus Christ as savior rather than merely a prophet. Conversion to Islam was thought by some to offer its believers a measure of protection from the slave trade, but slaving by Muslims in the interior had also pushed Indigenous people nearer the Americo-Liberian towns for protection, accelerating the blending of American and African culture. Some Indigenous converts were entering the ministry, Martha Erskine Harris Ricks wrote, including two she had heard herself, a Kru who took the eighth chapter of the Song of Solomon as his theme, and an elegant Bassa preacher. Her letters were filled with religious references that blended spiritual and earthly matters: "We are pilgrims in this wilderness that abounds with afflictions . . . but we have a home in Heaven if we only hold out faithful until death." Copeland attended an African church service and heard an Indigenous minister preach in his native language.[19]

Life was not easy even for successful people like Martha Ricks. Around the time of Copeland's visit, Ricks had heard rumors that an Indigenous uprising might threaten the farms on the St. Paul's, writing that she would put her faith in God. She said many people had already died in an outbreak of smallpox, including President Benson's wife while he was leading troops to put down an Indigenous revolt near Cape Palmas. Marrying Henry Ricks after first husband Sion Harris died, she'd lost a daughter who died soon after birth. Like Liberia itself, her letters mixed triumph with the tragedies. She'd raised two nieces Harris brought from Tennessee two years before and they were now grown, one married with a child of her own and the other a teacher. By August 1862, the most recent threat of war with the Indigenous people along the St. Paul's had passed, and she was thinking about the war in the United States: "What a pity that such a wise nation should act thus." But she didn't linger on problems abroad. Her second husband had "set out a beautiful Coffee orchard and is still planting; it seemeth these will be the life of Africa," and she had lived long enough to see steamboats coming up the river.[20]

By now, some high-ranking Americo-Liberians had come to resent the ACS's continued meddling in Liberian government matters. But even as Liberia asserted its independence and sought diplomatic recognition from the United States the settlers continued to rely on the ACS. Hopkins Erskine needed the chief ACS agent in Liberia, Henry W. Dennis, to secure supplies and trade goods including pork, flour, lard, butter, muslin, linen, flannel, and seed corn. Requests like these would be placed through Dennis and fulfilled with ACS assistance by a merchant in the United States. The emigrants then had to reimburse the ACS.

Erskine's purchases arrived on the same voyage of the *M.C. Stevens* that brought Copeland to Liberia, and on its return trip it carried some Liberian sugar and syrup ordered by a Lynchburg merchant, probably grocer Ambrose Rucker. The *Stevens* also brought Copeland himself back to America, but not before a final trip down the coast. Copeland accompanied colonization official Hall and some of the *Stevens* emigrants to Cape Palmas at the far southeastern end of Liberia, where C. C. Hoffman, their missionary shipmate, was also bound. Hall had been the first governor of Cape Palmas, and Hoffman preached and taught there for years, claiming the region was the most thriving part of Liberia after Monrovia and the St. Paul's. Cape Palmas had originally been a separate colony founded by the Maryland Colonization Society, and briefly became an independent state after Liberia declared independence in 1847. The previously friendly Grebo people objected to this further takeover of their lands and burned Hoffman's original mission and part of the town of Harper in 1856. Monrovia sent help, and Cape Palmas became an official part of Liberia shortly thereafter. Copeland and Hall didn't linger in Cape Palmas because the *Stevens* was due to sail for America in a few days. The colonization society had not agreed to pay for Copeland's return voyage, but he talked Hall into letting him return to America gratis on the *Stevens.* After his return, Copeland was confident enough of his free status that he planned to visit Virginia and Lynchburg to proselytize for Liberia, but the Civil War prevented that, and he lectured in Ohio instead: "I would never have left Liberia if I was ten years younger . . . it is the only home for the colored man . . . I intend to be a soldier in the field for Liberia for the balance of my days." In September 1861 he wrote that he had five people from Circleville interested in emigrating and asked Hall for help with arrangements. He also said he planned to emigrate himself, but the trip didn't materialize.[21]

The opportunity to own enough land to support a family, and a rising sense of Black nationhood, remained marketing points for Liberia in the early 1860s. The commissioners appointed by the Liberian government arrived in the United States in 1862 and promoted Liberia in several Northern cities. In his charge to them, President Benson wrote that Liberia wanted to push "the cause of African nationality and independence, by concentrating, as far as was possible, African talent, wealth, and enterprise in our fatherland." He also told them to emphasize the amount of land that was available (10 acres free to each family, 50 cents an acre for more), and foremost, "the blessings of a home of freedom and equal rights." For their part, the commissioners first assured the free Black people of Baltimore and other cities where they spoke that they did not question their right to remain in America. They were offering Liberia as a chance for betterment, not merely to escape degradation in America, and acknowledged that the very existence of Liberia and colonization was seen by some as a threat to the achievement of equality in America.[22]

Colonization, not necessarily in Liberia, came to be regarded by President Abraham Lincoln as a possible concession to border states who were loyal to the Union but might object to wholesale emancipation. Lincoln mentioned colonization in the Preliminary Emancipation Proclamation but not in the actual proclamation issued a few months later in 1863. Two of the Liberian commissioners met with Lincoln in August 1862 as the president considered various colonization proposals for free Black Americans. But Lincoln was more interested in Haiti and Latin America than Liberia, mentioning "compensated emancipation and colonization" in his December 1862 address to Congress. Earlier that year, Liberia and Haiti were finally recognized by the United States as sovereign nations. Southern congressmen had blocked previous attempts to recognize both because they believed "black envoys must not be allowed to mingle among white dignitaries," writes historian Eric Burin in *Slavery and the Peculiar Solution*. By the end of 1863, government enthusiasm for colonization had dropped to almost nil. Among the reasons, Burin concludes, were Black service in the Union Army; the success of reform in the Sea Islands of South Carolina once they fell under Union control; the calls by Radical Republicans for a Freedmen's Bureau to help the freed slaves; the use of Black people as a labor force in some Union-controlled parts of the South, and the failure of a federally-financed expedition to Haiti.[23]

Washington Copeland never stopped endorsing Liberia. He remarried in 1862 and tried again to emigrate in 1863. Instead of pleading his case to the ACS, he went directly to the US government, asking that it pay for himself and a Circleville minister to emigrate. The request attracted the attention of Secretary of War Edward Stanton, who asked the Interior Department if it would underwrite Copeland and McMillan's emigration. The pair hoped to benefit from a federal proposal to help slaves freed by the war, or living in Washington, DC, leave the country, although neither fell into that category. Mentioning them by name, Secretary of the Interior J.P. Usher wrote that they didn't qualify for the assistance. Colonization reached a new low of twenty-three emigrants in 1864, and the ACS couldn't afford to keep the *M.C. Stevens* docked and repaired, so it was sold.[24]

After his 1863 rebuff, Copeland disappears from the historical record. He was only in his mid-50s but sometimes wrote as if contemplating his eventual passing: "Now is my time . . ." There's no indication he ever emigrated, and I believe he died sometime between 1863 and 1870, because he isn't listed in the 1870 census. His second wife, Ronda Bond Copeland, was counted in 1870, with her two young daughters, Estelle, 7, and Nancy Copeland, 5, all apparently living with Ronda's mother in Circleville. His daughter was head of another household and widowed. Copeland didn't mention fever or sickness in his letters about his trip, but several weeks in Liberia was sufficient time to contract malaria. Staying only a few weeks meant he was less exposed to the mosquitos than the emigrants. Had he picked up the disease and returned stateside to suffer recurring bouts of fever? He didn't say, writing only, "If I had been 10 years younger I would never have left Liberia." Despite occasional references to his age and having only 10 years left to live, perhaps nothing killed him except cold Ohio.[25]

Copeland's legacy of determination for freedom, civil rights and dignity was passed to members of his family. Bucyrus Copeland, also a carpenter, spent the war years enslaved in Lynchburg and appears to have been one of the sons Washington Copeland mentioned in his letters. He would emigrate with the large Lynchburg group in 1865. James Copeland, Washington Copeland's grandson, was involved in one of the first protests by Black Americans denied their legal voting rights, in 1870. White poll workers told a group of Black men attempting to vote in a Circleville election that their ballots would not be counted, despite passage of the 14th and 15th Amendments. The would-be voters, including James Copeland, did not take no for an answer, held a community meeting, and petitioned their congressman, contributing to passage of the Enforcement Acts of 1870–71, which made interfering with the right to vote a federal crime. Washington Copeland would have approved.[26]

8

Banished from Old Virginny

1850-1860

> God knows I have tried. . . . The emigrants must suffer under this state of things.
>
> —Dr. Isaac Snowden, Liberia, 1858

DYLSIE BANKS was living in the stifling attic of a primitive log cabin deep in the Liberian forest as the 1858 rainy season wore on. She was sixty-two years old and had arrived in West Africa with her husband, daughter, and grandchildren just weeks earlier, enduring a hard passage from the Blue Ridge Mountains of Virginia northwest of Lynchburg. Her husband was with her in the attic, the others were crowded downstairs, and nearly everyone was sick with fever. It wasn't supposed to be like this, because they were in Careysburg, a new settlement on higher ground away from the pestilent coast. A few days later, Dylsie Banks would be dead, along with her daughter and two granddaughters. Seven years later, Careysburg would become the destination of the first emigration from the United States after the Civil War—the 172 people from Lynchburg and Piedmont Virginia.[1]

Other than the efforts of Washington Copeland, there wasn't a much of a "colonization movement" in Piedmont Virginia in the 1850s. The Banks and four other large Lynchburg-area families were sent to Liberia and Ohio following their owners' deaths. Enslavers' wills, helped by limited state aid and ministers working as part-time ACS representatives, sparked these emigrations. The only 1850s emigrants from the area not freed by wills were the young Miller women sent to Monrovia at Copeland's encouragement.

The white determination to treat Black people as property meant they were passed along as inheritances, with their owner's wishes and legalisms determining their fate. When freed by their owner's will, the 1806 state law required them to leave Virginia. The newly freed might protest via

Many of the Lynchburg emigrants worked in tobacco factories. This 1875 engraving from Edward King's *The Great South* shows men, women, and children inside a local factory where the leaf was processed into plugs for chewing, cigars, and later cigarettes. (The Library Company of Philadelphia, 3379.Q)

legal petition: One Black man in Amherst County successfully pleaded to remain in "the country where he was born and raised, in sight of the bigg mountains, and away from the Sea." Some went back into slavery to avoid banishment, exercising a measure of control over their own lives and staying in the place and among the people they knew.[2]

The Banks family travails are mentioned in ACS records, and a chancery case in Nelson County years later details their circumstances in Virginia. Their Nelson County owner, Nicholas Dettor, wrote in his will that he believed Liberia "would be better" for them than continued enslavement. Sending them to a free state wasn't mentioned and he and his wife had no children to inherit them. Dettor left money to send the Banks family to Liberia and get them established, and his executor suggested they would be more comfortable away from the coast since they were accustomed to living in the mountains. While Liberia is mountainless, the ACS had located a tall hill amid the densely forested countryside southeast of the St. Paul's River. The colonizationists believed a new settlement there would be healthier than low-lying Monrovia, and named it

Careysburg, after Richmond's Lott Cary, one of Liberia's founding fathers. The colonization society was continuing its version of US expansionism, establishing an American settlement in a foreign, sovereign nation where the land had been appropriated from its original inhabitants.[3]

The ACS touted the new settlement as a landmark achievement, but the Liberian government's superintendent in Careysburg, John H. Paxton, didn't learn the Banks and others were coming until the day before they arrived in Monrovia. They traveled up the St. Paul's to Millsburg by boat amid heavy rain, then trekked 10 miles from the river through the forest to Careysburg, with some, already sick, carried on hammocks, the children toted like cargo on the backs of Indigenous bearers. They enjoyed a brief respite as they neared their destination when Zodah Quee (probably a title, not a name), the local Queah ruler who had ceded the Careysburg land to the ACS, hosted them for about an hour and provided refreshment. But no preparations had been made for them in Careysburg, where they were scattered in various log or thatch houses.[4]

One of the first people the Banks met in Careysburg was the Harvard and Dartmouth-educated Black physician, Dr. Isaac H. Snowden, who cared for them under the auspices of the ACS. Snowden's father was an antislavery preacher in Boston. Snowden and his colleague, Dr. Daniel Laing, were two of the three first Black medical students admitted to Harvard College, in 1850, although all were soon expelled at the demand of white students. (The third student was Martin Delany, the abolitionist and future US Army surgeon who advocated Black emigration from the United States but not to Liberia.) In return for their agreeing to work in Liberia, the Massachusetts Colonization Society gave Snowden and Laing financial assistance to complete their training at Dartmouth College, Massachusetts General Hospital, and in Europe. Both practiced medicine in Liberia through the 1850s and 1860s, with alternating stints in Careysburg. The young doctors had been cautious about sailing to Liberia from Baltimore in 1854. They had heard that it wasn't safe for them to even set foot in Baltimore, because Southerners emboldened by the Fugitive Slave Act might kidnap them. The ACS acknowledged that Baltimore could be dangerous but said that emigrants to Liberia were generally not targeted. Snowden and Laing safely boarded the *Sophia Walker* as cabin passengers.[5]

The Banks from Nelson County arrived in Careysburg a few years later. The whole family was sick: Myra, one of Dylsie Banks's teen-age granddaughters, caught a cough and died of pneumonia almost immediately, and the others had the fever. The pervasive, tiny *anopheles* mosquitoes that carried malaria were taken for granted as mere annoyances. Both doctors subscribed to the prevailing theory that cold, damp, drafts, and exposure brought on the debilitating, recurring attacks of fever. Laing tied a number of 1860 cases to poorly-chinked log cabins, which may have been accurate, not because of drafts but because of mosquitoes flitting through the walls at night. Snowden did his best to help the Banks, although he lacked any effective treatments, especially quinine. Both doctors relied on herb tea, pepper poultices, calomel, ipecac, and laudanum when available. When the Banks arrived, Snowden didn't even have much of those medicines. Well-prepared, healthy food was also important for the emigrants' survival, and he had fired the ACS-employed cook for incompetence.

Snowden himself wasn't particularly enthusiastic about the ACS cause, saying he considered it a duty and pleasure to care for the emigrants, "though not strictly speaking as a colonizationist." His letters from Careysburg are full of such contrasts, and he grew increasingly pessimistic as time wore on. He wrote in 1858 that Careysburg had a sanitary reputation and only needed a good road to the St. Paul's to become the "Saratoga of Liberia." But a month later, he reported that as the settlers cleared land, they uncovered swampy and marshy areas, and there was not enough meat, flour or sugar to support them. Adding to his gloom was the fact that the ACS rarely paid him on time, and his own family was living many miles away. "God knows I have tried . . ." he wrote. "The emigrants must suffer under this state of things." Meanwhile, the ACS itself continued to blame sickness and death on the emigrants themselves. In spring 1854, a colonial agent had said some deaths were to be expected but that emigrants didn't need to worry about disease if they took care of themselves. The *African Repository* attributed deaths to causes such as "excessive or unnecessary effort in pulling a canoe 12 or 14 miles," "inflammation of the bowels produced by eating too much pine-apple and oranges," and "hard drink and exposure." The *African Repository* claimed the mortality rate was less than 3 percent among healthy emigrants who followed physicians' advice.[6]

The Nelson County emigrants' suffering had started even before they boarded their ship in Baltimore. Dylsie Bank's two-year-old grandson, Mitchell, died there the Saturday before they sailed. He may have had measles, which broke out among other children during the voyage. If he had lived, his life might have compared favorably with that of his contemporaries back home where he could have been tortured to death. Such was the fate of a young Nelson County field worker in 1854, who was beaten by an overseer and drenched with brine until he died. This was reported in the *Liberator*, just under an item which described the castration without trial of a free man in Bedford County who was accused of getting into bed with a white girl.[7]

The ACS wanted to send as many emigrants as possible to Careysburg, but the Liberian government favored a more measured approach, and they frequently clashed. The government re-iterated that the country needed educated, better-off emigrants, not unschooled laborers, like many of the recent Virginia people. Paxton, another ex-Virginian, wrote in early 1859 that the emigrants the ACS sent there were industrious but "not intelligent." President Stephen A. Benson remarked that many of the Indigenous people were more intellectually advanced than half of the annual emigrants from the US. Stubborn, determined against all odds, emigrants who arrived with at least modest means and survived the fever had a chance to achieve their liberty in Careysburg as it grew. An emigrant from South Carolina, Joseph Peacher, wrote that he was well-satisfied with his new home there, had cleared his land by early 1859, was building a house, and planning to give lectures on farming and agriculture, even as recent emigrants like the Banks continued to die. Peacher came to Liberia on his own, saving enough money to buy freedom for himself, his wife, and child. He was the type of emigrant the Liberian government wanted. [8]

People like Peacher sought independence on their own terms, using the resources of colonization for their own benefit, but they were the exceptions. Even after their eventual freedom was ordained, the Cheatwoods of Bedford County were enslaved for decades. The Davis family of Amherst County, encouraged by Washington Copeland, waited a year to learn their fate as relatives and lawyers made sure they were legally free on the date recent state aid went into effect. Like the Banks, these Piedmont Virginia emigrant families were mostly farm laborers and domestics and not welcomed by the Liberian government. The secretary of the Maryland Colonization Society lamented the lack of educated emigrants, especially from the North: "They cannot, will not, emigrate to such a country, with clod-hopping slaves, clad in linsey-woolsey and just redeemed from massa's plantation." Most abolitionists still opposed colonization, but a few had changed their minds after Liberia became an independent nation in 1847, so they made an uneasy peace with the colonization society. [9]

To maintain its limited white backing in the South, the ACS had to avoid anything that appeared to benefit the enslaved themselves or boost abolition, sometimes splitting up families with different owners. After they were freed by their owner's will, the Rogers families in Bedford spent nine years working for hire and protesting before they eventually were forced to emigrate. Working as domestics, nurturing orchards, and raising crops on Flat Top Mountain west of inappropriately named Liberty (today's town of Bedford), some of the Rogers were forced to go to Liberia in 1859 while their husbands or wives remained behind with other owners. Freed by the will of a former Quaker, Timothy Rogers, who died in 1850, they fought banishment from Virginia even as relatives of their deceased master protested that he was insane. After losing in court, Frances and Mary Rogers used money intended to sustain them in Liberia to buy passage with their children back to America. [10]

Timothy Rogers was raised a strict Quaker in Vermont and Canada but was expelled from the sect for joining a local militia. He soon moved to Piedmont Virginia, taught school in Lynchburg, married, and went to great lengths to gain ownership of the enslaved people who had belonged to his wife. Abandoning the Quaker precepts of his youth, the master of Wolf Creek plantation was known to be rough on his wife while drinking and once whipped an enslaved woman. His wife retaliated and had him held down by other enslaved while she whipped him. In spite of this humiliation, he devoted a large portion of his will to directions for the emigration of nearly 30 enslaved people and left ample money to support them in Liberia. They spent the years after his death in a kind of limbo, working for hire, their pay held by white people, pondering separation from their husbands, wives, and children as relatives' lawsuits dragged on. Daniel Rogers appears to have been the top hand on the Wolf Creek plantation, receiving a personal bequest of $100, but was more than ready to disobey his late master's wishes. He had an enslaved wife and family not owned by Rogers and refused to go to Liberia without them. Moreover, he convinced other Rogers enslaved to resist, fought his case through the courts, and eventually chose re-enslavement to remain near his family. Other family members were also married to enslaved people not owned by Rogers and had to leave them behind in Virginia.[11]

The Bedford County commonwealth's attorney had Timothy Rogers's will in his pocket when he approached a local minister representing the ACS in the spring of 1850. The ACS was enthusiastic but foresaw opposition to the will and tried to act quickly by raising $1,800 in New York City to finance the emigration: "We have sent this year already 393 emigrants, and we are now upwards of $26,000 in debt. Dare we say we will take them?" But the Rogers people would not comply. "They are not all willing to go," reported Jacob Mitchell, the white Presbyterian minister. "One, I understand, prefers remaining in slavery. But most or all the women who have husbands from whom they are unwilling to part, who are the property of three different masters. . . . The men are very valuable and would sell for $2,600. Their masters are much attached to them and would not consent to part with them under any other circumstances." The money the other Rogers earned by hiring themselves out in the interim was withheld until they reached Liberia.[12]

The ACS could no longer afford to employ full-time agents in the South, so Mitchell worked closely with the Reverend William McClain, the ACS financial secretary who ran the day-to-day logistics and apparatus of colonization. Both were determined to send the former Rogers enslaved to Liberia, but their motivations differed. McClain was a Northerner who was free of some of the personal prejudices that characterized other colonizationists. He was vexed that the ACS could not spend or raise money or even participate in the purchase of enslaved family members for fear of being branded as abolitionist. He expressed concern for the people themselves, describing the Rogerses' situation as stressful, noting that even if the families stayed together in Virginia, they could eventually be separated through future sale. But if the families went to Liberia without the men, he argued, they would lack the support needed to survive in a new country. McClain spent much time on the case: On May 29, 1850, he wrote five separate letters about the Rogers to people in New York, Boston, and Virginia. One of those letters was to Mitchell, a native New Yorker who studied at Princeton before coming to Virginia in 1830 to preach revival. By the 1850s, Mitchell was minister at Peaks Church in Liberty, fully invested in white Southern culture and an enslaver himself. Like his neighbors, he wanted free Black people out of Virginia but complained that the initial plan for the Rogers emigration was a "fast operation (for) those of us who are accustomed to move at our leisure."[13]

The colonization proponents did not move quickly enough to forestall the first lawsuit from Timothy Rogers's relatives. His brother-in-law and another Virginia relative wanted to keep some of the enslaved people for themselves. Mitchell and McClain worked with Rogers's executors, who suggested that the people harvest the current crop on the plantation, then be hired out until the lawsuit was settled, and that their accumulated wages go toward their eventual emigration. However, McClain advised against forcing the enslaved to emigrate: Unwilling or reluctant emigrants tended to suffer more during the acclamation process, and often didn't prosper in Liberia.

In 1854, the will's stipulations were upheld, and emigration plans resumed. The interrelationships of the Rogers families is unclear and their common surname comes from their enslaver. Researcher Randy Saylor, who made a detailed study of their genealogy, believes it's possible that some of the children were fathered by Timothy Rogers. He left $3,000 to support the families in Liberia, close to a fortune in rural Bedford County, so other relatives filed another lawsuit, claiming Rogers was out of his mind when he drew up the will. Insanity claims were not unusual from heirs of slaveowners hoping to keep property and money for themselves. Twenty-five of his acquaintances testified that while Rogers was a mean drunk, he was not insane. That case dragged on until 1859 while the families continued to work in virtual bondage. Again, the will was upheld. Daniel Rogers and three other men, London, Phil and Bob Rogers, remained steadfast and were indicted by the Bedford court for remaining as free men in Virginia, and were sentenced to be sold back into slavery. Daniel Rogers petitioned the court to remain in Virginia as a free man with his wife and five children. Bedford had more than 10,000 enslaved African Americans around this time, 40 percent of the population, and the white people were in no mood to add any additional free Black people to the numbers. His petition was turned down, he was indicted for remaining in the state illegally and finally had to re-enslave himself to the owner of his wife and children.[14]

But 27 former Rogers slaves did finally emigrate in 1859, and the colonization society acknowledged that the $2,355 they had earned in the interim was to be paid them, in gold coin, "for their own personal use" after they landed in Liberia. They left the country in spring and fall 1859 on two separate voyages of the *M.C. Stevens*. Both groups went to Greenville, down the coast from Monrovia. Greenville was founded by the Mississippi Colonization Society in 1838, but many American settlers had left after Indigenous wars depleted rice and bread supplies a few years before the Rogers arrived. By 1859 rice was plentiful and the colonization society was trying to repopulate the isolated community.[15]

Although Greenville needed able-bodied men to rebuild, enslavers were especially reluctant to free valuable working-age men needed to sustain the Southern economy. Out of the twenty-seven Bedford emigrants, only two were adult men, Frank and Tom Rogers. Two were teen-age boys, and the rest women and children. The first group of Rogers to emigrate included Frank, 46; Tom, 37; Sally, 50, Aberilla, 42; and their nine offspring. They sailed from Baltimore on May 12, 1859, with a large crowd and a reporter from the *Baltimore American* on hand. The *African Repository* referred to Africa as "the land of their fathers" although their families had been in America for generations. A Black missionary noted that he was not from Africa and had never seen it but was willing to go cheerfully "as a field of labor, where he could do good for his race." The religious ceremony included readings from the 35th chapter of Isaiah, the 46th Psalm, and preaching about Bible ministry to unknown lands.[16]

The second, even more reluctant, group of Rogers emigrated later in 1859. Mary and Frances Rogers had refused to go without their husbands and initially said they preferred to remain enslaved. Frances Rogers begged Mitchell to purchase her husband, a valuable worker who apparently belonged to a Rogers's relative, so he could go with them. That didn't happen, and the women changed their minds only a few weeks before their November departure, for a reason that later became evident. Dealing with a large group of Black people who declined to follow white direction was a new experience for John Sale, the will's executor. Although the women declared they didn't want to emigrate without their husbands, he attributed their refusal to "some mysterious cause." McClain of the ACS acknowledged the wrenching decision the families faced: "I am much troubled . . . it does not seem right . . . to separate man and wife, and leave the wife to take care of so many children, but what can we do. We have no funds to buy those men. Our Constitution will not allow us to use our monies for such purpose . . . it would at once raise the cry against us that we are interfering with slavery. That we are no better than abolitionists. . . . I have not the heart to advise the women to go without their husbands. Indeed, I understood last spring that those who then declined going, had determined to go back into slavery again rather than go."[17]

Leaving their husbands and homes in Bedford for Liberia on the second voyage in November were fifteen members of two families that included Frances Rogers, 40, and her nine children, ages 2–23; and Mary Rogers, 45, and her four children, ages 5–12. They landed in tiny Greenville, accessible to the ACS only by sea, less than a year before a major disruption of Liberian society, the arrival of the more than 3,500 Africans rescued from slave ships near Cuba and off the African coast. About half of them were detained in Key West until they could go to Liberia, including many hundreds sent to Greenville. Dr. John McCalla Jr., who would serve as a surgeon in the Union Army a few years later, had been hired by the ACS to tend to the Africans' needs and accompany them from Key West, and he left vivid descriptions of Greenville in his journal. Viewed from the sea, it was a beautiful place with white beaches and rich green foliage. The village itself was small with a few nice dwellings where officials lived, and multiple small frame houses for emigrants. In one of those, McCalla met a couple who had emigrated from Georgia and knew his mother and grandmother. Oranges, bananas, guava, lemon and plantain grew in abundance, along with coffee plants. Near the colonial town was a Kru village of thatched houses. McCalla remained in Greenville a couple of weeks, entertained almost every night by ACS and Liberian government representatives, eating apple pie and drinking East India pale ale.[18]

But by then, Frances and Mary Rogers and their children from the first Rogers's emigration were on the move again. The women hatched a plan before they arrived in Liberia to use their earned money to pay for their passage back to the United States and maybe even buy their husbands' freedom. Dr. Henry J. Roberts, brother of ex-President Joseph J. Roberts, was in Greenville in 1860 and wrote that Frances and Mary Rogers "are of the opinion that men can live and do well in Liberia, but they do not think indeed they say they know that women . . . with . . . four (and) nine children to provide for cannot do well. They are determined to return to the United States, and their minds are fully made up to return by the first favorable opportunity unless they can be convinced their husbands will be sent out." Roberts continued, "They made up their minds to this before they landed here and they have never wavered in their determination. It appears when they left the United States they were under the impression that there was sufficient means for them to . . . purchase their husbands but finding themselves disappointed in this particular, Liberia has no charms for them and they make themselves miserable deploring the severity of their lot. They appear to be worthy women and have a fine lot of children that may prove of service to Liberia and it is a great pity that some means could not have been devised to have had their husbands gone along with them."[19]

Roberts said the women had enough money to purchase passage back to the US for their families, but not enough to buy their husbands and return with them to Liberia. He asked McClain: "Will you not my dear sir exert your influence to give these women the desire of their hearts, to embrace their companions on free soil and to raise their children in a free country where none dare molest them or make them afraid?" The ACS rarely publicized the return of dissatisfied emigrants, and the trail of the Rogers disappears after the Greenville agent wrote that he had not had time to prepare an accounting of their ship's departure for America due to the overwhelming job of dealing with the hundreds of unexpected Africans from Key West. Where did they go when they returned to America? I was unable to determine this, but they apparently are not listed in the 1870 census or among the people receiving rations from the Freedmen's Bureau in Bedford after the Civil War.[20]

ALSO FREED by will was the Davis family from Amherst County, who chose migration to Liberia rather than a free state or re-enslavement after their owner died in the early 1850s. Washington Copeland reported that he talked with them and influenced them to emigrate. The group had a healthy component of six younger, able-bodied men. Except for one, all the family members were under 40, including two infants, James and Paulina. Eady Davis, 78, was the senior member of the Davis family, born around the same year as the United States itself. He and other members of his family were freed in 1854 and emigrated aboard the *Sophia Walker*. Traveling with them were three free Black Amherst residents: Susan F. Johnson, 18, who was married to one of the Davis men, and her daughter Francis A. Johnson, 3, both born free; and Ann Eliza Wilson, 28, who Copeland had urged to accompany them. The Davis enslaver was Arthur B. Davis, an attorney, who built a brick mansion, Edgewood—nicknamed "Arthur's Folly"—in 1818 on the stage road through Amherst County, with walls later hand-painted to resemble French wallpaper. He had been Amherst County's clerk of court, the most powerful figure in the day-to-day government of nineteenth-century Virginia counties, later moving to a plantation near the mountains. His former slaves' choice of emigration to Liberia was unusual enough to be reported in the *New York Times:* "A gentleman of Amherst County, lately deceased, has left $6,000 for the settlement of his negroes in a free State. The heirs of the gentleman being willing that the slaves should be sent to Liberia, application is to be made . . . to this effect."[21]

A month before their ship was to sail, the ACS wrote to Davis's brother, requesting more details including a death certificate and documentation of the date the Davis's were freed, to ensure the state would reimburse the ACS. The legislature had recently set up the new Virginia Colonization Board and authorized modest state aid for individual emigrants. The infant board embraced old ideas: "It is an obvious truth that there is now a very extended and growing sentiment in Virginia that the free negro population is injurious to the country; and there is a strong desire felt by many that they should be removed, if it could be done in a manner consistent with the claims of justice and humanity." The board's first report noted that the number of free Black people in Virginia was continuing to increase, before plunging into a mix of math, fantasy, and wishful thinking, declaring that the relatively small numbers of free Black people exiled to Africa would somehow end this growth. Only Black people who were free as of April 6, 1853, were eligible for state aid, with official documents and certifications from lawyers required. Once the legalities had been observed, the Virginia Colonization Board reimbursed the ACS $50 for each member of the Davis party except Ann Wilson, who may have lacked proper free papers.[22]

Theirs was another overcrowded voyage. The *Sophia Walker* sailed from Norfolk on May 14, 1854, then went to Savannah to pick up more emigrants and didn't reach Liberia until the end of July. Even before the ship left Norfolk, ACS organizer McClain said he was "almost dead with troubles, fatigue and anxiety." He'd booked too many emigrants and ended up hiring a second, smaller ship to handle the overflow. About twenty children died on the ship, as well as eight or nine more shortly after arrival. The water went bad, contributing to the onboard deaths. The eighteen-member Davis group went to Buchanan, one of three small towns near Bassa Cove about halfway down the Liberian coast from Monrovia. The Buchanan region had originally been colonized by Black Quakers from Philadelphia, and when the Davises arrived, it was home to Vice President Stephen A. Benson, who would be elected Liberia's second president in 1856. The nineteenth-century obsession with race was evident in ACS founder Ralph R. Gurley's description of him: "Mr. Benson is of purely African descent: but through his dark features beams a mind of great intelligence."[23]

Bassa was nowhere near as populous as the St. Paul's region. Still, the newly named town of Buchanan boasted not only a day school and a Sunday school, but also a steam sawmill, one of the few in the country. Benson had also arranged for the donation of an oil press, used to make oil from palm nuts, peanuts, and castor beans, but as usual in Liberia a key part of the process was in short supply—casks to contain the pressed oil. In nearby Fishtown, he built a large building for the ACS where new emigrants could live for their first few months. There were several of these soon-dilapidated buildings around the country, called "Receptacles."[24]

When the Davis group arrived, many people from a previous emigration were sick in the Receptacle with fever. The Buchanan region was developing a reputation for mortality and some emigrants arriving in Monrovia a few months after the Davis group refused to go there. There are fewer ACS mentions of the Buchanan people than those in Monrovia or the St. Paul's River settlements, and the Davis family disappears from the historical record after their arrival.

Other emigrants from the Davis voyage were sent to the St. Paul's region, including a young couple from Kentucky, Carey and Nancy Bell. They didn't like Liberia and managed to return to the US a couple years later. Nancy Bell was interviewed about her life when she was an elderly woman. She provided a gruesome account of burials at sea on the way to Liberia: "The bodies were weighted with sand so they would sink. But I saw the sharks nab the bodies no more than they struck the water. The sharks do certainly know when there is a dead body on the ship." Her husband served as a cook for three years in the Union army during the Civil War and later was elected to a town council in Kentucky but wasn't allowed to serve because his white opponents discovered that he was still technically a citizen of Liberia.[25]

THE CHEATWOODS from Bedford County went to Liberia in 1853, even though only a few had been born when their enslaver died in 1828. The twenty-two family members included only two men over eighteen and endured a hellish voyage across the Atlantic on the appropriately named *Banshee*. They were packed aboard "like swine" in conditions one white colonizationist traveling with them compared to the Middle Passage that brought their ancestors to America.[26]

The Cheatwoods' late owner, John Cheatwood, was a Revolutionary War veteran who fought the British with Morgan's Virginia Riflemen. His will set in motion a complicated arrangement to pass along some enslaved to his sister while eventually freeing them all. He also designated six men to be manumitted after his death, but only after they had been hired out for a total of $750. That $750 was to be used to support of the rest of the enslaved, whom he willed to his sister, Alice, for the rest of her life. By the time she died in 1851, the Black families had grown, with 15 children born after John Cheatwood wrote his will in 1821.[27]

Part of the Virginia-Liberian tragedy is that poor people like the Cheatwoods who had spent their lives working and raising children in Virginia were not wanted by the governments in America or in Liberia. In the early 1850s, three separate organizations wanted to move Black people out of Virginia: The American Colonization Society; the Virginia Colonization Society; and the similarly named Virginia Colonization Board. George Leyburn, a white minister in Bedford County who also preached to Black congregations, represented both the ACS and the Virginia Colonization Society. Referring to the Cheatwoods, Leyburn wrote in summer 1853 that he was pushing "emigration with a number of the best-looking and most respected colored people in this quarter" but needed to provide them with facts about their chief concern, the fever.[28]

The parsimonious state aid from the Virginia Colonization Board was to be financed by a $1 annual tax levied on each free Black male in Virginia. Leyburn did not like this, believing that the state should pay for colonization, not tax the freemen. The almost-powerless Virginia Colonization Board devoted most of its next annual report to complaining about its lack of resources "for diminishing this species of obnoxious population" in Virginia. State law forbade it from recruiting or assisting with the logistics of colonization, other than through the ACS. The Cheatwoods were among only 68 of the 154 Black Virginians aboard the *Banshee* who had sufficient paperwork to prove they were free as of April 6, 1853, and therefore qualified for the state aid.[29]

They traveled by steamboat from Richmond to the Norfolk docks, where colonization officials could not locate enough fresh water to supply the month-long voyage. Eventually, they turned to a US Navy commander, who had some water not fit for a warship, but suitable for an African passage. Among the 277 emigrants with the Cheatwoods on the *Banshee* were William and Rosabella Burke of Fairfax County, and their four children, all just-freed slaves of the family of Col. Robert E. Lee. Others came from Maryland, North Carolina, Kentucky and Indiana. Unlike the Burkes, many of the emigrants arrived with very little and were given clothing in Norfolk.[30]

The *Banshee* first took on emigrants and cargo in Baltimore, where the departure was delayed overnight because the crew was drunk. This was a bad omen and ACS officials were worried beyond their normal fretting. However, the risks were viewed as acceptable, and the ACS needed to remove as many Black Americans as possible from the US, so the ship left supplies behind in Norfolk to crowd on more passengers. "Oh me, she is not half big enough," wrote McClain. Still, sending this many people to Africa was viewed as a major success for the organization, boosting the number of emigrants to 783 in 1853, the most of any year since 1832.[31]

Whooping cough broke out among the ship's children and some died. The survivors arrived in Monrovia on New Year's Day, 1854. How most of the Cheatwoods fared isn't clear, but Caroline, nineteen, and Elizabeth/Eliza, seven, both died within months of their arrival, along with twenty-six others from the *Banshee*. William Burke picked up the story of the Virginians in a letter home. He said the voyage was rough but added, "This certainly is a fine place for anyone who has money or goods to sell to get along very fast. At the same time, I am happy to say that a poor man may also live if he has health and if he is industrious . . ." Burke went on to scout the countryside, studied Latin and Greek at the seminary in Monrovia and became a Presbyterian minister in 1857. He and his wife kept in contact with the Lees for years, and like other emigrants, they took Indigenous children into their home.[32]

Although the colonization society boasted that new emigrants were free to live wherever they wanted, the reality was different. Many of the Virginians from the *Banshee* settled along the St. Paul's River at the direction of the society. The 1855 ACS annual report combined cynical honesty about emigration with grotesque hope: "Some of them will doubtless not live through the acclimating process. They will go to an early tomb! But the mould shall live fresh upon their graves, and the flowers planted over them shall flourish in perpetual bloom, for they died in a holy endeavor to rekindle the extinguished fires, and rebuild the shattered fortunes of their race."[33]

Rhetoric like this triggered the Reverend E.W. Stokes and other ministers in Monrovia who saw colonization as anything but a "holy endeavor." Stokes, from Baltimore, was among the first Black men ordained by the Protestant Episcopal Church. In a formal letter to the ACS in 1853, the ministers protested emigrants being sent hither and yon amid rampant fever, "dragged like galley slaves to a place they do not like and to which they had no intention of going." One ACS agent in Liberia had even bragged that he persuaded some emigrants that "fever is the handmaid of health." With each new settlement established, the ACS renewed its claim that it was in a healthy locale, but the ministers said many of the settlements were in "very unhealthy, yea, sickly places." The powerful letter charged that the society was actually committing "the wholesale murder of innocent human beings, for though men may be reared in the degradation of slavery, they have immortal souls."[34]

The cruel choices facing anyone freed in Virginia in the 1850s were exemplified by the Shacklefords. As North and South edged toward war in 1859, the will of an Amherst County woman, who had died four years earlier, Frances B. Shackleford, ordained the destiny of nearly 50 Black Virginians. Her will stated she wanted them sent to Liberia, but only if they agreed, and if not, to a free state. The will directed that most of the enslaved be hired out for four years after her death, and the proceeds used to settle them in Liberia or a free state. Shackleford made her preference clear: "It is my wish that my slaves elect to go to Liberia, believing that it will be most conducive to their happiness, which is my object and desire." The enslaved spoke up for themselves and all refused to go to Liberia, objected to leaving Virginia, and were ordered to go to Ohio.[35]

Seven of the Shacklefords chose to remain enslaved in Virginia and the others were banished. Their departure via James River canal boats from the Lynchburg basin turned out to be quite a spectacle. "Some . . . were thrown on the boat by main force, so much opposed were they to leaving," reported the *Lynchburg Republican* in a story published as far away as Salt Lake City and recounted in the *Liberator*. About 1,000 Black people gathered on Lynchburg's waterfront to watch and wish them well. The deportees vowed to return to Virginia as soon as they could. As the canal boats pulled away from the Lynchburg docks, the unwilling deportees began singing an early version of "Carry Me Back To Old Virginny." A few days later, half of them ran away before reaching the Ohio border.[36]

9

The More Things Change . . .

1860–1865

> We are willing to venture upon the land of Africa and there put our trust in almighty providence.
>
> —Levi Norvell, Lynchburg, 1865

In October 1859, the same month Lynchburg's main Liberia advocate, Washington Copeland, moved to Ohio, abolitionist John Brown raided Harper's Ferry. The Reverend W. Asbury Christian, born only a few years later, mused about the eve of the Civil War in his 1900 history of Lynchburg, claiming that "Many discussions were going on in regard to slavery . . . Lynchburg was deeply interested in it, but was not much exercised over it as the abolitionists were. Little apprehension was felt that the property in slaves was in danger. The buying and selling of negroes was going on as if nothing was being said. . . . Some feared trouble, but if it came, it would be in the next generation."[1]

The belief that Lynchburg was a genteel town which only wanted to be left alone to continue its commerce with the North and treat the enslaved in a kindly fashion was part of the Lost Cause myth, perpetuated by writers like Christian. After the South lost, Virginia teachers were armed with textbooks written to hide the truth of slavery, glorify the Confederacy, and normalize the continued treatment of Black Americans as inferior. It's no coincidence that Lynchburg's Confederate soldier monument, which still looms over downtown, was erected in 1899 by the United Daughters of the Confederacy as the old rebels, but not their beliefs, were passing away. Its cornerstone was dedicated in 1900, the same year Christian's book was published. Confederate memorabilia inside the cornerstone includes a poem entitled, "The Nation's Ward, A Nigger."[2]

Christian's *Lynchburg and Its People* didn't mention that some local white people in 1860 supported a secret Southern movement, the Knights of the Golden Circle, founded to preserve slavery and extend it by

A Confederate soldier facing south toward the old City Courthouse towers over Lynchburg's Monument Terrace, up a steep hill from the location of the nineteenth-century slave market. The statue was erected in 1899 and dedicated in 1900 by the United Daughters of the Confederacy during the Lost Cause era. (Author's photo)

colonizing Mexico and the West Indies. John Wilkes Booth was a member. A Lynchburg Methodist minister, J. R. S. Clark, was chaplain of the national organization and traveled around the state in the summer of 1860 with the founder of the group, writer, public speaker and phrenologist George Bickley, who proclaimed in Lynchburg that the Knights' flag would soon be hoisted in Mexico, claiming that the Knights had been preparing for war in Lynchburg and other cities. Bickley and Booth had also been members of the secretive Know Nothing society (later the American Party) which had a strong presence in Lynchburg in the mid-1850s. Chaplain Clark was seen walking around town "with his beard fully grown and a pair of revolvers in his pocket," and withstood a challenge to his reappointment to the Methodist clergy because the presiding bishop, local colonizationist John Early, took a lenient view of such conduct. Violence against Black people was commonplace and authorized by the Lynchburg courts. An enslaved man, Wesley, received 25 lashes in the summer of 1859 after he was convicted of passing a counterfeit 50-cent piece to another enslaved person, even though Wesley had a speech impediment making defending himself difficult. [3]

By January 1861, some unidentified men in Lynchburg were talking about going to Washington and assassinating President-elect Abraham Lincoln should he be inaugurated, according to a letter to Lincoln signed by R.A. Hunt of Lynchburg. Hunt said he was a "proud friend" of Lincoln and offered to go to Washington to raise a body of men to defend Lincoln. That slavery was the cause of the Civil War was rarely disputed among the white elites at the time, especially the educated women. Longtime Fredericksburg colonization supporter Mary B. Blackford wrote in early 1861 to the American Colonization Society's William McClain from Lynchburg, where she was visiting relatives: "Some of our earliest . . . patriot[s] expressed the belief that slavery threatened us as a nation with mighty evils, though they did not foresee them in this form. All of the quarrels that have shaken this country to its foundations, have grown out of this fatal cause, and now, it is destroying us as a great people."[4]

A Lynchburg resident wrote in the mid-1850s, "We hear a great deal said about 'Big Richmond,' 'Little Petersburg,' and 'aristocratic Lynchburg,'" and the city was reputed to be the second wealthiest per capita in the United States. With fine buildings among high hills, it reminded a northern reporter of Albany, NY. Railroads had begun to eclipse the James River and Kanawha Canal, with converging lines running to the North, South, East, and West. Mr. and Mrs. Samuel Garland Jr. were among the leading members of society, with old white Virginia credentials that were impeccable: An enslaver and great-grandnephew of President James Madison, he was a graduate of Virginia Military Institute and studied law at the University of Virginia. Elizabeth Garland was the daughter of local merchant and art lover John G. Meem, and their 1856 wedding was described as one of the most brilliant social events ever held in Lynchburg. They lived in a two-story brick home in the Garland Hill neighborhood, where Garland enslaved six men and four women, including several teenagers. Their last winter of peace, 1860–61, was one of "unprecedented gaiety," featuring grand costume balls, one hosted by wealthy neighbor, Dr. Edward Murrell, who had freed and sent Jack and Patience Murrell and their son to Liberia in 1847. His costume ball featured revelers dressed as lower-class Irish immigrants, many of whom came to the city to help build the canal and railroads.[5]

More than 70 stores, banks, and other businesses lined both sides of Main Street. Locals enjoyed the theater, including a performance of *Richard III* in November 1860 at Dudley Hall. Early in the war, advertisements for plays, lectures and musical performances were frequent. Downtown, readers could buy a volume of Thackeray or a pamphlet with a neatly printed local sermon. Another bookstore advertised books on cavalry tactics, dime novels, and justifications for slavery. Kyle's Gallery offered portrait photographs. Two daily newspapers reported local, national and international news, and one sold the *Southern Literary Messenger.* Before the war, the wealthy toured Europe. During the war, businesses advertised European goods received via blockade runners. Multiple brick mansions dotted the hills above the riverfront along streets named for the US presidents through James Buchanan. "The telegraph is getting to be a more and more popular institution . . . It has become one of the necessities of the age," the *Daily Virginian* noted in 1859.[6]

As the Civil War began, more than 72,000 people lived in the city and the three surrounding counties. About 30,700 were enslaved, roughly 43 percent, compared to the state average of about 30 percent. Many of these African Americans were rented by their owners to the city's tobacco factories, where the leaf was made into plugs and cigars. Others were field hands and domestics and laborers, and some were skilled craftsmen like Washington Copeland—carpenters, bricklayers, plasterers. In Lynchburg, Black people made up 60 percent of the total number of workingmen in 1860, a higher percentage than in Richmond, Charleston, Mobile, Nashville, or Baton Rouge. Southern-born white people comprised only 24 percent of the workingmen, with foreign-born white people (mostly Irish), free Black people, and white people born in northern states making up the rest. The enslaved workingmen were mostly laborers rather than artisans as they had been in the Revolutionary Period. Men who were able to maintain and learn craft skills as slavery hardened were highly valued by their white owners, and Mac Nuckles, leader of the 1865 expedition, was said to be the most valuable enslaved man in Lynchburg. As fighting began in 1861, the enslaved were still selling for high prices: "It certainly does not look like Negro property [is] depreciating much," reported the *Daily Virginian* after multiple children, teenagers, and a man and woman were auctioned to the highest bidder downtown at the city Market House.[7]

Despite their non-status as citizens, the important role Black Americans like Nuckles (soon to be McNuckles) played in the life of the city

Joseph Jenkins Roberts's mid-1860s attire, that of a planter or Richmond lawyer, reflected the Virginia emigrants' hope to create a replica of Southern-style culture in West Africa, minus enslavement. He was president of Liberia from 1848 to 1856, and again from 1872 to 1876. (Library of Congress Prints and Photographs Division, Washington, DC, LC-DIG-cwpbh-01792)

was apparent every day and reflected in newspaper advertisements, ranging from businesses seeking hundreds of enslaved laborers to build and maintain the railroads to individuals seeking a family cook. About 800 of the enslaved in the city were house servants, nurses, cooks and domestics. The community was a close one—both races lived and worked together and knew each other. Poor Black and white people gambled and drank and frequented prostitutes together. Laborers might be personally acquainted with the tobacco factory owners. Most of the watermen who crewed the canal boats carrying freight and passengers between Lynchburg and Richmond were Black, including William P. Moseley of Goochland, who captained a freight boat during the war, served in the State Senate in 1869, and ended up owning his former master's house.

Enslaved people in Lynchburg might occupy tiny rooms, kitchen corners, lofts or small apartments near tobacco factories. In the counties around Lynchburg, they generally lived in small cabins on their owners' property. When country freedmen moved into Lynchburg after the war, they sometimes had to sleep on the ground or sidewalk, in abandoned buildings, or in shacks of wood, metal and newsprint with not even a chair or table, let alone a bed.[8]

The *Daily Virginian's* publisher and editor, Charles Button, did not own slaves himself but profited from slavery, selling frequent advertisements for slave auctions and running daily ads from people and businesses who wanted to buy or rent slaves, sell them, or recover runaways. Lynchburg dealers Seth Woodruff, Bryan Akers, and J. B. Hargrove supplied slave traders from the Deep South who regularly came to Lynchburg and then herded the newly purchased Virginians away like livestock. Woodruff had been buying and selling Black people up to 150 at a time since the 1840s, keeping them locked up as if they were in jail. Hargrove offered advance payment for enslaved he could confine in his own lockup on Market Street across from the *Lynchburg Republican* office. The domestic slave trade was "a commerce in which Lynchburg participated to an embarrassing degree" wrote local historian S. Allen Chambers Jr. who noted a significant drop in the city's enslaved population between 1850 and 1860.[9]

Thanks to the Depression-era Federal Writer's Project, the observations of several formerly enslaved men who experienced Lynchburg slavery firsthand were documented. Most of the project's employees who interviewed the formerly enslaved in Virginia were Black themselves. They transcribed the interviews using the project's detailed guidance about dialect. Robert Williams, born in 1843, recalled in 1937: "I seen dem sell slaves on de block down on Ninth Street in Lynchburg. . . . De block was a big rock dat slaves would stand on so dey would be up over de crowd. . . . De women would just have a piece around her waist . . . her breast an thighs would be bare. De seller would turn her around and plump her to show how fat she was and her general condition. Dey would also take her by her breasts and pull dem to show how good she was built for raisin' chillun . . . Dey sold my cousin and sent her down in de cotton fields of de deep South, because master got short of money . . ." Williams noted other class distinctions, putting himself and his fellow enslaved above the poor white people, whom he said "were just like stray goats."[10]

Lynchburg's Charley Mitchell, born in 1852, was an old man living in Texas when he recalled his hometown: "Lynchburg was good sized when war come on and Woodruff's nigger tradin' yard was 'bout the bigges' thing there. . . . They got a big price for 'em and handcuffed and chained 'em together and led 'em off like convicts. That yard was full of Louisiana and Texas slave buyers mos' all the time. None of the niggers wanted to be sold to Louisiana, 'cause that's where they beat 'em till the hide was raw, and salted 'em and beat 'em some more. . . . Course us slaves of white folks what lived in town wasn't treated like they was on most plantations. . . . most of the folks we was hired out to was good to us. Lynchburg was full of pattyrollers, jus' like the country, though, and they had a fenced in whippin' post there in town and the pattyrollers sho' put it on a nigger iffen they cotch him without a pass." Pattyrollers were white men—patrollers—who looked for runaway or delinquent slaves.[11]

While Lynchburg's civic leaders were advocates of slavery, they were not early advocates of secession. The *Daily Virginian*'s front-page slogan was "The Rights of the States, and the Union of the States." As a border state, poking up from the South on the map, Lynchburg had vital business dealings with the North, and wanted to keep both its enslaved and its ties to Baltimore, New York, and other port cities. Button did not want the state to leave the Union, but he got in line when it happened. A native of Harpers Ferry, the *Daily Virginian* editor was self-educated, business-oriented, prolific, and fond of classical allusions. Button was also a devout Methodist amid the casual violence of the times, surviving an 1860 gunfight on the streets of Lynchburg when he, his brother and a local minister were ambushed by editors of the rival paper. Button's brother was killed. Throughout the war, Button wrote editorials endorsing slavery and providing economic, social, and religious justifications. In his news and advertising columns, the horrors of slavery were taken for granted. When a Black youngster stole some newspapers, Button asked the mayor to whip him. Conversely, he exposed his readers to frequent Northern denunciations of slavery, especially early in the war. He referred to African Americans as "blacks," or "negroes," or "colored," and sometimes "darkeys." He almost never used the n-word. The *Virginian's* editorials took a sharper tone when the Union began allowing African Americans to fight the Confederates in 1863. A modern reader senses that Button believed the United States Colored Troops were not worthy opponents and that the white Northerners had broken an unspoken code by allowing them to enlist. He once called for the execution of white officers leading Black units. Did Button really believe what he was publishing in the paper? A couple months after Appomattox, he saw the roads at City Point outside Petersburg filled with columns of United States Colored Troops, and termed their movements admirable, adding that the Confederacy made a great mistake by not trying to draft Black soldiers until the war was nearly over.[12]

The *Daily Virginian* held nothing back in its response to the 1863 Emancipation Proclamation. The newspaper called President Abraham Lincoln a monster (twice), an incarnate fiend, an outlaw, a miserable creature and a negro generalissimo—all in one editorial. The editor urged Confederate President Jefferson Davis to put a bounty on Lincoln's head, because he "does not deserve to live another day . . . We sincerely trust that if he ever ventures to set foot on Virginia soil again, there will be found some heroic [Stonewall] Jackson . . . to rid the world of such a monster."[13]

But some white people in the North would come to believe that Black Americans deserved not only freedom but citizenship, based on the performance of the United States Colored Troops. Radical Republicans in Congress pushed to establish a department to help former slaves. The Black convention movement revived in 1863 in New York, with African American activists gathering to press for reform and equal rights. Conventions were held in Richmond and Norfolk soon after the surrender at Appomattox. Most African Americans still remained firmly opposed to leaving their homeland, although some abolitionists, like Alexander Crummell, had reversed course and were supporting emigration. By then, Lynchburg socialites Elizabeth and Samuel Garland of Lynchburg were dead, along with their young son. Mother and son had died during an influenza epidemic in 1861; after his promotion to brigadier general in the Confederate army, Sam Garland was killed in action in Maryland in 1862. Hundreds of other soldiers from Lynchburg and the surrounding area were killed and wounded in battles large and small, or died from disease. An Amherst County unit, the 19th Virginia, was on the front line of Pickett's Charge at Gettysburg. The railroads turned Lynchburg into a mustering point and then a Confederate hospital center, where Black orderlies and domestics cared for wounded white soldiers from the Northern Virginia battlefields. The city also became a food and supply hub for the Confederate Army of Northern Virginia, thanks to its railroads and relatively remote location. The fairgrounds became a prisoner of war camp, earning Lynchburg another mention in the *Liberator*, quoting a returned prisoner who said five or six Union soldiers died there every day from exhaustion, insufficient food, and water contaminated with river sewage.[14]

The city escaped destruction in the 1864 Battle of Lynchburg, when Gen. David Hunter's army, fresh from burning Virginia Military Institute just over the Blue Ridge Mountains in Lexington, was driven off by Gen. Jubal Early. With the freedom offered by the Union lines only about a week's walk north or east, more and more of Piedmont Virginia's enslaved ran away. Slave dealer Hargrove's office helper, Ferdinand, a mixed-race youngster, bolted in 1865. Only 12 or 13 years old, he could read, and was described as sprightly, intelligent, and light-skinned. Hargrove expected that he would try to pass as white. An advertisement offering a $100 reward for Ferdinand was published directly under Hargrove's regular advertisement touting the security of his lockup. By now, poor people were foraging for wood, coal was not available, and the gas works were closed. Enslaved laborers had been forced to strengthen earthen fortifications on the north side of the James River against further attacks. The *Daily Virginian* published one of its final advertisements for slaves on March 24, 1865: Bryan Akers was selling two women and two girls, along with some fruit trees.[15]

Around this time, US cavalry troops led by Gens. Phillip Sheridan and George Custer ransacked counties north of Lynchburg but then swerved east toward Richmond. Sheridan's main army was trailed by hundreds of Black Americans leaving behind enslavers in the Shenandoah Valley and Charlottesville. If Confederate Gen. Robert E. Lee had been successful in reaching Lynchburg during his retreat from Richmond a few weeks later, the city could have been destroyed by federal troops. But he surrendered his army to Gen. Ulysses S. Grant at the village of Appomattox, about twenty miles east, and US Cavalry troops rode into Lynchburg a few days later. Fittingly, perhaps the last local casualty of the Civil War in Lynchburg was Ferdinand's owner Hargrove, who had advocated whipping the enslaved to keep them in line but was referred to as a kind-hearted man by the white people. Drunk, depressed over the loss of his business, he shot himself in the head in front of his young son in a downtown store on July 5, 1865.[16]

By then, freedmen Mac Nuckles, who had renamed himself John McNuckles, and Levi Norvell were deep into plans for a fall emigration. Trying to jump-start the movement in the South, ACS officials were anxious to find a large group of Black people to send to Liberia, which coalesced perfectly with the Lynchburg men's plan. McNuckles wrote to the colonization society in Washington, DC, on July 10, saying he was assembling a high-quality group including many of "the very first class of colored people," church members who could bring "the light of the Gospel" to Africa, some with a "good common education" and trade skills. Old colonizationist Charles L. Mosby, the well-known Lynchburg lawyer and likely McNuckles's former owner, forwarded the letter to the ACS: "He is a freed man, and they all feel it."[17]

Local Black people wanted citizenship, education for their children, jobs and their own land to farm. But living and working conditions in immediate postwar Lynchburg resembled those of slavery and the white people wanted to keep it that way. The reality of the Southern microcosm in 1865 Piedmont Virginia is far different from the version Virginia's public schools still taught well into the twentieth century. The summer of 1865 in and around Lynchburg saw as many if not more idle white people than Black people. Many white people hoped to re-create a forced labor system, by physical abuse if necessary. White people thought Black people were lazy and ungrateful because they didn't want to work for little or no pay. Former masters only wanted to provide them with food, clothing and a place to stay, essentially what they gave them as slaves. White people were nearly unanimous about denying any rights of citizenship to freed slaves and in some instances, shot and killed their former slaves over perceived insults.

The local newspapers did their part to shape how generations of white Southerners would view the Civil War, with frequent postwar editorials and commentaries on race and slavery. One said that Virginia had seceded from the Union not over slavery, but for honor. Another argued that despite their defeat and the end of slavery, Southern men were not in a mood to meekly accept their fate. As former slaveholders, wrote the editor, taking orders from someone else was harder for them than for those who had owned no slaves. This was part of a longer editorial arguing that North and South should move forward as if the war had never happened.[18]

But it had happened and now the US Army was in control of the old Quaker town where nearly half the population was Black. Gen. John I. Gregg was federal commander of the Military Subdistrict of Lynchburg, and Lt. Col. Alexander P. Duncan was provost marshal. About a month after the Confederate surrender Appomattox, they issued orders that dealt with the general establishment of order and restricted the movements of the newly freed Black Americans. Their former owners had no obligation to support or help them; they had no right to any of the masters' property; they needed to continue to work, sometimes even harder than when they were enslaved; they were forbidden to gather in groups except on weekends, and if they gathered on the street they would be arrested. Finally, they had to stay away from the Army camps unless they were officers' servants or selling cakes, pies and vegetables to the troops. Gregg's order was reprinted approvingly across the South, but a New York newspaper termed it merely a re-enactment of previous Virginia slave codes.[19]

Initially, Gregg did not concern himself with pleasing either race. He was trying to keep order amid confusion, shortages, fear, and resentment on all sides. He was a lifelong Army man, a cavalry officer from Pennsylvania, a Mexican War veteran who was wounded during the Civil War, captured, and released a few days before Lee's surrender. Lt. Col. Duncan, who had served under him with the Fourth Pennsylvania at Appomattox, announced on May 27 that all Black people employed in Lynchburg were required to have passes from their employers or face arrest. Under slavery, they had been more or less able to walk the streets during the day and go about their business, subject to their owners' whims. Gregg warned in his orders that they ought to stay on their plantations and work, and that they would starve if they moved in large groups to cities and towns.[20]

Stories about the misdeeds of newly freed African Americans cropped up immediately. By summer, the Leftwich's Row neighborhood had been "made hideous with their orgies," the *Daily Virginian* declared. While continuing to maintain that Black people were inferior to white people, Editor Button accepted the fact that slavery was no more after Appomattox. As John McNuckles and Levi Norvell began arranging with the ACS to leave Lynchburg, Button's newspaper deployed a quasi-intellectual assertion to justify white attitudes, asserting that freedmen were not actually free men, merely former slaves. This July editorial so irritated Gregg that he nearly forced the paper to stop publishing. The controversy began when two Black preachers, who were minding their own business and walking quietly, were put to work sweeping the streets as a result of the ordinance against idlers. In response, Gregg issued an order noting that both races now had exactly the same rights (this wasn't accurate) and that in fact many white layabouts were filling the streets and stealing. Calling the arrest of the Black preachers an "outrage against the rights of citizens," he said that instead, habitual white loafers obstructing the sidewalks should be arrested and put to work.[21]

Gregg's declaration that the preachers were citizens was getting ahead of what the federal government favored at this time. Button had already written that the military commander did not understand Black people and that he would soon learn that they were better suited for slavery than freedom. Apparently Lynchburg sharing a nickname, "The Hill City," with ancient Rome, had gone to his head: Quoting Daniel Webster, he wrote, "The freedman is one who has been a slave and is manumitted simply; while the freeman is one who is not only not slave or vassal, but 'who enjoys or is entitled to a franchise or peculiar privilege; as the freemen of a city or State." He later published a grudging clarification to mollify Gregg.[22]

In late 1865 and into 1866, legislatures across the South began to enact new Black Codes to prohibit freedmen from owning land and ensure that they remained poorly paid laborers. Vagrancy laws aimed to keep Black people working on farms and plantations rather than moving about wherever they wished. Black men and women who left Piedmont Virginia plantations were blamed for damage to the common good. The expectations of the two races were opposites: Black people sometimes asked that ownership of farms be turned over to them, while some white people believed the Freedmen's Bureau could more or less help them re-enslave the African Americans. Two Mississippi planters came to Lynchburg in July 1865, requesting the bureau to assign them 100 laborers to take south to the cotton fields. They didn't seem to understand that the African Americans could no longer be compelled to labor for white people and expressed their belief that Black people would not work at all unless faced with physical punishment. Said one, "If you'll let me tie him up by the thumbs, or keep him on bread and water, that will do." Lynchburg-area farmers faced an agricultural dilemma of their own. How would they harvest the current crops of wheat, corn and other staples that both Black and white depended on to survive, without enslaved labor?[23]

The initial solution was virtual re-enslavement of Black farmhands. Farmers north of Lynchburg colluded to set wages and limit employment itself. They met in June at New Market, a James River village, and agreed to fix wages for an individual field hand at $5 per month from which he had to buy clothing for himself and his family; provide lodging, fuel and rations "as heretofore," i.e., during slavery, and to prohibit formerly enslaved people from switching to a different employer without a "certificate of permission" from their current employer. Finally, the field hands were to be "entirely subject to the orders of the employers." The "deluded" negroes were told they were liable to go hungry because of "a life of indolence," when in actuality most wanted to work, but expected to be paid a fair wage, be able to come and go, move around, and to be treated as employees, not slaves. The army disallowed the forced-labor restrictions and prohibited planters from denying the freedmen room and board, reasoning that a good crop was coming in and the enslaved had helped produce it so should benefit from it.[24]

Button, who rarely bucked the local trends, wrote in July that Black people must always be "hewers of wood and drawers of water" for the white people. For them to compete for jobs with white people was unthinkable and would mean that the Black Americans would either be crowded out of the country or out of existence. Such thinking wasn't limited to the South. The same editorial quoted at length from the *New York Herald,* which predicted that like the American Indians, the Black race would disappear from the United States, with Irish and German immigrants elbowing them out in the competition for jobs. Delving deeper into what he presented as a racial competition based in science and statistics, the *Herald* writer said the moral deterioration that would come from mixed-race marriages was entirely the fault of "colored" blood, not white, and from the maternal line. Indirectly referring to the many mixed-race children fathered by white slaveowners, he wrote that few mixed race-people had white mothers. His newspaper was reputed to sell more copies than any other paper in the country, hawked by newsboys in Richmond, and delivered to Lynchburg by rail. But in 1865, a new journal was founded in New York, *The Nation,* to consider topics of the day "with greater accuracy and moderation than are now to be found in the daily press." One of its goals was to promote education and justice for the laboring class of the South and to report on the progress made by the Black population. Among its writers would be a recent Harvard graduate, John R. Dennett.[25]

The Nation dispatched Dennett, 26, to spend eight months in the South in 1865–66. His reports were published weekly, and he spent part of the summer of 1865 in and around Lynchburg. He was class poet at Harvard, but in *The South As It Is,* he turned a Northern reporter's eye on the racial landscape of Lynchburg and the surrounding countryside. Dennett said he found local Black people were "orderly, industrious, and self-supporting." He noted that only a few freedmen out in the country had applied for assistance, speculating that they were remaining on their home plantations, disagreeing with local reports of streets crowded with freedmen who were abandoning their slave jobs. He also said the US Freedmen's Bureau in Campbell and Bedford counties was feeding more white than Black people in June 1865. Southern states showed little interest in helping the formerly enslaved: "Not a dam[n] bite will I give them. I would choose hell first," said the president of the overseers of the poor in a Northern Virginia county. By October when the McNuckles group departed, the Freedmen's Bureau was feeding and clothing a thousand freedmen a week in Lynchburg. The Bureau eventually came to be regarded as an ally of the white people rather than the freedmen, according to historian Stephen Tripp, and the Army's efforts to protect property and rebuild the economy brought approval from white civic leaders. By January 1866, the Bureau was pushing unemployed Black people in Lynchburg to sign labor contracts with farmers. Tripp also noted distinctions between African Americans who already lived in Lynchburg, and those who moved in after the war, quoting an agent in 1867 who said resident Black people wanted the new arrivals gone to lessen competition for work.[26]

Dennett found Lynchburg a "rough little city" with "dirty and ill-paved streets" that were unsafe at night and was surprised that it was second only to New Bedford, Mass., as the wealthiest city per capita in the US before the war. In the neighboring counties, he wrote, white farmers who might be willing to pay the formerly enslaved had no money to provide anything other than food and clothing. Some had turned to sharecropping arrangements with their former slaves, with the farmers agreeing to feed and clothe the Black families, allow them a bit of land for a garden, and divide a small portion of farm produce with them. With no land of their own and no prospects for getting any without any money, that was the best the freedmen could expect if they stayed in Virginia. Dennett was not without his own prejudice—he referred to two children carrying their primers to a newly established Black school in an old tobacco factory as "grotesque-looking little creatures." But he also wrote that paying free people of color a fair wage in his home state of Massachusetts had lifted them into an estimable class of citizens.[27]

In Bedford County, Dennett listened to an exchange between an Army sergeant in charge of freedmen's affairs and "a very good looking" mixed-race man wearing a Confederate officer's uniform coat. The man was representing a number of African Americans and wanted to know if they would be forced to sign labor contracts, could rent or buy property, and if the government would help them buy mules or plows. The sergeant told him they could not be forced to sign labor contracts, but that the government could not help them get land or a mule to plow it. He did give the man a paper authorizing him to buy or rent property.[28]

An unnamed Bedford white man announcing for Congress saw colonization as the solution to the white dilemma of living among Black people who were not subservient, Dennett wrote, but most farmers wanted to keep their laborers in Virginia. Everywhere he went in the Virginia countryside, Dennett saw idle white men. One group in Appomattox was drinking apple brandy and watching soldiers at the courthouse. "It is the custom of the country, which throws all work upon the Negroes . . ." The *Daily Virginian* agreed, more or less. The paper reported on Aug. 21 that the lack of work for white men was one of the worst aspects of the times, and the writer speculated that some of the jobless white men were former Confederate soldiers. "Many of these young men seem to have lost much of their self-reliance, and seem willing that others may care for them, without making a corresponding effort themselves." The solution, according to the paper? Employers should give preference to white workers "in all cases." This set the stage for a century of racial discrimination in hiring.[29]

Dennett rode out to a 1,200-acre plantation 20 miles from Lynchburg in Campbell County for another look at race relations. He had a gift for eliciting revealing statements from the white elites, and his visit to the plantation reveals much about the conditions that influenced the Lynchburg emigrants to leave Virginia for Liberia. The unnamed plantation owner was a former member of Congress whom Dennett referred to as "the Colonel." The Colonel told the reporter that he had owned slaves for forty-five years but "I never bought a nigger in my life." This may have been true, given the natural increase in the numbers of enslaved Virginia people over the previous decades. The Colonel recalled life before the war, saying he had only ordered one man whipped, for stealing sheep, and bragged to Dennett about the grotesque punishment he'd had in mind. In addition to the whipping, the Colonel ordered a ram's skin tied to the man's back with the horns over his head and a rope around his neck. His overseer refused to lead the man to the auction block in the ram's skin, so he was sold as is. Now, the former congressman told Dennett, "The bad niggers spoil the rest." He blamed all the postwar trouble in Virginia on anarchy among the Black population. He'd offered to let his former slaves stay on the farm with food and clothing provided, if they worked for no pay.[30]

Across the South, the previously enslaved wanted to assert their freedom, and they wanted white people to acknowledge their new status, to feel it just as they did. But the Colonel declared, "Since mine are freed, they have become lazy, stubborn and impudent . . . they are not like white people. I begin to believe they are without gratitude." The freed people should be grateful for their treatment while enslaved, he believed, not anxious to demonstrate their freedom. Recently, he'd banished one woman, Elsie, to a remote cabin for refusing to hang out his daughter-in-law's washing. His son had recently twice slapped another Black woman, Rose, for disobedience. The overseer drew his pistol on another "sassy" ex-slave and threatened to blow his brains out.[31]

The Colonel said he would like to throw all the Black people off the plantation rather than endure their insolence. They numbered about sixty, including twenty-one able-bodied men and women. The rest were children, and the old and infirm who cooked and cared for the others and worked as his domestics. Fed up with the freedmen, the Colonel had recently leased the plantation to his overseer who prepared a sharecropping contract for the freedmen. The overseer would pay the expenses of planting and in return for their labor, the freedmen would receive half of the crop. They would also receive rations from the overseer but would have to repay him from their portion of the crop. The freed people still lived in their cabins, Dennett reported, while the overseer's quarters were little better: a mud-plastered two-room cabin. Having nowhere else to go, with almost no paid work available, only two freedmen had refused the Colonel's original offer to stay on at the plantation.

The Colonel told Dennett that he feared the freed people of the surrounding countryside, who far outnumbered the white people, would rise up and attack his family: "The Government has taken away all coercive power from us; a Negro does what he likes and I cannot inflict adequate punishment." Dennett got to the heart of the situation around Lynchburg and throughout the South as he reflected on his visit with the Colonel. He found the Colonel, despite his racist attitudes, to be a humane man, possibly even viewed as kind and indulgent by the enslaved. His problem, Dennett wrote, was "He believes that the blacks were born for slavery, and is intolerant of anything resembling independence and self-reliance in them . . . he still wishes to be master, is willing to be a kind master, but will not be a just employer." The Colonel said abolitionists had a right to think that Black Americans were the equal of white people, but that white Virginians knew God had made Black people inferior.[32]

The Colonel and his overseer might not have carried through on all their threats, but other former enslavers were not as hesitant. A military commission made up of officers from New York and Connecticut put a respected member of the Lynchburg community, Gilbert Haythe, on trial a few days after the 1865 emigrants left for killing a freedman. Haythe had chastised the man's young son for repeated disobedience. The father complained, then argued with Haythe and they got into a scuffle in the yard. Haythe ran into his house, got a gun, and shot and killed the freedman. "The principal witnesses are negroes, and the clearness, intelligence and evident truthfulness with which they testify had been a subject of remark by both the court and counsel," the newspaper reported in a rare bit of praise for the freedmen.[33]

Part of Haythe's defense was that the freedman had used language Haythe would not have tolerated, even from a white man. Haythe was convicted and jailed, triggering the white community to get up a petition to President Andrew Johnson seeking his release, saying punishing a white man for killing a Black man could upset the fragile state of postwar race relations. About a month before, another Lynchburg white man had shot and killed a freedwoman and her son after the white man's children and her children had argued. The fatal mistake in that incident was language as well: "The woman it is said, used abusive words toward [the white man], when he got his gun loaded with ball and buckshot, and fired on her. She was hit in the heart, her son, in the head."[34]

The Lynchburg prosecutor in these cases was Commonwealth's Attorney James Garland, seventy-five, the former congressman who had addressed the American Colonization Society's annual meeting in 1837. He was named an honorary vice president of the ACS after the war. In his acceptance letter, Garland wrote that if all Black people had been sent overseas, the Civil War could have been prevented. As his former Lynchburg neighbors were struggling to establish themselves in West Africa in early 1866, Garland wrote: "To separate the colored from the white . . . and to plant them on their native continent, will be the most glorious achievement of modern philanthropy." Of course, the emigrants' native continent was North America, not Africa.[35]

10

Coming Into the New Country

1866

> God has suffered me to pass through the fire but has not permitted me to be burned. He has carried me through deep waters but the rivers of sorrow [have] not yet overflown me.
>
> —John R. Freeman on behalf of John McNuckles, Liberia, 1866

As THE *Henry P. Russell* sailed toward Cape Henry and the Atlantic from Baltimore, John McNuckles was almost giddy with excitement and religious fervor. Local Methodists and Baptists were leading singing and prayer twice a day. Even the food was delightful. Writing from the Chesapeake Bay, he bid farewell to Lynchburg: "God bless you all, may you all prosper in business and not forget to pray unto God, the author of every good thing, for all of us, and if we never more see each other again on earth, I hope that we all shall meet in Heaven at last, where partings are no more . . ."[1]

After 40 days at sea, sleeping on their mattresses in the cargo hold, the people of the Lynchburg exodus caught sight of West Africa on Dec. 14, 1865. Some had been seasick, but most arrived in good health. During the voyage, Julia Waller, 22, gave birth to "a fine baby boy" and named him Henry P. Russell Waller after the ship. The colonization society's wharf was on the Mesurado River, which separated the cape at Monrovia from mainland Liberia. Near the wharf, on Water Street, stood the colonization society's stone warehouse, with cracked walls, rotten woodwork, and a leaking basement. It was part of a row of frame and brick buildings, the emigrants' first view of the capital of their new country. They walked along the streets of a town smaller than Lynchburg, with about 2,000 residents compared to Lynchburg's 6,853 in 1860. As in Lynchburg, social life, complexion, and class distinctions were important here. A few weeks after the Lynchburg emigrants passed through, a Russian Navy steam frigate docked for four days. President Daniel Warner, his cabinet, and other Americo-Liberians entertained the officers at a reception, and the Russians invited two dozen prominent women to the ship for music and dining. Maintaining their American ways helped emigrants at the top of the social order distinguish themselves from the West African people, as well as the poorer colonists, often darker skinned, whom they considered less refined than themselves.[2]

Unfortunately, this class included most of the Americo-Liberian population. Colonization society physician Dr. Daniel Laing wrote: "There is not sufficient variety of employment in Liberia to enable the communities to thrive or even keep their own. The hard, outdoor labor and consequent exposure, the excessive wear and tear of the system; falling mostly upon the male head of the family . . . is sapping the life of our communities and as our numbers increase the difficulties increase, and the waste of energy becomes greater, from the increased demand of the weak and feeble, who are unable to contribute to the common stock. The country is without capital; we have no manufactories, and as a consequence no indoor work for women and children. Youths from twelve years upward who might be earning something to help support the family, go about dirty, ragged, half fed, idle but to their credit not half so vicious as one would suppose."[3]

A day or two after arriving in Monrovia, John McNuckles introduced himself to Warner at the president's brick mansion on Ashmun Street. While many of Monrovia's public buildings and wharves were in the same shape as the American Colonization Society warehouse, the homes of government officials were better maintained. The president's house included folding doors, oil portraits, embroidered curtains, books, and a tapestry curtain. Liberia's third president, Warner had been born free in Maryland in 1815 and was one of the earliest emigrants, arriving in Liberia with his family when he was 8 and growing up to become a businessman and shipyard owner.[4]

Warner wrote, "Mr. McNuckols and a fellow emigrant called to see me a day or two after their arrival here and expressed themselves in the most encouraging manner respecting the general aspect of the country so far as they have been able to observe it." Other parts of Warner's letter describing his meeting with McNuckles could have been written by a Virginia enslaver of the 1850s. Not particularly popular in Liberia, Warner referred to the mass of Americo-Liberians as "men of poorly developed and educated minds—minds still dizzy and distracted by the innervating effects of two and a half centuries' servitude and degradation." Status and class were complicated in Liberia. Sometimes, they reflected beliefs which placed light-skinned men who were already free in America at the top of the social hierarchy. Alexander Crummell said his "Black face" was regarded as a disgrace in both church and civic affairs by "half-caste" (mixed race) people there. The West Africans still referred to the Americo-Liberians as "white," because their culture resembled that of white Americans and Europeans.[5]

But as with all things Liberian, it wasn't that simple. Americans thought mixed-race Black people were more intelligent and more refined, more like white people but still not white. Originally, the ACS had preferred the lightest-skinned emigrants it could find, like the country's first president, Joseph Jenkins Roberts, whom New York colonizationists referred to as "a slightly colored gentleman of good appearance." This racial thinking meant that the emigrants with lighter skin tended to rise higher and more quickly than those with dark skin who were thought to be more like Africans than Americans. "The very few souls who embraced relocating to Liberia were usually people of color most able to take advantage of the ambiguity wrought by Atlantic mobility and Liberia's 'in-between' racialized space," writes Robert Murray in *Atlantic Passages.* Skin color didn't always hold emigrants back once Liberia became its own country in 1847. The American Colonization Society's manager and Corresponding Secretary William Coppinger described President Warner himself as racially pure, of "unmixed African blood."[6]

The Lynchburg people stayed in Monrovia only a few days, long enough to send some letters home saying they had arrived safely. To lessen their exposure to possible fever, some remained on board the *Russell* for a few days, and then all went upriver in boats. They sailed along the wide, shallow St. Paul's past farmland, forest, and small settlements named for US states—Kentucky, Louisiana, Virginia—and West African towns like King Peter's. On the twenty-mile journey, they passed several large coffee and sugar farms, one employing fifty to sixty people.[7]

The twelve communities along the St. Paul's, including Careysburg, had about 3,000 acres under cultivation in 1865, including 682 acres of sugarcane, 46,000 coffee trees, 28 acres of cotton, 26 acres of peanuts (called "groundnuts"), 16 acres of arrowroot, and 1,800 cocoa trees. This was reported approvingly in the *Liberia Herald,* but the acreage was minuscule compared to farms in Virginia. The *Herald* also claimed the

Americo-Liberians had built 147 frame, 44 brick and 25 log houses in the St. Paul's region; 30 brick kilns; 24 saw pits; two steam mills, and 13 water mills. William Eubanks, one of the Lynchburg carpenters, offered a thoughtful impression a few months later: "I am much pleased with the country, and so far as I have been able to observe, consider it a delightful place. It is true things are not altogether as they are at home, and not altogether as I would like to see them. But a stranger often looks for, and expects to find things in a strange [land], that he would not and could not find in his own home."[8]

The navigable portion of the river ended at rocky falls about twenty miles upstream from Monrovia at Millsburg, the terminus of a Manding trading route from Bopolu. After a long day on the river, the Lynchburg settlers landed across from Millsburg at the Careysburg wharf, where some of their baggage was stolen. Seeking compensation from the ACS, Levi Norvell said his losses would hardly encourage further emigration from Lynchburg. He was missing a gallon jar of spices, a large slate, leather, a blanket, a yellow cotton shirt, a pair of his wife's shoes, and some other items, valued at a total of $17. Not a man to be trifled with, Norvell went over the head of the ACS's top man in Liberia, Agent Henry Dennis, to demand compensation directly from the ACS in Washington. Dennis grumbled that such losses were not the fault of the ACS and could hardly be prevented, with the emigrants themselves sometimes stealing from each other, but finally gave Norvell twenty-five pounds of tobacco in compensation.[9]

From the wharf, the emigrants set out with their baggage and mattresses along a winding road through dense tropical forest, crossing a dozen creeks and dilapidated bridges on the 10-mile trek southeast to Careysburg. A hand-drawn map which McNuckles and Norvell may have seen refers to the Careysburg area as "Fine Mountainous Country," appealing to people who grew up in the foothills of the Blue Ridge. Arriving at Careysburg a few days before Christmas, their first community activities could have been held back in Virginia—a Sunday School picnic and a New Year's Day church service—although the tropical December weather was warm and damp. New emigrants lived at the colonization society's three-story frame dormitory, the Receptacle, just outside Careysburg. The Lynchburg group was to stay there until they received their land, but they immediately got busy cutting trees and clearing brush. About thirty or forty men went out in a group each morning, worked all day,

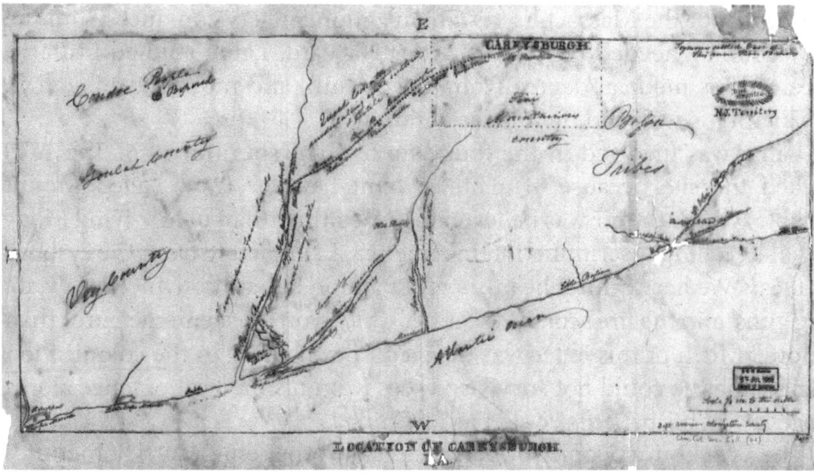

Missionary, explorer, and colonization proponent John Seys suggested the Careysburg region for a new settlement in the 1850s after locating a hilly region there, believing the higher elevation would be healthier than low-lying Monrovia. He drew this map showing a proposed route up the St. Paul's River and through the forest to Careysburg. (Library of Congress Geography and Map Division, Washington, DC, 96684982)

and returned in the evening, a sharp contrast with the white stereotype in Lynchburg about the formerly enslaved being too lazy or ignorant or to work for themselves. "It is true we are poor, we came to the country poor; but by labor and perseverance, we can better our condition," wrote McNuckles's brother Woodson. Careysburg had grown since Nelson County's Dylsie Banks, her daughter, and granddaughters, died there in 1858. A few months before the Lynchburg group's appearance in 1866, a Lutheran missionary passed through on a donkey and described the town favorably: "Carysburg is regularly laid out, has broad streets, some fine houses, three or four churches and a population of six or eight hundred. Its location is fine." One of the oldest buildings in Careysburg was a log church put up in 1857 by emigrants from Albemarle County. A Presbyterian church was under construction in 1865, and Norvell would join at least three other Baptist preachers there.[10]

Dr. Daniel Laing, expelled from Harvard for being Black, had practiced off and on in Careysburg since it was founded in 1856. Like Dr. Isaac Snowden, he was technically an employee of the ACS, which often could not afford to pay him. He had originally wanted to emigrate to Liberia as a printer, but the Massachusetts Colonization Society convinced him the new country needed physicians. After Harvard, Laing studied in Paris, received his medical degree from Dartmouth, and moved to Liberia in 1854 with his wife and their three children.[11]

Laing was involved in the founding of Careysburg in 1856. The ACS picked the site because of a hill, Mount Fawblee (now called Mount Vouble) where the air was believed to be healthier than in low-lying Monrovia. Recalling discrimination in America, Laing wrote from Careysburg in 1863: "We here cannot hear . . . your cannon but are convinced they are 'big guns' and the fire scorching; out of which you must emerge purer than before." Much of this letter was devoted to explaining to the colonization society that he could not survive on fees from his medical practice alone, since few of his patients could pay anything.[12]

The Lynchburg people soon met multiple other emigrants. Sometimes assisting Laing was John R. Freeman, who had arrived in Liberia in 1860. A free man, he was a descendant of a personal servant enslaved by Presidents Thomas Jefferson and James Madison. A merchant and teacher, Freeman would later become the country's comptroller. His business card resembled that of any American businessman: "Freeman, Hyde, & Co./ Auctioneers, and Commission Merchants, and Dealers/In Liberia Produce/Seys Avenue, Careysburg." William Douglass, formerly enslaved in Albemarle County, represented the ACS and assisted the Lynchburg group. He was a sugarcane farmer and had built a two-story, eight-room, frame house in Careysburg and also owned a rental house. Now, he and his wife were hoping the ACS would send over their three adult daughters and seven grandchildren still in Virginia. Douglass had learned to write, his sugar business was profitable, he had a small mill to grind cane, and he had sent $20 in gold to his children, whom he hadn't been able to contact throughout the war. Two officials of the Liberian government, Charles Deputie and John H. Paxton, a former Virginian, also lived in Careysburg. Paxton was a member of the Liberian Senate and former postmaster general, and rival of ACS agent Henry Dennis. Deputie was a free man from Pennsylvania who came to Liberia in 1853, volunteered to help establish Careysburg, and moved there with his family in 1858. He was the town's top law officer, justice of the peace and magistrate, as well as a teacher and Presbyterian church elder. Letters from all these men include frequent references to heated disagreements between the Liberian government, the ACS, and the Americo-Liberians.[13]

They rarely considered the wishes of Indigenous people like the Queah who had inhabited the region for hundreds of years. West Africans like those around Careysburg lived in villages and towns governed by "almost an unmitigated democracy," according to Protestant Episcopal Bishop John Payne, a Virginia missionary who spent many years in Liberia. Their houses were also generally round with thatched roofs, as small as six feet in diameter and as large as thirty feet. While a council of elders and patriarchs was nominally in charge, the residents generally deferred to a council of all the men in town who could pay a fee to qualify. Payne wrote that Indigenous religion was based on spirits of the dead taking on the same roles they had in life—trade, war, agriculture. This was a Western view and calling these beliefs "ancestor worship" is wrong, writes modern Liberian scholar Carl P. Burrowes. The spirit of a venerated male ancestor who had lived a good long life in the mortal realm was thought to continue into the slower, more peaceful afterlife where he could watch over and influence his descendants: "Like saints in Catholicism, ancestors were intermediaries between their descendants and God. They helped to safeguard the community and its moral order. The norms or 'ways' passed on by them formed the foundation of law, religion, and morality." West Africans believed they could communicate with these ancestors through various rituals including animal sacrifice. West Africans could not become citizens of Liberia unless they converted to Christianity and acculturated themselves to Western ways, and the country's 1847 constitution also limited citizenship to Black men who owned real estate. Despite this, President Benson once said that many of the Indigenous people were more intellectually advanced than many of the emigrants from the US. The ACS hoped to prevent the local Queah people from living in Careysburg itself until they became acculturated.[14]

In many respects, the remote, heavily forested Careysburg region was what the Virginia group had expected. McNuckles picked a site for the Lynchburg settlement in a "beautiful locality" a mile or two southwest of Careysburg itself, "well pleasing to the entire company." The area resembled Piedmont Virginia, or western New York, with a succession of hills and valleys. The soil was good, and the timber was plentiful with abundant mahogany. They would live along Zodah Creek, with plenty of room for the anticipated second group of Lynchburg emigrants to expand downstream. Nearby was the town of Queah leader Zodah who had ceded the Careysburg area lands to the ACS in the 1850s. During a trip to Careysburg in 1859, former President Roberts dined with him and gave him a silver medal from the ACS, just as American presidents gave impressive medals to American Indian leaders after seizing their territory. Zodah had since died, and ruling in his place in 1866 was his more-acculturated brother, John Wilson, who had recently sent a son to live at the Lutheran mission house in nearby Muhlenberg.[15]

Surrounded by an undulating "deep green sea of uninterrupted foliage," Careysburg was said to be "healthier than any spot on the coast, the air is lighter and the water is purer, the seclusion from various misdoings is favorable." Lynchburg carpenter William Eubanks wrote that Zodah's Creek offered a perfect location for a sawmill, and McNuckles planned to procure the saw and fixtures for the mill when he returned to the States to lead the second emigration. Milled lumber was a valuable commodity in Liberia, necessary for building frame houses instead of cabins, and the group had several experienced carpenters in addition to McNuckles and Eubanks. With a sawmill and frame houses the Lynchburg emigrants planned to create a rural Virginia-style community in Africa. Some nineteenth-century Western accounts stress the exotic nature of the region—elephants, leopards, giant snakes, chimpanzees, mound-building ants. But the influx of settlers, combined with hunting by the West Africans, had driven the elephants and predators like the big cats farther into the interior. The Lynchburg emigrants focused on clearing land, hewing trees, and planting.[16]

While the Careysburg hill itself was at a higher elevation than the pestilent coast, Zodah Creek—needed to power the mill wheel—was in a lower-lying section. With no knowledge of what caused malaria, McNuckles may have selected the worst location possible. Americo-Liberian and former Virginian William C. Burke, previously enslaved by Confederate Gen. Robert E. Lee, traveled extensively in the region. Earlier in 1865, he had expressed doubts about Careysburg's location in a letter to Lee's wife. "I . . . do not see why it should be more healthy than anywhere else. The hill or mountain . . . is quite high; but . . . it is very small, and the country all around it is very low, and wet during the rainy season; and besides it is not far enough in the interior to make any difference." While no one knew that mosquitos were the chief threat, plenty of tangible problems soon became apparent for the latest arrivals. The American Colonization Society's attitude was that somehow emigrants could prosper amid a weak economy in a frontier town with little assistance after their initial support, and the Lynchburg settlers soon found themselves without sufficient medicine or healthy food. Even the most commonplace things that Virginians took for granted, like lamp oil, were in short supply. The shortages weakened the emigrants' resistance to disease and made attacks of fever—which were nearly universal—more fatal. The land the Lynchburg people had dreamed of owning and farming was readily available around Careysburg, but money was not. A lack of capital to develop the country, devalued currency, and few jobs for those without craft or business skills were endemic.[17]

Despite Coppinger and McClain's diligence in getting the Lynchburg emigrants to West Africa, the ACS was ill-prepared for their arrival. When they reached their temporary home, the Careysburg Receptacle, they found it still occupied by recent emigrants from Barbados, whom the ACS turned out in favor of the Lynchburg group. The new year of 1866 began gloomily with the Jan. 3 death of little Henry P. Russell Waller, born aboard the ship. The next day, tragedy struck the family of tobacco worker Henry and Susan Moore. Susan, who had been injured in a fall on the ship, died in childbirth. Their daughter Cornelia, 5, died, probably from fever, a couple weeks later. Four other Lynchburg emigrants became sick in early January. By the end of the month, Peyton Christian, 43, a blacksmith; one of his children, four-month-old Ida; and the newborn daughter of Addison and Amelia Banks had died, and Norvell and McNuckles were questioning the amount of rations the emigrants were allowed by the ACS. Each emigrant received a half pound of beef and fish a day, which they said would be sufficient if it was all bacon. But they only received pork about once a week and had begun trying to conserve food. Each family cooked for itself outside, like camping out, because cooking fires weren't allowed in the wooden Receptacle building. Norvell and McNuckles continued to encourage emigration, endorse reports in the *African Repository,* and comment on the US political situation: "There [is] room enough [for] all colored friends to get their full growth, all their heart can wish in freedom will be seen . . . Nothing that President Johnson or the US Congress can [do] can make you such men as you can be [in] Liberia in the way of lawful, legal or law-abiding men."[18]

Much of what is known about the group's first weeks in Careysburg comes from a Jan. 5, 1866, letter signed by McNuckles and Norvell, and sent to Coppinger in Washington. It was dated the same day as a similar but shorter letter published in the *African Repository* and attributed only to McNuckles. The longer letter contains much more objective information about deaths, lack of healthy food, and other problems, and its handwriting resembles that of Norvell. The shorter letter, apparently sent to the *Daily Virginian* by Coppinger and in a different hand, was upbeat and boosterish. Mentioning the Sunday School picnic, plentiful iron ore, and men in fine spirits, it said nothing about illness, death, or meager rations and reads like an attempt to present a glowing account of a tough situation. Both are written in the first person. McNuckles notes in the longer letter that he is writing "again." Perhaps the short letter was written for publication and publicity purposes, the longer one to inform Coppinger of the actual situation. McNuckles was purposeful, the ACS was misleading, and both wanted to encourage emigration. Then, on March 1, 1866, a long letter purportedly signed by McNuckles was written to the "Mr. Editor" of an unnamed publication and included in ACS records with concurrent letters from Liberia to the ACS. It described in great detail the Dec. 26 Sunday School picnic in a Careysburg grove, referring to it as "a most exquisite picture." The language of this letter is much more elaborate than previous McNuckles's letters, and it was also written in a different hand. It appears to be another piece of publicity to encourage Liberian emigration. "McNuckles" does not mention any sickness or deaths—by now six people had died—but says, "we as an emigration are all well." The colonization society was using him in its propaganda efforts. Further casting doubt on this March 1 letter, two months later Coppinger wrote to McNuckles that he had not heard from him since Jan. 6.[19]

The Lynchburg emigrants finally received their land around March 1, with the rainy season approaching. No serious farming could get under way until their heavily forested acreage was cleared. As in Virginia, clearing raw land meant back-breaking labor—cutting trees and brush with hand tools, then burning to create open fields. Fever continued to ravage the emigrants, especially children: George and Louisa Rose's newborn baby died March 4, and their daughter, Eliza Ann, died March 16. David Johnson, 39, an unmarried farmer, died on April 5. By mid-April, the emigrants had managed to build a few cabins along the creek, and some people were eating potatoes they had planted. Without the sawmill, they were hewing logs by hand for cabins. While primitive, these cabins were likely not much different from the homes of many rural people in Virginia. Norvell described the agricultural situation after a few months in country. Rice, potatoes, and tobacco grew well. Corn was "half a leg" high by late

April. Oranges, coconuts, and pineapples were plentiful. Local coffee and sugar were of high quality. The fish were biting. The local cattle were "fat and fine," but they didn't produce much milk; the sheep had no wool; and the goats didn't smell. Wild hogs, deer, and parrots were abundant.[20]

Amid the struggle to recreate Piedmont Virginia in Africa, McNuckles made arrangements to travel back to the US as the ACS pressed for more emigration from Lynchburg. Coppinger asked the Reverend Jacob Mitchell how many were expected in the second group. Mitchell, who assisted the 1850s Rogers emigrations from Bedford, replied with bad news: The mood had changed. The widespread Southern rumor that emigrating freedmen would be taken to Cuba or South America and re-enslaved was circulating in Piedmont Virginia. For people who had been enslaved their entire lives, and only freed a few months before, this was believable. Although some of the 1865 emigrants had written back to Lynchburg from Liberia, rumors that they had been re-enslaved were pervasive. Soldiers stationed in Lynchburg were urging local African Americans to stay put. Some locals also believed another rumor, that McNuckles had received a bribe in gold to take the emigrants not to Liberia, but to the West Indies, where they had been sold.[21]

Jack Averitt, planning the second emigration, had heard directly from McNuckles and tried to convince his Lynchburg friends and acquaintances that the emigrants had arrived safely in Liberia. But a colonization agent, the Reverend John Orcutt, visited the city in early April 1866 and found the prospects depressing. Pastors of two Black churches in Lynchburg refused to let him speak from their pulpits, much less encourage emigration themselves. "They are Northern negroes," grumbled Orcutt, himself from Massachusetts. He blamed anti-emigration sentiment in Lynchburg on Freedmen's Bureau employees and federal soldiers, who were telling prospective emigrants they would never reach Liberia but would be sold into slavery in Cuba. Orcutt's reception had been more encouraging a few days before in Richmond, where he spoke to 1,200 people at First Baptist African Church. As usual when white colonization agents spoke in Black churches, the parishioners were polite and encouraging as a group, but in private, expressed doubt. Averitt said Lynchburg families wanted more than reassurance from ACS bureaucrats and brochures, and that not being able to talk face-to-face with McNuckles was a problem. Some said they might "bundle up and go" if they could receive assurances from him, or their friends Addison Banks, George Waller, and Alex Crawford of the first emigration. Averitt tried to persuade Black ministers to put Orcutt in their Lynchburg pulpits to push colonization, but they refused.[22]

Coppinger sent the *Daily Virginian* another publicity piece about Liberia on April 9, 1866. But the complex influences on both continents that spurred the first Lynchburg emigration and squelched the second collided on that same day. In Africa, McNuckles began to get sick, and in America, overriding a veto by President Andrew Johnson, the Republican-controlled Congress enacted the first Civil Rights Bill. It said that all people born in the US, except American Indians, were citizens, regardless of race, and aimed to negate the Black Codes which Southern localities like Lynchburg were enacting to keep the freedmen in semi-bondage. While it did not grant them voting rights, the act meant the Southern freedmen had other civic rights like buying and selling property and giving evidence in court.[23]

The opportunity to gain rights of citizenship in Liberia had long been one of the primary inducements for Black Americans considering emigration. Coppinger told ACS President John Latrobe, "The passage of the 'Civil Rights' Act has done more than any or all the other things combined to prevent emigration this spring." Freedmen's Bureau agents, American Missionary Society abolitionists, schoolteachers and Black ministers in Lynchburg were also telling the African Americans that voting rights were coming. Blaming "the new element of population in Virginia from the North, white and colored alike," the state was a disappointment, Coppinger wrote to a friend in Philadelphia. He mused that 10,000 freedmen were needed in Liberia to strengthen the new country and to help spread civilization and Christianity in Africa.[24]

Sometimes, Coppinger appeared resigned to the situation: "We and Liberia must bide our time." He viewed rights granted to Black Americans through the lens of how those rights affected his cause and still believed in racial separation: "I feel greatly interested in the welfare of the colored people and conscientiously believe that it matters not what rights are accorded them by legislation, they will be far better off in their own land and under their own government." The ACS man also predicted, correctly as it turned out, that if African Americans presented a united front in demanding equal rights, they would provoke severe pushback from the white people and lose the very rights they were seeking to exercise. Coppinger told Jack Averitt he would come to Lynchburg again himself, to meet privately with influential African Americans, "if you think I can do any good for Africa."[25]

Rumors that former slaves would receive their former owners' Virginia lands also helped discourage emigration from Lynchburg. Local freedmen were hearing they would get not only land in America but also $100 each. Averitt said he had eighty people convinced to emigrate in the fall until they heard this. Nonetheless, he was still planning to emigrate himself: "If I was to get a hundred [acres] of land and bounty, I would not want to stay here."[26]

The freedmen had to endure the disdain of some educated men of color like Alexander Crummell, who had by now arrived back in Liberia. With a rare bit of imagery, Coppinger told him that hopes for large Virginia emigrations had vanished with "the ice and cold of winter." A complicated man, Crummell was a former opponent of colonization turned supporter. Sounding a different tone from his original warm encouragement of the Lynchburg emigrants, he wrote that he didn't believe newly freed slaves were capable of realizing they could better themselves by emigrating: "Present impressions are always the strongest with infantile minds." Averitt's mind was hardly infantile: He did not believe the rumors, saying the false information about slavery in Cuba had been spread by both races. He inquired about another rumor, that the land the emigrants were to receive would only be theirs temporarily. Coppinger assured him that the emigrants received deeds, that the land was given to them free of charge, and that they could sell it or do whatever they wanted with it. But the actual number of those committed to the second emigration never exceeded thirty, Averitt said in mid-April, and his own wife didn't want to go. The second emigration was off.[27]

The possibility of dying from disease was well-known and reported in the Lynchburg newspapers. By mid-April, more emigrants had died, Norvell wrote: Two children, the adults Gilbert Dudley, David Leftwich, Joseph Jones, and one other. Information took at least a month to go from one continent to the other, and when McNuckles went to Monrovia in early April to make final plans for his voyage back to the US, he did not know that the second emigration was falling apart. Still buoyant, he told Henry Dennis, the top ACS agent in Liberia, that he was over his acclimatization process and that the Lynchburg company was "driving ahead" in clearing their land and building their houses.[28]

McNuckles was ill when he returned to Careysburg from Monrovia on Monday, April 9, the day Congress overturned the presidential veto of the Civil Rights Bill. Laing advised the hyperactive McNuckles to slow down until he became more used to the climate and country but on Thursday,

April 12, the doctor readmitted McNuckles to the Receptacle, which doubled as a hospital, and told him not to leave Careysburg without permission. McNuckles felt well enough the following Saturday to approve a four-page letter from his sick bed boosting Careysburg, Liberia, and emigration in general. He wanted an independent, official endorsement of his plan for the second emigration, requesting it from John Freeman, the Monticello family descendant who was assisting Laing on behalf of the Careysburg Medical Department.[29]

Freeman wrote that the Lynchburg emigrants were "ingenious mechanics and practical agriculturalists" who did not expect to find life easy in Liberia—no "down beds"—but had set to work to build a settlement that would bless them in their old age and provide a legacy for their children. On arrival, they were as "robust and healthy" a group as had ever come to Careysburg, he wrote, acknowledging the prevalence of fever while praising their medical care. Mentioning that old settlers sometimes advised new emigrants to move away from Careysburg, he said the majority of Careysburg's population wanted the Lynchburg emigrants "to enjoy with us the happiness found alone in a 'Black Nationality.'" He addressed the lack of assistance for emigrants in-country by noting that the colonization society had to spend so much on transportation and the first six months' food that it might be ungenerous to ask for more.[30]

After his first bout with illness, McNuckles began to recover and was anxious to go out to check on his friends' progress before leaving for the states. Disregarding Laing's advice, he left the doctor's care on Monday, April 16, returned to his property on Zodah Creek, and cleared trees and burned brush in the hot sun. He became overheated and "took fever in its worst stage." He died the next afternoon, with family and friends at his bedside. Without much medicine, Laing had tried to keep McNuckles healthy according to the best practices of the times. But he did not know that the tiny mosquitoes breeding in the swampy environment were causing the on-again, off-again fever, and the ACS lacked money to keep him supplied with anything that would have eased its effects. In a detailed letter, Laing said the Lynchburg leader had caused his own death, through "needless exposure. He went to the Cape, returned sick. I took him in charge and cautioned him particularly not to go out of town for several days, and not without first consulting me. I put him under treatment on Thursday, and on Monday, he went to his farm, and commenced clearing up and burning and was brought home in a very weak condition." Like everyone who met McNuckles, Laing praised him: "He was a man of a great deal of energy and good sense, and was much respected; and would have been of great service to the country." The Lynchburg emigrants were "a thrifty set of people, and in my estimation, the immigration is one of the best we have ever had," wrote Laing. He would change his mind as the months and years passed in West Africa.[31]

Omitting several pages that revealed how precarious the situation in Liberia was, Coppinger published the letter about McNuckles's causing his own death in the *African Repository* a few months later. Reading the multiple letters about John McNuckles's life and death, it's hard not to think of someone like Moses or Martin Luther King Jr. leading their people to the promised land but not living to enjoy it. The ACS records include a religious mediation on death in an intriguing addendum to McNuckles's endorsement letter. It was signed by Freeman but reads as if it could be McNuckles's last words: "God has suffered me to pass through the fire but has not permitted me to be burned. He has carried me through deep waters but the rivers of sorrow [have] not yet overflown me. . . . Pray for me, make me the object of a special petition that God may be around me as the walls 'round about Jericho that in my last hours I may cry out in victory.' When I am dead then bury me in the sepulcher wherein the man of God is buried, lay my bones beside his bones.'" A partial paraphrase from 1 Kings in the Old Testament, it's a testament to the faith that had helped the enslaved endure centuries of bondage in old Virginia.[32]

The death of the Lynchburg company's leader was lamented by President Warner, who termed it "a dark and singular dispensation" from God, targeting someone who had seemed especially fit to carry out the Lord's work in Africa. Despite previous comments about the lack of emigration being a good thing, Warner said he had been looking forward to the second emigration from Lynchburg. When he died, McNuckles had already booked passage to America to help organize the second expedition. Instead, the ship carried at least five letters about his death. One was from William Eubanks, terming the cause a short illness of lung fever. "We expected much from him, and had he lived, we would not have been disappointed." The news took months to reach Lynchburg, and Averitt wrote on June 1: "The people are looking for Mac here and are looking to hear some great news from him." McNuckles's death shook Coppinger, who believed that McNuckles could have squelched re-enslavement rumors and personified the benefits of emigration. Now, any remaining confidence among prospective Lynchburg emigrants would be extinguished. Still maintaining that McNuckles caused his own death, Coppinger mourned him in several letters: "He seemed to be more free from the imperfections of human nature than most men, and to be animated by a strong desire to be useful in his day and generation." McNuckles's death was "a dark, sad Providence . . . It is a curious fact that those who we expect the most from always fall early. Why is it?"[33]

11

The Not-as-Promised Land

1866–1867

> A gloom seemed to overspread us, and how could it be otherwise?
>
> —Woodson McNuckles, Liberia

INITIALLY, THE death of his brother did not cool Woodson McNuckles's fervor for Liberia, despite his grief: "If our folks in America had a correct idea of this country and the advantages that would in time accrue to them by coming, nothing would stop them from emigrating here." He said he accepted his brother's death as God's will and with a wistful sentence asked William Coppinger of the ACS to pass his consolations to John McNuckles's wife: "Remember us all." He did not know that she had married one of McNuckles's friends just weeks before, an event which scandalized the strait-laced ACS officials. One speculated that perhaps God had taken McNuckles to keep him from witnessing her "wickedness."[1]

Although Woodson reported that building and planting continued at the beautiful Zodah Creek location, the Lynchburg emigrants made little impact on the tropical countryside, where tall cotton trees, oil palms, and pineapples proliferated in the forest and bush. Darting near the creek were birds including malachite kingfishers, resembling the familiar bluebirds of Virginia but with long reddish-orange beaks. Vipers, mambas, and cobras prowled the undergrowth instead of rattlesnakes and copperheads. Here, the crawfish were big enough to eat. The mahogany trees would be flowering in a few months, but their struggles left the Lynchburg emigrants little time to appreciate the environment. They had been cast back into a pre-industrial era, and without a sawmill trees were of limited practical value. They'd erected six or seven cabins by mid-April 1866 and might have been further along if they hadn't had to wait two months to receive their land. The rainy season was beginning, the settlers had much acreage to burn off before they could begin planting rice in earnest, and more of them were beginning to fall ill.[2]

In Monrovia, ACS agent Henry Dennis was suffering from fever. He heard from Careysburg that a number of the Lynchburg emigrants were sick, a change from just weeks before. John McNuckles may have had a premonition of all this, because he had given Dennis $40 in gold coin, possibly an ACS reimbursement for leading the emigration, with instructions that it be sent to his wife in case fever killed him. (Coppinger did not publish this dismal letter from Dennis in the *African Repository.*) By the end of April, Gilbert Dudley, the Lynchburg farmer formerly enslaved by the wealthy Murrell family, had died, leaving his wife, Jennie, with multiple children to care for. Teenager Joe Smith, 17, had also died.[3]

Despite pleas from Dr. Daniel Laing, the ACS couldn't afford to send Careysburg much medicine to ease the symptoms of fever. Laing had received no salary since the beginning of the Civil War. He was paying for medicines for the emigrants out of his own pocket and no one would accept his checks unless they were endorsed by the colonization society. He devoted the first page of his letter about John McNuckles's illness and death to a polite but pointed demand for some type of compensation, in tobacco if not money. He received neither. Isolated in the West African forest, Laing had little of the most important medicines: castor oil, sweet spirits of nitre, ipecac, and snake root. He also needed strong ale or brandy for his patients. Laing also wanted potash to make soap. The role cleanliness played in good health was not well understood, but the doctor knew it was important, as did settlers like Charles Lewis who brought a large quantity of soap with him. Remarking on great mortality among the emigrants from Barbados, Laing blamed it chiefly on uncleanliness. The lack of light also hampered medical treatment because Laing could barely see his patients inside dim cabins. He needed forty gallons of kerosene for oil lamps and lanterns. Laing said he had tried to assist the sick at no charge even after their official support from the ACS ran out but was no longer able to do that.[4]

Still optimistic with potential emigrants and in public, colonization officials were less so with associates. In June 1866, Coppinger blasted the Philadelphia and the Richmond ACS efforts in a letter to John Orcutt, who had just returned from his recruiting trip to Lynchburg. Coppinger was worn out and traveled by train to Bedford County near Lynchburg on June 28, apparently to recuperate. He met with Jack Averitt, who had tried to organize the second emigration, at the Lynchburg train depot that evening. No doubt they discussed both McNuckles's death and the dismal prospect of further emigration from the city.[5]

Hope and faith that endured after McNuckles's death was fading at the Zodah Creek settlement. Around twenty-five Lynchburg people had died. Parents were watching children, damp with sweat, shaking with chills, lying on soiled mattresses inside the Receptacle and dim cabins far from home. Sick themselves, many were becoming dissatisfied with the country. They badly needed sawmill equipment and now, their six month's support, mainly food, from the ACS had run out. "I am almost induced to say that I despair of Liberia," wrote Lynchburg emigrant William Eubanks, who would no longer advise others to emigrate because little paid work was available. He still viewed Liberia as the best place for the Black man but said the country did not need further emigration, because the West Africans themselves could be educated and become valuable citizens. On behalf of the Lynchburg survivors, he asked for flour, pork, fish, scrapple (pork scraps mixed with cornmeal), and nails, as well as leaf tobacco and cloth for trading.[6]

By August 1866, Eubanks himself had suffered several bouts of fever. "We are doing as best we can under the circumstances. Our health is somewhat improved from the last attacks of fever, and we indulge the hope that ere this reaches you we may be more improved. We have lost a good number of our most able-bodied men, not from fever exclusively, but much exposure . . . most of the survivors are in a convalescent state . . ." The Lynchburg adults were used to hard work and probably could have survived the heat and damp if they had not been weakened by malaria. By September 1866, the Lynchburg company had already suffered more deaths than any other emigrant group in Careysburg's short history. So far, Woodson McNuckles and family were an exception, all living and "well-satisfied."[7]

The *African Repository* picked up the story of Careysburg in September 1866, reprinting an inaccurate report from the *Liberia Herald* that the Lynchburg group had cleared its allotted properties and built sixty houses: "The mortality from fever has been quite small." Actually, the Lynchburg emigrants had managed to build only fourteen houses, on both sides of the creek, nearly a year after they arrived. Still American, some were beginning to assimilate into West African culture, and vice-versa. One family was living in a thatched house similar to the homes of the Queah. By the following spring, two local West Africans had been ordained elders of the Methodist church, with one running for a seat in the House of Representatives. The local emigrants from Barbados had begun moving out of the country, to neighboring Sierra Leone. President Warner, as anxious as the colonization society to blame any failure on emigrants themselves, said that the Barbadians were disappointed that "gold could not be dug up here so easily" and were leaving the country as fast as they could get away. Then, one of the few Barbadian families still living in the Careysburg Receptacle accidentally burned it to ashes with an indoor cooking fire.[8]

Many of the letters sent to America from Liberia were pleas for help. One was particularly poignant. Settler Jonas Carey had come to West Africa from Richmond aboard the *Nautilus* in 1821 with the first American emigrants. He was a relative of Virginian Lott Cary, a founding father of the country and the namesake of Careysburg. Jonas Carey had fought in battles against the West Africans and done everything he could to help plant the new country. Now, he was old and sick, his house in the Junk River region had burned, and he was desperate for assistance from the ACS: "As a last resort I apply to my old friends for assistance." I found no record that the ACS ever responded.[9]

The colonization society continued to borrow and scrape together enough money to charter ships to send more settlers to a country that could not support those who were already there. The ACS had little left over to help emigrants like Carey, or even pay its own employees, like Dr. Laing. Financial contributions had mostly dried up. Without emigrations to prove that the effort was still viable, and attract donations, the organization might not have survived the aftermath of the Civil War. The enslaved were now free, at least officially, yet the society continued to target Lynchburg's Black community, sometimes using information it knew to be false. In August 1866, Coppinger wrote to Averitt in Lynchburg, again asking about the prospects for further emigration. Almost like the reverse of a slave trader who wanted a shipful of West Africans to send to the Americas, the ACS man was trying to round up enough Black Americans to justify another voyage to Liberia. By then, Coppinger had received letters from not only the emigrants but also Laing and ACS agents describing the deaths and deadly conditions in the Careysburg country. But in this letter to Averitt, Coppinger stressed instead the erroneous June report in the *Liberia Herald*, quoting that the emigrants "are getting along prosperously, and that they have cut, cleaned and planted their land and erected thirty houses." Averitt wasn't buying it, and most local Black people had no interest in going to Liberia in the first place, encouraging their friends to stay put in Piedmont Virginia.[10]

As the one-year anniversary of their January arrival in Careysburg passed, the Lynchburg emigrants continued to sicken and die, with the ACS and the Liberian government in denial of the actual conditions. Liberia's treasury secretary, Frederick Hyde of Careysburg, an 1859 emigrant from New Orleans, insisted that the Lynchburg survivors were doing "tolerably well" on their farms and blamed some of the deaths on "imprudence." He wrote with an emerging sense of Black nationalism, mixed with the old Southern ethos of Christianity and racial separation: "It is impossible for the White man, and negro, to live on the same soil, in terms of equality. God never designed that the negro should enjoy social, and political rights, with the White race, while there is an Africa to Christianize and civilize . . . It is unfair of the negro to expect the whites to accord to them privileges, that they would not be willing to allow the whites . . . As to my part, I will never give my consent, for the whites to enjoy the same political rights in this county as we do. I shall speak boldly on the subject when I visit the United States . . . I am a Liberian and proud of the title . . . this is the only home for the negro, let him [come here] and assist in building up a firm nationality instead of quibbling and contending for what the Supreme Judge of the universe never intended they should enjoy in America."[11]

Lynchburg's George M. Wheaton, 32, was still doing his part to build up the nation. He did not regret coming to Liberia and had not given up on Careysburg. A carpenter, he was making a living "pushing my Jack plane" as he plied his trade with his Lynchburg friend, William Eubanks, "with whom I delight to work." He'd also planted coffee, which was growing well in early February 1867. He asked the ACS to send him a drill press—which he would pay for in Liberian currency—along with a dozen files to sharpen his saws. To identify himself in case Coppinger had forgotten, Wheaton noted that he was 6 feet tall, and that the ACS man had given him a few carpenter's tools in Baltimore. Wheaton, a Baptist, also wanted a suit to wear to church. He had come to Liberia with his wife, Louisa, 25, and three children. Now, he needed cloth, needles and thread for his children's garments, and some flannel shirts for himself. Wheaton also asked for trade cloth to barter with the West Africans. The emigrants often requested cloth in their letters to America. Like lumber, it was a manufactured staple of day-to-day existence that was taken for granted in America but valuable in Liberia. Obtaining cloth from America undercut the Manding suppliers and was another way Americans interfered with the West African economy. William Eubanks renewed his plea for iron, nails, and the mill saw. Surviving the fever which had him in despair the previous year, he wrote, "I am in good health now and hard at work . . ." But the ACS never sent the mill equipment, nor the iron or nails.[12]

In their letters, the Lynchburg emigrants portrayed themselves as devout and hardworking, attending church, clearing land, hewing wood, building cabins, planting rice, sewing clothes. No doubt many were, but by now Dr. Laing believed some of the Lynchburg emigrants themselves could be blamed for their problems: "They were generally intemperate, both in eating and drinking." Town constable Deputie, a sometimes-paid ACS employee, went further regarding the emigrants' prodigious consumption of local liquor: "Those that had money would [buy], others would sell their [clothes] to get it. They would drink it hot from the still. They all drank. I do not know if there was any effort to prevent it." He said several of the Lynchburg people had been convicted of stealing, and some for insubordination and riot. Sick or well, the restless emigrants did not linger along the wide, shallow creek. "They have died everywhere, and almost under all circumstances; at Careysburg, at their own settlement, on the road, and at the Cape [Monrovia]," Laing wrote in February 1867. Building up a remote settlement like Careysburg with only new emigrants, as the ACS was attempting to do, was impossible, wrote John D. Moore of Monrovia, the surveyor who laid off the emigrants' acreage. Referring to the Lynchburg group, he said, "It seems as if they become discouraged and give up."[13]

Painting a large group of people with such a broad brush denies their individuality. The Lynchburg emigrants were unable to overcome cascading setbacks including continuing illness, the delay in receiving their land, the deaths of McNuckles and many others, the lack of a sawmill to build their own houses and create a livelihood, the remoteness of the settlement, and insufficient food and medicine. The toddling Liberian government was of little help, sometimes encouraging further emigration, sometimes opposing it, but never able to offer much support to its citizens or even keep the economy viable, alternating between resenting and craving the parochial influence of the ACS. The ultimate success or failure of Liberia rested entirely on the efforts of the emigrants themselves, Moore wrote. Careysburg was essentially a company town, a venture of the ACS, not the government itself, so it suffered from the love-hate relationship between the two. Letters from the Liberian government to the

ACS and vice-versa in this period mingled praise and veiled, sometimes outright, criticism of the other.

Laing continued to criticize the ACS for not sending him the medicine and salary he needed to live and practice in Liberia. "You speak of the Lynchburg people and the mortality [large] among them. They were allowed their full rations; cooked for themselves and ate and drank (new rum not excepted) as they pleased. I had a very poor supply of medicines, not sufficient for their wants; and could not obtain what I needed, and asked for . . ." Laing finally received most of the medicine he had requested, but only after the Lynchburg emigrants had been in the country for more than a year. By that time, early 1867, nearly a third of the Lynchburg emigrants were dead, including many of the strong, talented men the group was depending on. Life in Careysburg got harder, not easier, as US emigrants continued to arrive, increasing the numbers of the weak and feeble who needed support. The country had no factories, no capital, no indoor work for women, and little work for adult men other than field labor in excessive heat, which increased their chances of falling sick. The situation worsened as more emigrants arrived but were unable to contribute to the common good. The plight of the day laborers, who ought to have been the bone and sinew of the country, was particularly bleak and it was little wonder some drank excessively. When they could get work, they might earn fifty cents a day, find themselves in debt for necessities at the end of the week, and then be paid in tobacco or cloth. This crushed their spirits and made them anxious to return to the US. Writing in beautiful script in January 1868, John Freeman, who had nursed John McNuckles, believed that some emigrants lacked personal energy and enterprise because of their enslaved heritage, when for generations the main responsibility of the enslaved was following orders, not planning and organizing.[14]

Nevertheless, the ACS, which had hoped to send more than 1,000 emigrants to Liberia on two voyages in 1866, rustled up enough support to send 600, none from Lynchburg, but including 144 from the Knoxville area. The Knoxville group was led by Hopkins W. Erskine, who had emigrated through Lynchburg in 1830 with his sister, Martha Erskine Harris Ricks, and her future husband, Sion Harris. (In 1853, both Erskine and Harris had been elected to the House of Representatives.) Now Liberia's attorney general, Erskine wanted to bring over another sister and her husband, children and grandchildren, all enslaved until the end of the war. The 1865 Lynchburg group had passed his farm on the St. Paul's on the way to Careysburg.[15]

Arriving in Tennessee in the summer of 1866, Erskine recruited throughout Tennessee and in Georgia. He faced some resistance at first, but human nature prevailed: "As soon as I became known to our people and informed them that I was born in Knoxville . . . both black and white crowded around me, seeking information." He met many people who remembered his father, the Reverend George Erskine, who like McNuckles died soon after arriving in Liberia. Erskine said most Black Tennesseans were waiting to see what the next Congress would provide them in the way of equal rights. He also said emigration was opposed by two classes of people: The "would-be ruling class of negroes styling themselves the intelligent ones," and large planters who didn't want to lose their labor force. But he finished his trip with the names of more than 200 people who had agreed to emigrate, and 144 did emigrate. Unlike typical prewar emigrations where the emigrants received short notice of upcoming voyages, his recruits had two months to prepare to go to Africa, and he was far more successful than most white emigration agents. Like his sister Martha, Erskine was a favorite of the colonization society, which sent him $30 while he was in Knoxville, and he praised its "persistent and arduous labors" on behalf of Liberia.[16]

Erskine also met with Tennessee's Gov. William "Parson" Brownlow, who urged him to travel the state pushing colonization. In Knoxville, where he was born, Erskine posed for a tintype photograph, wearing his suit, waistcoat, bow tie, and white shirt, with a mustache and chin-strap beard. He's looking directly into the lens with a determined, "Let's get on with it" expression, arms folded. Leaving Tennessee, he passed through Lynchburg on his way back to Liberia. Erskine spoke twice at the city auditorium and was on hand for the laying of the cornerstone at the new Colored Methodist Church on Oct. 2, 1866. This church is today's Jackson Street United Methodist Church and presumably Erskine's business card remains in the cornerstone, along with some coins, a hymn book, a Bible, copies of the Lynchburg newspapers, a *Christian Advocate* newspaper, and the names of contributors to the building. The Reverend Jacob Mitchell, Coppinger's friend, offered the opening prayers, and ceremonies were conducted by the local Masonic lodge, including "a mounted detachment of Knights Templar, in full regalia." Much of the city's clergy was in attendance. Erskine is the only African American mentioned by name in the patronizing account of the ceremony published in a national Masonic newsletter. The church was established by the Black community, not the whites, but the *Daily Virginian* editorialized about how white financial contributions to the church "put to shame the endless cry of the radical fanatics that nothing but hostility and bitterness is now manifested by the whites of the South towards the Blacks." Accounts like this made the white citizens of Lynchburg feel better about themselves, but they didn't reflect reality. "Outrages on freedmen are of daily occurrence," an Army lieutenant in Lynchburg wrote. Another officer reported increased, not decreased, complaints of cruelty and whippings: "The feeling toward government is bitter and civil war is discussed in public places."[17]

In his speech at the Lynchburg auditorium, Erskine addressed 100 people of both races on the "Condition, Prospects, Climate and Productions of Liberia." Oddly, the 1865 emigrants from Lynchburg were not mentioned in Lynchburg newspaper stories. The *Daily Virginian's* writer

Hopkins Erskine and his sister, Martha Erskine Harris Ricks, survived the deaths of their parents and harsh poverty in Liberia to rise into the Americo-Liberian elite. Erskine was a minister and teacher who returned to Lynchburg and Tennessee to recruit more emigrants in 1866. (Library of Congress Prints and Photographs Division, Washington, DC, LC-USZ62-56012)

praised Erskine's rhetoric, saying his points were "well put and strongly urged. He speaks well, with force, clearness and facility." Erskine said racial prejudice was a barrier to Black progress in the US and also talked about Liberia's climate, soil, schools and government, claiming the country was prosperous, except along the swampy, fever-ridden coast. After recounting Erskine's speech, the newspaper writer reassured his readers that the ACS acknowledged "the inferiority of the Black race." Lynchburg Black people were often told to stay in their place, and since Erskine's "place" was Liberia, he was no threat. The newspaper story exemplified the persistent white Southern dichotomy: Praise for some individual African Americans, but disdain for the race in general.[18]

Erskine was back in Liberia by January 1867. A few of his Tennessee emigrants went to Careysburg but were unhappy because of its remoteness and because they were frightened by the high mortality among the Lynchburg emigrants. As with the Lynchburg people the year before, Tennessee children began to die almost immediately, more than usual this early in the rainy season. Their voyage over had been so bad that one passenger said if the true details were published in America, it would stop emigration in its tracks. A fire, quickly extinguished, broke out aboard ship when a lamp overturned, causing panic. The captain was a "worthless . . . drunken beast" and he fumigated the ship with smoke, again terrorizing the passengers. At one point while intoxicated, reported Erskine, he physically assaulted Dr. Isaac Snowden, Laing's partner, who was returning to Liberia. "The doctor gave the Captain a decent pummeling which sobered him considerably," Erskine wrote.[19]

Erskine and the ACS continued to praise Liberia, but the Tennessee emigrants found it a hard country. Earlier emigrants were dressed in rags, everything was expensive, and merchants would not accept Liberian currency. "The agents out here are just like a lot of land Sharks they get all they possibly can out of the emigrants and then turn them adrift," wrote one passenger, who said even the distribution of provisions when the emigrants reached Liberia was handled with incompetence. Although new settlers now received twenty-five acres of land instead of ten, old Careysburg settler and constable Deputie wrote that few families had the wherewithal to cultivate ten acres of land, let alone twenty-five.[20]

John McNuckles's dream of helping create a community of freedmen—citizens—had faded in the bright light of West Africa. His brother Woodson McNuckles died in late April 1867. "Sun struck," he only outlived

Mack by about a year. As many as 85 of the Lynchburg emigrants had died by the start of the 1867 rainy season. With nearly all the "mechanics" dead, many of the surviving Lynchburg people began moving away from Zodah Creek. George W. Rose, 30, and his family relocated to Monrovia to practice his trade of shoemaking. A fever survivor, Rose built a house and shoe shop in Monrovia and planted 300 coffee plants on his farm. He wrote that while he himself was getting along well, he despaired for the country: "The way looks very dark but yet I am a free man." It's unknown if his wife or one of his children had died because the ACS stopped recording the deaths of individuals after the first six months. The Careysburg graveyard had been established almost exactly ten years before, with the first person interred there an infant who died in 1857.[21]

William Eubanks wrote, "Many of the Lynchburg emigrants died. I think . . . [Word] has gotten out in the United States that Liberia is not the place where the colored man should go but I say that Liberia is the place and country for the man of color. [If he can keep his health] then I think it is the best country in the world for the colored man." The remainder of the Lynchburg emigrants are getting along "tolerable well," meaning mediocre. Few had money to buy medicine for themselves. Among the dead he mentioned was Bucyrus Copeland, who passed away in the land his father had dreamed about for decades. Rose wanted to be remembered to J. W. Murrell in Lynchburg, his former enslaver, and also wrote to his mother, Linda Murrell, living in Washington. He continued to correspond with Coppinger into the 1870s. Also living in Monrovia by 1867 was Charles Lewis, another Lynchburg shoemaker and a signer of the original letter to the newspaper. He was in good health, but the possessions he brought with him to Liberia had gone missing the year before and he was still seeking compensation.[22]

In Careysburg, the initial sympathy and support for the remaining Lynchburg emigrants had evaporated as they demanded more, and better, food. They insisted that they receive food intended for newer emigrants, complained Douglass, the settler from Albemarle County who had helped establish the town nearly 10 years before. Douglass was relatively well-off but the emotional damage of enslavement lingered. Two of his adult children arrived in Liberia in August 1867, but they didn't recognize their father. The Douglass family was reunited in a country and region whose economic stress was worse than the postwar South. Even those who came to Liberia with a skill like shoemaking were hard-pressed to thrive in the backcountry. Careysburg still lacked a decent road for settlers to send their products to market. Imported goods were expensive, and Liberian currency depreciated. Agent Henry Dennis himself was a trader on behalf of the ACS, but he hadn't been able to do more than break even. He said money "and everything good" was more plentiful in America. Laing, a civic booster as well as physician, mentioned a couple of feasible but never enacted improvements, including setting up a foundry at Careysburg, which would provide work and much-needed bar iron, and distributing hand looms to provide indoor work for women.[23]

June 1867 marked 18 months since the Lynchburg emigrants had come to Careysburg. What was left of the Zodah Creek settlement remained unhealthy, with "considerable sickness" and nine more deaths since April. Deputie, Careysburg's law officer since its founding, had soured on the Lynchburg group: "They were a bad set. The half of them are dead. Some [are] among the worst set that ever came to this place." Deputie, who accepted the fever as a matter of course, was sick himself and would die in a few months. He blamed the failure of the Lynchburg settlement on drinking and poor nutrition. The first six month's food had been brought over on their ship, and they had no fresh meat.[24]

A few of the surviving Careysburg emigrants were able to return to Lynchburg after corresponding with their old masters. It's another example of how white people could like individual Black people, while considering their race inferior. A Lynchburg banker sent $50 in December 1867 to a woman he had enslaved, Fanny Proffitt, to pay for her voyage back to the states. She had emigrated at age 23 with her husband, Jacob, 25, a carpenter who had died. Also hoping to return from Liberia to Lynchburg were Jennie Dudley and her four surviving children, all under 12. Her husband, Gilbert, and two other children had died. A white Lynchburg woman still had kindly feelings toward the Dudleys, formerly enslaved by her family, and wrote to the ACS in October 1867 inquiring about how much she should send to pay for their passage back home. In November 1867, another former Lynchburg slaveowner, T.H. Ivey, a lawyer and railroad official, wrote to the ACS asking if he could make arrangements to finance the return of an unnamed emigrant and his children. The man's wife had formerly belonged to Ivey, but she and one child had died, and her husband was anxious to return to the states.[25]

In the time since the emigrants left, little had changed for freedmen in Lynchburg, despite receiving received some civil rights from the federal government. They deserved forbearance, wrote the editor of the *Lynchburg Republican,* who said they were not to blame for their emancipation, urging Lynchburg citizens to treat them with kindness and friendship to avoid the consequences of future Black empowerment. But belying any kindness to a few individuals were multiple acts of violence against desperately poor Black people in Lynchburg. The Lynchburg courts instituted whipping as a punishment for petty larceny in an attempt to discourage them from stealing food to feed themselves and their families. While the *News* was careful to note that this punishment would be extended to both races, no white people were whipped during the first week it was enforced in October 1866, only Black men and women. Among them were "Louisa Manson, negress," 15 lashes; "negro James Wright," 25 lashes; and the unfortunate "Frederick Jones, negro," who received 30 lashes, was sent to jail for 10 days, and was to receive another 30 lashes at the end of his sentence.[26]

The same week as these whippings, a white youth shot and killed a Black man who was taking sweet potatoes from another man's garden. The killing was ruled justifiable homicide, and the *News* opined that white people were right to "take the law into their own hands . . . even at the expense of shedding blood." The unstated root of the rampant thievery was deemed to be something in the Black nature that made them steal, not the fact that many had no jobs, no chance of getting a job, no money, no house of their own and no chance of buying any land on which to raise their own food. The solution was to shoot and whip them to discourage the symptoms of the problem, not fix the problem itself. The *New York Times* reported an unprovoked attack by two white men armed with a whip and a knife on freedman Reuben Jackson of Lynchburg in spring 1867. These attacks were common, and local white people had formed clubs to pay bail for the attackers. In this case, the military commander ordered the white men held without bond to prevent that. The situation was so bad in Danville, about sixty miles south of Lynchburg, that Black people were trying to organize their own military companies.[27]

The reconstruction of Lynchburg and its tobacco trade was important to Northern readers, and newspapers dispatched multiple writers to get a firsthand glimpse. What they found two years after the Civil War ended was not encouraging. "Among a large class of the inhabitants a most squalid form of poverty seems to prevail," reported a correspondent who detailed the situation around Lynchburg in spring 1867. He talked with someone who blamed the malaise on several factors: The white people were not accustomed to working themselves and hadn't enough money to hire Black people; the Black people were not used to working unless forced to work, and they wanted to be paid daily or weekly, not following harvest season. The reporter said the only people he actually saw working on farms or in the city were Black.[28]

Another *New York Times* writer, byline "Libra," arrived in Lynchburg in summer 1867, riding the rough rails from Petersburg near Richmond. The writer said for the first fifty miles of his Virginia journey, he did not see "three houses in which a Massachusetts or Ohio farmer would dream of lodging his family." Both the Black and white people he saw from the train looked alike, "ill-conditioned and miserable." Things began to improve as he got closer to Lynchburg. In Farmville, a former Confederate hospital had been converted to a Freedmen's Bureau school—"and out of one of the buildings there come trooping a pack of bright-faced Black children with their schoolbooks under their arms." Reaching Lynchburg, he was fascinated by the hilly city, a "queer anomalous burg" with steep streets. The tobacco factories and warehouses were busy, and demand for labor outstripped the supply, the only place in Virginia where he observed that. Libra attributed the labor shortage to "idle negroes" but inadvertently revealed the real reason: The factory owners weren't paying fair wages. Showing the writer his account books, a tobacco man acknowledged that during slavery, the factory hands generally completed their assigned tasks by about 1 p.m. each day. Then, they were paid for their additional daily time, "over-work." But that overwork pay, basically an afternoon's wages, equaled what they now earned in an entire day. Not surprisingly, the reporter observed, "they have not so much rush and spirit in their work."[29]

An 1866 story in the *New York Times* reported that Lynchburg had three schools for Black people, partially supported by the white citizenry, and that education of young African Americans was seen as key to making them better workers for the white people. The writer met with several leading white citizens, unnamed. He reported that they had kindly feelings for the freedmen but said that the "poorer class" of white people wanted to continue oppressing Black people, and that Black people preferred to work for the wealthy. Inclined to think well of the local African Americans, the *New York Times* correspondent still could not conceive of them as independent citizens. He concluded that while the freedmen had much to learn, good Freedmen's Bureau officers could teach them "their new responsibilities in a very short time."[30]

One thing had changed for the better: The US Congress had ordered that freedmen be allowed to participate in an 1867 vote on whether to hold a state convention to craft a new Virginia constitution. The results of this, the first multiracial election in Virginia's history, reflected the stark divide between the races in Virginia. Some whites boycotted the election because they didn't think Black Americans should be allowed to vote, and some were still disenfranchised for serving the Confederacy. The new Black voters turned out in large numbers and prevailed. In an election later that year to select delegates to the convention, Lynchburg Black people were told the only issue they should concern themselves with was the state's readmission to the union. Some whites threatened to fire anyone who didn't vote for an old Virginia Democrat. Nonetheless local African American Samuel Kelso, a Radical Republican and associate of Jack Averitt who had planned the aborted second emigration, was elected, and introduced a resolution authorizing Virginia's first public school system. The new ability of Black people to participate in civic life in the United States sparked a bit of nonsensical optimism from ACS agent Henry Dennis in Monrovia, who predicted that once the "colored" population became conversant with the ways of citizenship in the US, "Providence would so control events as to have them come to Africa." Maybe he was in a good mood because the always-tight ACS had just sent him $500 in cash.[31]

Along the James River, other Black Americans continued to fill traditional roles. Pulled by three horses in tandem, packet boats were again running west from Lynchburg up the James River and Kanawha Canal toward Lexington. Aboard one day was yet another New York reporter, who watched as a Black driver rode one horse and controlled the team. The driver had a horn slung over his shoulder, sounding it to alert keepers ahead to open their locks. Two small Black boys helped open one lock gate. At another, a strong dwarf was in charge. The writer mocked him as "a short dumpy Caliban . . . the model of Scott's Black Dwarf . . . the monster." But this man rose to the challenge each time a packet boat came through. He muscled his back against the lock's beam, pushing with his legs and short sticks held in each hand. At one point, straining against the lock, he lost his balance and toppled into the canal, watched by passengers ranging from mountain whiskey makers returning from a

Lynchburg spree to a freedman cultivating a large farm with his former master. The reporter was impressed by the freedman-farmer and said lumping all Black people into one category was incorrect. "They represent all varieties of individuality, and this is especially true in Virginia where they have had the advantage of a breeding greatly superior to those of the far Southern states." The freedman had better judgment than his old master. They split their profit in shares, but he had to supply the white man with extra corn to get through the winter.[32]

The writer interviewed former Confederate general Robert E. Lee, president of Washington College (now Washington & Lee University) in Lexington, saying the region was bursting like a rose. For Lynchburg, the tobacco flower would have been a more apt analogy. If any returning emigrants wanted to resume work in a tobacco factory, they would have been welcomed. The golden leaf was once again generating money, and J.W. Carroll and Co. of Lynchburg won the bronze medal for smoking tobacco in the American awards at the 1867 Paris Exposition.[33]

Around this time, the settlers near Careysburg had finished cleaning their arrowroot, a starch made from a yam-like tuber and used in cooking, only to find merchants and ship captains either did not want it or were willing to pay only low prices in depreciated Liberian currency. John Freeman, sick himself, wasn't sure the town would survive. In spring 1868, several more Lynchburg emigrants left Careysburg and returned to Virginia, reporting that only about 60 of the original 172 were left alive. Who these returnees were is not documented, and the only record of them is a brief item in a couple of out-of-town newspapers. They were said to harbor "disgust and hatred" for Liberia. The writer speculated that those reports were exaggerated and that they were simply so lazy they would not be happy anywhere they had to work for a living. This was the same year that the Ku Klux Klan established itself in Lynchburg. For the returnees it was a sour welcome back to old Virginia.[34]

12

Those Who Carried On

1868–1892

> Although I was not born here, I have lived here so long I have forgotten any other homes I may have had.
>
> —George Rose, Liberia, 1869

WHEN 1869 dawned over West Africa, only about 30 of the 172 emigrants from the 1865 Lynchburg expedition were alive in Liberia, and most—but not all—were desperately poor. "They have no money and as a matter of course it is very hard for them to get along," wrote George Rose, one of the survivors in Monrovia. The Zodah Creek settlement near Careysburg was almost abandoned. For some of the Lynchburg emigrants, the only extant written record that they ever lived was the list of passengers on the ship that took them away from Virginia.[1]

The high death rate among the 1865 group surprised even the ACS. Accustomed to the smothering blanket of enslavement, some of the emigrants were not able to live on their own in a tough place, but malaria killed many of them, not hard living. Perhaps generations of slavery and discrimination had beaten them down to the point they couldn't cope with a new set of seemingly insurmountable challenges while trying to live through an often-fatal disease. Mere survival was a triumph in Liberia. That a few of the early emigrants from Lynchburg—two of the Lynch brothers, and Martha and Hopkins Erskine—rose into the Liberian elite was all the more remarkable.

A Sierra Leone newspaper, the *West African Record,* published a look at Liberia in 1870, calling out exaggerations and misstatements by American Colonization Society supporters. Liberia was "small and weak and poor, we all know that out here . . . the citizens, as a rule, are rather unwilling to teach their trades to natives . . . there is not much love lost—in any country—between colonist settlers and natives." On the other hand, the *Record* noted, Liberia was a boon to the West Coast of Africa: "Slavery ceased, civilizing powers are at work . . ."[2]

Rose was making a living for himself and his family in Liberia, which he called "my native land," writing: "Although I was not born here, I have lived here so long I have forgotten any other homes that I may have had." He had opened a shoe business in Monrovia and his family was well. He loved Liberia, although its lack of raw materials hit him in the pocketbook when he had to import leather since the country had few cattle or tanneries. The ACS sent him a stock of leather in 1869 and by 1871 he had built a house in Monrovia and taken on an apprentice, although the society was unwilling to become a permanent source of his raw materials. Rose, a patient negotiator, told William Coppinger that this would cripple his business but continued to correspond, requesting six hymn books the following month and not mentioning more leather, which Coppinger eventually sent anyway. A planned trip to the United States did not materialize, and he asked Coppinger to forward a letter to his mother, who he had not seen in six years.[3]

By 1873 Rose had two apprentices but still needed leather. Coppinger turned him down on the grounds that it was not fair to favor one shoemaker over others just as deserving. Rose argued that no one would be of greater benefit to the youth of Monrovia than himself, and that others wanted to apprentice themselves, but he needed more leather to take them on. He also mentioned a rare upswing in the Liberian business climate, with more Liberian currency available. He enclosed a $25 bill of exchange drawn on a London bank to pay for the items he needed. The list began with a dozen calfskins and included hemlock and oak wood for soles, hammers, two dozen awls, and other supplies. Coppinger told him $25 wouldn't cover that much and Rose dutifully sent him $60 more in bills of exchange drawn on New York banks. A couple of years later, Rose asked Coppinger to vouch for him at a Baltimore wholesaler so he could order what he needed himself: "I have always tried to be faithful in my business dealings, and will thank you for whatever service you may render me." Rose had signed the original letter to the Lynchburg paper announcing the emigration in 1865 and this 1875 letter is the last I found from the 1865 emigrants.[4]

Rose's requests for raw materials and tools illustrated the problems faced by the struggling little country. What infrastructure there was in Monrovia itself had been in decline for years. Once-handsome brick and stone buildings were even more rundown than they were before the Civil War. A. B. Williams, a Charleston, SC, reporter, accompanied some South Carolina emigrants in 1878 and wrote: "Nearly all of the old houses are two-story ones, well-built of stone or brick, and arranged with an eye to architectural beauty, and about most of them were once neat stone fences surrounding large yards and gardens. These buildings are, however, fast going to rack and ruin, and the more modern, though hardly less dilapidated, edifices are of wood . . ." Weeds choked the walkway to the Customhouse and its broken windows and falling plaster, with all business conducted in one room. The brick courthouse was in similar condition. Wild verbena, green and purple, had overrun the way up from the ACS wharf, and tall cotton trees gave the whole place a wooded appearance. Williams wrote that the Executive Mansion was in relatively good repair, and that the homes of well-off Monrovians were similar to those of white people in the Southern US. He was served fresh fish and Liberian coffee, but the rest of his first meal in Monrovia consisted of canned meat, oysters and vegetables, all imported from England.[5]

Among the several thousand residents of the dilapidated capital city were other Lynchburg survivors, including carpenter George Wheaton, who had persevered in Careysburg for several years. By 1869, he was living in Monrovia and wanted to expand his carpentry business and train some youngsters in his trade, but needed Coppinger to send him tools and other supplies, promising to pay more than $200. He included a specific list of everything from screws and glue to hammers, planes, and screwdrivers, all not available in Monrovia or priced beyond his reach. Coppinger filled his order for tools. Considering the cooperation Wheaton and Rose received, perhaps the ACS at last was trying to help those who helped themselves, who were often the least likely to need help in the first place.[6]

The exodus from Careysburg to Monrovia also included the Braxton family. Shoemaker Carter Braxton, and his wife, Adeline, came from Lynchburg with their two sons, Joseph and James, on the 1865 voyage. In 1869, their third child, Sarah, was born in Monrovia: She grew up there, married at age 21, and became a leader in the Pentecostal Church. After her first husband died, she married Arthur Barclay, a former president of Liberia. He had been one of the Barbadian youngsters who lived near the Lynchburg emigrants around Careysburg, but he too moved to Monrovia where, according to one story, he sold salt on the streets, eventually earning enough money to go to school and become a lawyer. He died in 1938, but Sarah lived until 1955.[7]

John McNuckles's associate, preacher and tobacconist Levi Norvell, among the most independent of the Lynchburg emigrants, wrote back to the colonization society in September 1866 from Monrovia, noting he had survived the fever and was "creeping about again thanks to the Lord." Norvell mentioned that none of his family members had died although they had been very sick. He'd come with his pregnant wife who had been reluctant to travel, and their four children. He'd also brought his grandmother, at seventy-three, the oldest of the Lynchburg group. I found no further records of Levi Norvell's eventual fate, or that of his family.[8]

After the collapse of the second Lynchburg emigration in 1866, organizer Jack Averitt turned his activism to improving the lot of the freedmen in their hometown, not overseas. He encouraged people to have patience with their former masters but finally became fed up, quit his job, and joined the Radical Republicans who were arguing against handing control of the state to the former Confederates. He became known for sharp criticism of how the local white people exploited the labor of Black people. The late 1860s were contentious across Piedmont Virginia: In nearby Rustburg in 1868, some drunken white people tore down a United States flag at a Republican meeting at the courthouse and, guns drawn, ordered a Black speaker to sit down. That was observed by both Averitt and Samuel Kelso, one of the first African American teachers in the city. Both said that two magistrates did nothing to stop the white men. A Staunton newspaper correspondent complained that everywhere he went in Amherst, Rockbridge and Augusta in December 1867, "every other negro we met was armed with a U.S. musket." In January 1869, Averitt testified to the House Select Committee on Reconstruction in Washington, DC, confirming to the congressmen that white citizens colluded to lower wages and raise rents for Black people after the war. Black people were also arrested frequently for petty crimes, then imprisoned for long sentences on little evidence, suffering punishment for little or no cause. Averitt told the congressional committee that any Black man arrested in Lynchburg stood little chance of being cleared.[9]

Averitt's friends in Monrovia were doing their best to keep what little they had and get by day to day, while the Liberian government dreamed of expanding the country into the interior and taking over its mysterious sources of gold, iron and cotton cloth. However, the Mandings, whose territory stretched toward the old empires in the Sahara region, had long discouraged travel to the region. Benjamin Anderson, the first Americo-Liberian to explore their lands, wrote in 1870, "No one has passed unnoticed these tall black men from the eastern interior, in whose countenances spirit and intellect are strongly featured. Their avidity for trade has brought them from their treeless plains to the Atlantic Ocean." Anderson's expedition found a rich, thickly populated countryside where almost everyone was spinning cotton to manufacture "country cloth," a trade mainstay. He said most of the West Africans enslaved at Bopolu were engaged in carrying this cloth to the coast after it had been cut into smaller pieces to increase its profitability. Bopolu marked an invisible line northeast of Monrovia beyond which the Mandings strongly discouraged travel, to block access to their sources of commodities and to keep traders away from Musardu (in today's Guinea), the capitol of the western Mandings.[10]

Anderson's journey required multiple negotiations with people of varied ethnic groups and cultures, including Momolu Sao, the Bopolu ruler and son of Sao Boso. At least seven languages were spoken in Bopolu, although Vai was the shared tongue. As his chief negotiator for the journey, Anderson relied on a Manding, Kaifal, who mixed Islam and traditional West African beliefs, at one point "practicing certain rites, such as the interment of beef-bones bound round with transcripts from the Koran." Later he impressed Anderson by showing him how to conjugate a verb in Arabic. Momolu Sao's decision to let Anderson travel beyond Bopolu was controversial and not approved until a sand doctor was summoned to perform another ritual involving casting sand onto the ground and interpreting the resulting pattern. The people who accompanied Anderson from Bopolu to Musardu were an Atlantic world mixture: Anderson was a Black man born in America; his interpreter was Chancellor, a Gola and cousin of Momolu Sao; his guide was Beah, a Manding; and serving as bearers were three recaptives with American names, Jim, Alex and Pickanninny.[11]

Anderson wrote that the West Africans near Musardu were raising rice and cotton and living in densely populated, clay-and-earth walled towns. Elephants were rarely seen in the coastal forests anymore, but were plentiful in the Loma town of Ballatah, where a drawing from Anderson's book shows five elephants eating young cotton plants just outside the town's walls. Inside the walls, round houses with conical thatched roofs lined the streets, with a few cattle among the passersby.[12]

In 1870 another Americo-Liberian explorer intent on expanding the Liberian government's domination of Indigenous lands headed northeast from Careysburg into the Barline country. W.S. Anderson (no relation to Benjamin Anderson) traveled with twenty-five guards and thirty-five baggage carriers and was authorized by the Liberian government to purchase territory, enact treaties, and build block houses for military stations. About eight days' trek northeast of Careysburg he reached a town called Palaka, "a very ancient city" encircled by eighteen-foot-high stone and clay walls with watchtowers at the gates. Anderson claimed he secured by purchase and treaty agreements the entire region and what he estimated at 150,000 inhabitants for the Liberian government. He left a Liberian flag flying on the walls of Palaka. The Barline region, in today's Guinea, was well-watered, cultivated, mostly self-sufficient, and "much drier and freer from the miasmatic influence than the coast." The Barline people played musical instruments made from elephant tusks and raised cattle, sheep, goats and fowl. Although this region bordered the Mandings, W. S. Anderson found it to be "entirely free from Mohammaden influence" and thus suitable for "civilizing" influences from the Americo-Liberians, but that never happened.[13]

Back in Lynchburg, people were hot, and not just because of a July 1869 heatwave that hit 102 degrees in the shade. Virginia's conservative white people and former Confederates were waging a successful campaign based on racial discrimination to shove their way back into power. A torchlight parade of Black people in Lynchburg supporting the Radical Republican candidate for governor months earlier had so alarmed white people that the commander of the town's military garrison directed that police and soldiers guard the procession. Just as Washington Copeland and John McNuckles had feared, elite white attitudes were unchanged from slavery days. The *Daily Virginian* framed the election, for governor and state legislature, in stark racial terms, calling Black Americans' demands for equal rights a "horrid monster" which needed to be crushed before Virginia became unfit "for any respectable white man." The paper opined that Northerners who had come South to help were vermin and that the freedmen were deluded. Turning the reality of the situation upside down, the *Daily Virginian* said Black people needed to rally to the side of the white men who had always been their best friends, and that all white men needed to vote for conservatives to achieve "Virginia's emancipation." Businesses were encouraged to close on Election Day to increase the turnout, and fifty extra men were hired to police Black voters. Newspapers made little pretense of objectivity in the nineteenth century and the *Daily Virginian* distributed sample ballots for the white ticket. The paper also claimed that some Black residents who wanted to vote Conservative were afraid of being killed by other Black people. It printed a letter signed by "Anty Q. Klux" as evidence and endorsed an order from the military commander threatening the arrest of any voter who intimidated another.[14]

The newspaper summoned echoes of the English Civil War in "The Argument Closed" on July 3, 1869: "But the contest is now one of race. It must determine whether the proud Anglo-Saxon, with the blood of Virginia's cavaliers in his veins, shall rule this State; or, whether it shall be dominated over by 'American citizens of African descent,' officered and led by the very meanest types of the fanatical, malignant Roundhead, that have been 'a stone of stumbling and a rock of offense' in every land where they have inhabited."[15]

On Election Day, July 6, 1869, the white tide against equal rights for African Americans in Lynchburg and Virginia was running high. The Radical Republicans lost the governorship, and conservative candidates were elected to local seats in the state Senate and House of Delegates. Black educator Samuel Kelso of Lynchburg lost a bid for the legislature. John W. Daniel, an avowed racist and former Confederate officer, was one of three white candidates elected instead. Known as the "Lame Lion of Lynchburg," he would go on to a long political career, serve in the US Senate, and help write the Black disenfranchisement portion of the 1902 Virginia constitution. He died in 1910, and Lynchburg memorialized him in 1915 with a large statue by Moses Ezekiel, a noted sculptor and Confederate veteran. Black youngsters still had to walk it past on their way to segregated schools many years later. Kelso is now regarded as a founder of public education in the state but after the 1869 election, he and Averitt were among the local Black activists urged to get out of town by the newspaper.[16]

Piedmont Virginia depended on Black labor, and once the white conservatives were back in power, the *Daily Virginian* urged that most freedmen be treated kindly and educated, although not in integrated schools. The paper also said Virginia had far too many freedmen in the cities and that those who couldn't find a job should move to the country and work in the wheat and cornfields. The editor suggested that Black leaders like Averitt and Kelso should be ostracized and leave Lynchburg, equating their work for equal rights as an effort to spread enmity between the races. Black fraternal and civic groups were springing up after the war, and the *Daily Virginian* called for disbanding these "wicked organizations," asserting that membership meant that freedmen were not free, and further, "debars [them] from the sympathy and friendship of the white people."[17]

Many of the freedmen were unwilling to forgive and forget. The paper claimed no Black preacher could be found to officiate at the funeral of a railroad worker who had voted the Conservative ticket in 1869, "and the colored people refused to bury the dead man." A week after the election, Lynchburg's favorite orator, Charles L. Mosby, the old colonizationist and McNuckles's white sympathizer, was asked to speak on Black-white relations. Moderate for the times, Mosby counseled Black patience, and said Black people needed to be satisfied with "rights of citizenship" they had received in the Reconstruction amendments to the US Constitution. But "rights of civilization" were the result of white labor and sacrifice, he wrote, adding Black people hadn't earned those and could not vote themselves into actual equality. He urged his "colored friends" to abandon politics and resign themselves to racial separation.[18]

The editor of Lynchburg's newest newspaper, the *News*, was not as conciliatory heading into the November 1870 Congressional elections. Col. Robert E. Withers was a physician, farmer, and virulent racist. He blamed Black voters for his loss in the election for a seat at the 1867 constitutional convention. In the 1870 election, Withers advocated using the issue of race to ensure future Conservative victories statewide. He later wrote that Southwest Virginia had more Unionists than the rest of the state, and with the "immense negro vote" farther east, might overpower the white conservatives. He said boosting white turnout in the old slave lands by stoking white fears would tip the scales toward the Conservatives.[19]

That's exactly what happened, wrote Harry S. Ferguson many years later. Like Kelso, Ferguson was a Black Lynchburg educator. In his 1950 thesis, *The Participation of the Lynchburg, Virginia Negro in Politics,* he examined the 1870 local and congressional elections: "The effectiveness of an appeal by the local press to the emotions of many whites that they were in danger of being ruled by Negroes appeared to have won the election of 1870 for the Conservatives." An ACS prediction had come true: Black people who stayed in the US and asserted their rights had triggered a powerful white backlash that further restricted their liberties. Five Black men were elected to Lynchburg City Council in the 1880s, but white conservatives eventually re-asserted their prewar power, with Daniel mentoring future US Senator Carter Glass of Lynchburg to help disenfranchise most Black people statewide in 1902. Segregation and racial discrimination were enforced in Lynchburg and Virginia until overturned by Congress and the federal courts in the 1960s. No more Black residents served on city council until 1970.[20]

As in Lynchburg, the political situation in Liberia was in turmoil as the 1870s began. Civil unrest began with a complicated dispute between political parties over a constitutional amendment extending the term of the president, Edward Roye, admired for his wealth by Lynchburg's Washington Copeland ten years earlier. A second election was held, and Roye refused to participate. Virginia native Joseph J. Roberts, the country's first president, was re-elected and returned to power in 1872; Roye died in custody after being charged with keeping the proceeds from a British loan; intellectual and former Secretary of State Edward Blyden narrowly escaped hanging, and the postmaster general was killed. As in the Virginia elections, complexion played an important role, "the question of color privilege," as scholar Claude Clegg calls it. The dark-skinned Roye was a member of the Whig party. Roberts was of mixed race as were many of the former Virginians in positions of power, who were Republicans.[21]

Hopkins W. Erskine, who had visited Lynchburg five years earlier encouraging emigration, had become less optimistic and alarmed by the bitter politics. The former attorney general was superintendent of the Presbyterian Mission in Liberia and wrote from his home in 1871 on the St. Paul's River, "We are in a state of anarchy and confusion out here—one hardly knows when he lies down at night whether he will not be murdered before morning. Thousands would gladly return to America if they had the means to do so. Military arrests are the usual sights nowadays. Men are arrested and imprisoned for no cause other than they differ from the dominant party who deposed President Roye." Former president Roberts eventually restored order and life went on.[22]

Erskine and his sister, Martha Erskine Harris Ricks, were well-connected in the small world of families atop nineteenth-century Americo-Liberian society. Commenting on the American Civil War, Ricks asserted in 1865 that it had forced Liberians to learn to do for themselves, something they should have realized long before. She herself had begun weaving: "I have learned enough to weave cloth to help clothe my family. No doubt if the

Martha Erskine Harris Ricks spent a year in Lynchburg with her family waiting to emigrate, survived an Indigenous attack on a missionary outpost where she was teaching, and spent much of her long life on her farm on the St. Paul's River. She gained worldwide notice by presenting a handmade quilt to Queen Victoria in 1892, and was photographed for this cabinet card in London. (© National Portrait Gallery, London, x38887)

war had not of been I would not have learned . . . we are spinning and weaving, just what we ought to have done years ago, instead of waiting and depending on America." As always, she mentioned her faith in the same letter, asking Ralph Gurley, who was by now semi-retired from his colonization work, to pray for her as she prepared "to step down to Jordan, where there is no war, or death."[23]

But she wasn't ready to die yet: A trip to England in 1892 brought her worldwide recognition after she met Queen Victoria at Windsor Castle and gave her a handmade quilt of Liberian cotton, depicting a coffee tree. Her month-long visit to England was covered in British newspapers, which reported she had long wanted to meet the Queen but arrived in Liverpool without an appointment or invitation. She used her knowledge of influential Britishers who traded with West Africa to meet someone who knew someone, as the story goes, and met the Queen less than a week later. The *London Standard* reported "she was a shrewd old lady to get interviewed so promptly." Actually, her friend Jane Roberts had moved to London after former President Roberts died and was living with the family of the first Black Lord Mayor of London, so the introduction to the Queen was not that far-fetched. Before she left the country, she had a portrait photograph taken, a copy of which is owned by London's National Portrait Gallery. She died in 1901, at age 92.[24]

The Erskine family had other ties to influential Liberians. Blyden, nearly lynched in the 1870 uproar, was an early advocate of African nationalism and as the Liberian ambassador to England, accompanied Martha Ricks when she met the Queen in 1892. By then Blyden was living in Sierra Leone with Rick's niece, Anna Erskine, Hopkins W. Erskine's daughter, while married to another woman. Polygamy was part of some African cultures, and Blyden opposed missionaries forcing moral precepts on the West Africans. Blyden's views on racial separation and African nationalism coincided with those of the ACS, minus the belief that Black people were inferior. Anna Erskine, a teacher, grew up in Caldwell, the St. Paul's River settlement where "a uniquely Liberian personality developed blending both settler standards and local African standards," according to historian Nemata Blyden, a descendant. In 1878, yet another Virginia native, Anthony W. Gardiner, was elected as the first True Whig president of Liberia, and the party would rule the country without interruption until a coup in 1980 deposed the old Americo-Liberian families. A. B. Williams, a white reporter who accompanied a group of 1878 emigrants from South Carolina, wrote, "Virginians seem to about run the machine here. I expect that from them the Liberians inherit the delusion they are constantly occupying a large share of the world's attention, that being a weakness of the Old Dominion."[25]

One of those successful Virginians was Lynchburg native William H. Lynch. He had come to Liberia at age 6 in 1843 with his family, freed by the grandson of the city's founder on the condition they emigrate. His brother, John H. Lynch, had written back to Lynchburg in 1865 seeking to buy tobacco to trade in Liberia. William Lynch was secretary of treasury in the late 1850s and was a member of the Liberian House of Representatives. He wrote to a member of the white Stabler family (Robinson Stabler was his former owner's best friend), in 1866, expressing a Southern viewpoint on the US Civil War, saying he felt "no small degree of respect for the land that gave me birth . . . Nor do I see any just cause why Lincoln deserves more praise for what has been done for my race than Jeff. Davis."[26]

Lynchburg's twenty-first-century Silent Witnesses project memorializes enslavement in Lynchburg. This is one of the markers in the heart of downtown, embedded in the Ninth Street sidewalk near the site of nineteenth-century slave auctions. (Author photo)

Lynch also sent along a few copies of the *Liberia Herald* and asked for copies of the Lynchburg paper. By the 1870s, he'd become a successful businessman and a newspaper publisher who needed a new press. He wrote to the colonization society in 1873 asking it to procure one for him, saying a used hand press would be sufficient for his small newspaper, the *Republican*, and some job printing work. He said he was "endeavoring to get up and keep up a commendable line of public spirit here, and to stimulate . . . a correct sentiment on our behalf abroad." Lynch also chaired a committee planning the 1872 observation of Monrovia's semi-centennial. As a member of the House of Representatives, he addressed the crowd at Roberts's 1872 inauguration.[27]

The successful Americo-Liberians like the Lynches and Erskines couldn't advance the country beyond an agrarian replica of old white Southern society, minus the money and the slave trading. A. B. Williams, the South Carolina reporter, could have been writing about farmers along the James River in Virginia: "The general life of the older and wealthier . . . along the St. Paul's resembles in many particulars that of the Southern planter in the 'good old days.' Having a good brick house built, and his coffee, or sugar plantation . . . the tiller of the soil generally takes his ease, wears good clothes, and smokes, only exercising a supervision of his affairs. The spirit or wine decanter is almost invariably at the service of his guests." A Lynchburg survivor was among the first to greet the

South Carolina newspaper man's ship, the *Azor*, when it arrived in Monrovia in 1878 following a voyage that saw twenty-four deaths. After docking at Monrovia, the reporter chatted with "a strange colored man" who had just come aboard and who offered his impressions of the country. He said he had emigrated to Liberia from Lynchburg just after the war. The man, whom the reporter did not name, was pleased with Liberia, even though he had come over with nothing. In fact, he was on "the high road to wealth," clearing as much as $2,000 some years. (The Liberian president's salary was $2,500 in 1878.) The reporter had been worried about how the South Carolina emigrants would fare in their new country and was relieved to hear this. Then, one more question. "'What is your occupation?' I asked. 'An undertaker,' was the cheerful response."[28]

Afterword

THE STORY of the McNuckles family continued into the twentieth century, when they would again be known as Knuckles. I believe that at least one of the McNuckles children survived to become the progenitors of the Knuckles family in Careysburg and around Liberia today. While writing this book, I contacted a member of the Knuckles family, a native of Liberia living in Indiana. He said that five brothers went to Liberia, and three returned to the United States. As family history passes down through centuries, specific generations are often difficult to distinguish. The two adult men, John and Woodson McNuckles, plus Woodson's three sons, equals five—not five brothers, but three brothers, a father, and an uncle. Robert Knuckles, born around 1900 in Careysburg, is listed in twentieth-century family obituaries and appears to be the ancestor of many of the Knuckles of today. He was the father of another Mack Knuckles, as well as several other sons and daughters.

The Knuckles became well-known citizens of Careysburg. Three were mayors of Careysburg—Gabriel E. Knuckles Sr., Willis D. Knuckles, and Daniel Knuckles—in its first 100 or so years. Jonathan Knuckles was a prosperous sugarcane farmer for much of the twentieth century. Willis D. Knuckles Jr., who died in 2014, was an advisor to President Eleanor Sirleaf. She attended his funeral and cried over his casket, and he is buried across the street from his home in Careysburg in the Knuckles family cemetery. He was a former minister of state for presidential affairs, minister of public works, and chief executive administrator of the vice-president's office. Benjamin Freeman's *Careysburg* includes a wonderful Knuckles family snapshot from the 1960s that could have been taken anywhere in rural Virginia. The adult men are wearing suits, and the children and toddlers are clustered around two elderly women, apparently grandmothers: Emma Knuckles, b. 1887, and Etta Knuckles, b. 1891. It's not much of a stretch to imagine that their parents were born in Lynchburg.[1]

The Liberian economy never recovered from its heavy burden of foreign debt, focus on agriculture rather than manufacturing, many years of corrupt, one-party rule and the unhealthy climate. Historian Marie Tyler-McGraw summarized the country after the passing of the founding generations: "The arc of progress peaked in the 1890s, and the twentieth century produced little but tired rhetoric to inspire pride." The Americo-Liberians never fully bought into the culture and society they found in West Africa, leaving them forever between two worlds. An Indigenous coup in 1980 ended the reign of the Americo-Liberian descendants in Liberia, followed by rebellion and civil wars between 1990 and 2003. Indigenous leaders came to the fore, although Liberia and its institutions and infrastructure still suffered from the devastation many years later. Reconciliation efforts in 2025 included state funerals for both President William Tolbert, who was executed in 1980, and President Samuel Doe, who deposed him and was in turn deposed in 1990. [2]

Careysburg survived the first months of the Liberian civil wars, partly because rebels mistakenly believed a Voice of America base nearby was protected by US Marines. But later the base was ransacked and by 2003 most of the colonial style-houses in Careysburg as well as newer homes had been destroyed. By 2005, the town had lost 90 percent of its population, mostly to the United States, Benjamin Freeman wrote. Estimates vary, but across Liberia between 150,000 and 200,000 people were killed, many others were displaced, and the average income fell to about 12 percent of 1980 levels. President Sirleaf tried to move the country forward and won the Nobel Peace Prize in 2011. President Joseph Bokai, elected in 2024, pushed reconciliation and reform. Descendants of the West African ethnic groups make up 95 percent of Liberians. Descendants of the American colonists, and the recaptive Africans, constituted only about 2.5 percent of the country's population of about 5.3 million in 2022.[3]

No one else from Lynchburg is known to have emigrated after 1865, and the ACS stopped most emigration activities by 1900, noting in 1903, "It is now regarded as chimerical to attempt to send the entire mass of Negroes back to their native land." Reality had finally set in but not quite; Africa was certainly not the native land of Black Americans in 1903. After 1872, fewer than 200 people a year from the United States emigrated to Liberia, most years far less. The 1887 edition of the *African Repository* claimed that the Society had sent a total of 3,900 emigrants since the Civil War, making a total of 15,898 since its founding, and added 5,722 recaptive Africans, for a total of 21,620 persons "to whom the society has given homes in Africa." The Society's archives were donated to the Library of Congress in 1964.[4]

While I was working on this book, the *New York Times* did a small travel piece on the nightlife scene in a revived part of Monrovia, and it sounded a bit like hipster Brooklyn. The story was written by the *Times*' Helene Cooper. The daughter of a Liberian businessman, as a child she had to flee the country—her uncle was among the government officials tied to telephone poles on the beach and executed by the new government in 1980. In addition to a biography of former President Sirleaf, she's the author of a wonderful book about her up-to-then happy childhood in Liberia and her move to America, *The House on Sugar Beach*. Two of her great-great-great-grandfathers were emigrants from America. One, Randolph Cooper from Norfolk, arrived on the *Harriet,* the same ship that brought the first emigrants from Lynchburg.[5]

Amid the colonialism, death and poverty that characterizes Liberia's history, it's easy to overlook that regardless of whether they even wanted to emigrate in the first place, the Black Americans who went to West Africa in the nineteenth century hoped for freedom and liberty and a better life for their children and they risked everything to achieve it. Many died, but their words, and their struggle and perseverance against overwhelming odds, are worth remembering.

NOTES

Notes on Terminology

1. Dunn, D. Elwood, Beyan, Amos J., Burrowes, Carl Patrick, *Historical Dictionary of Liberia;* Burrowes, *Between the Kola Forest and the Salty Sea;* Holsoe, Svend E. "The Manding in Western Liberia: An Overview," *Liberian Studies Journal 7;* Leopold, Robert, "A Brief History of the Loma People." *Liberian Studies Journal 31.*

Introduction

1. Elson, *Lynchburg Virginia,* 111, quotation.
2. Jefferson to John Lynch, Jan. 21, 1811, Jefferson papers, Founders Online/National Archives; *The first annual report of the American Society for Colonizing the Free People of Color . . .* Washington: Printed by D. Rapine, 1819, LOC.
3. Moses, *Liberian Dreams,* xxxii–xxxiv.
4. Levi Norvell to the Colonization Society, Aug. 26, 1865.

1. From Many an Ancient River

1. John Mack Nuckles and Levi M. Norvell to William McClain, Jan. 6, 1866, quotations.
2. Chambers, *Architectural History,* 299. 1860 "Blackford map of Lynchburg," Edward Beyer's 1855 "Panoramic of Downtown Lynchburg," lynchburghistory.com.
3. Jordan, *19th Virginia Infantry,* 27; Nicholas, *Sheridan's James River Campaign,* 30; Tripp, *Yankee Town,* 157–61.
4. Houck, *Confederate Hospital Center,* 110, 115, 126, 131.
5. Nicholas, *Sheridan's James River Campaign,* 58–59; Tripp, *Yankee Town,* 161, quotation.
6. Tyler-McGraw, *African Republic,* 128–29.
7. *African Repository* 41 (1865), 362–65, 369–71; Author's compilation based on Emigrants Database, *Virginia Emigrants to Liberia,* Virginia Center for Digital History, University of Virginia.
8. *African Repository* 41 (1865), 370.
9. William Coppinger to James May, Oct. 8, 1865; Levi M. Norvell, Lynchburg, to William Coppinger, Oct. 17, 1865, quotation; *Daily Virginian,*

July 18, 1865. Over the years, this Lynchburg newspaper's nameplate also used *The Virginian* and the *Tri-Weekly Virginian* on various days of the week and later the *Lynchburg Virginian*. For simplicity, I refer to it throughout as the *Daily Virginian*.

10. Page, *Black Resettlement*, 56–57, quotation, 8.
11. C. L. Mosby to McClain, July 10, 1865, quotation.
12. John Orcutt to Coppinger, June 30, 1865, quotation.
13. *Daily Virginian*, June 15, 1865; Tripp, *Yankee Town, Southern City*, 165, 172; Suzanne Ramsey, "The Charley Mitchell Story," 2016 blog post drawn from Federal Writer's Project interview with Mitchell, https://appetite4history.com, quotation.
14. Lindsay, *Atlantic Bonds*, 48; J.M Goldberry to William Coppinger, Dec. 13, 1865, LOC, ACS domestic letters, Series I, incoming. Tyler-McGraw, *African Republic*, 174; Levi M. Norvell to the ACS, August 26, 1865, quotations.
15. Mills, "Situating African Colonization within the History of U.S. Expansion," in *New Directions*, 166–83, 169, quotation. Ericson, "The American Colonization Society's Not-So-Private Colonization Project," in *New Directions*, 112–28. Lindsay, *Atlantic Bonds*, 46; *Daily Virginian*, Aug. 31, 1831.
16. Dunn, *Historical Dictionary*, 328–29; Burrowes, *Kola Forest*, 217–34.
17. Burrowes, *Kola Forest*, 45–54; Leopold, *Brief History of the Loma*, 5–30.
18. *African Repository* 42 (1865), 42–43, first quotation; Freeman, *Careysburg*, 95–100; Murray, *Atlantic Passages*, 3,81, 98; Page, *Black Resettlement*, 8.
19. *African Repository* 37 (1861), 282, 283, quotation; Lindsay, *Atlantic Bonds*, 98–100.
20. Mack Nuckles to McClain, July 10, 1865.
21. Mack Nuckles to William McClain, July 10, 1865, first quotations; William Coppinger to Alexander Crummell, Sept. 22, 1865, final quotation.
22. William Coppinger to Mack Nuckles, Aug. 12, 1865, first quotation; William McClain to Mack Nuckles, Aug. 1, 1865, second quotation; Hine, *Crossing Boundaries*, 225–27.
23. Ramsey, "Charley Mitchell,"; Egerton, *Wars of Reconstruction*, 101–7; Gates, "40 Acres and a Mule."
24. *Daily Virginian*, Sept. 26, 1865, first quotation; *New York Times*, Nov. 26, 1865, second quotation; Ramsey, "Charley Mitchell," third quotation.
25. *Daily Virginian*, Aug. 9, 1865; Tripp, *Yankee Town*, 174.
26. *Daily Virginian*, July 6 ,1865, first quotation; Reid, *After the War*, second quotation, 336–37.
27. Tripp, *Yankee Town*, 184, freedmen's houses; William Coppinger to unnamed recipient (John McClain), Sept. 7, 1865.
28. Charles L. Mosby to William McClain, July 10, 1865, "freed man" quotation; *Daily Virginian*, Aug. 18, 1831, Mosby address to Lynchburg Colonization Society; Coppinger to McClain, Sept. 7, 1865, final quotation.

29. Sanneh, *Abolitionists Abroad,* 223–30. Alexander Crummell to "Dear Brethren," Oct. 19, 1865, *African Repository* 41 (1865), 371–72.
30. Mack Nuchols to O.O. Howard, Lynchburg, Oct. 8, 1865. LOC, ACS domestic letters, Series I, incoming; William McClain to John Orcutt, Oct. 4, 1865, quotation. William Coppinger to Dr. James May, Oct. 23, 1865; *African Repository* 41 (1865) 362, ship's list.
31. *Daily Virginian,* Oct. 19, 1865. Charles Mosby may have helped write this letter. The conciliatory language resembles published comments from him about the freedmen.
32. *New York Times,* Oct. 22, 1865; William Coppinger to John McClain, Oct. 25, 1865.
33. *African Repository* 41 (1865) 363, ship's list; Charles Lewis to William Coppinger, Aug. 18, 1867.
34. G. W. Rose to William Coppinger, Oct. 12, 1871; *African Repository* 23 (1847), 307.
35. Miller, *Liberia Described,* 10–11.
36. *Daily Virginian,* Nov. 1, 1865; William Coppinger to Levi M. Norvell, Oct. 20, 1865; William Coppinger to Franklin Butler, Nov. 18, 1865; William Coppinger to Daniel Warner, Oct. 27, 1865.
37. Mac Knuckles to Charles L. Mosby, Nov. 6, 1865; *African Repository* 41 (1865), 369.

2. Quakers and Colonizers

1. Morgan and Nicholls, "Slaves in Piedmont Virginia," 217; Chambers, *Architectural History,* 29.
2. Chambers, *Architectural History,* 29, 31, quotation.
3. Delaney and Rhodes, *Free Blacks,* 31, population; "Letter from Bishop Allen," *Freedom's Journal,* New York, Nov. 2, 1827, quotation.
4. Robert, *Tobacco Kingdom,* 21–25, 183; Jefferson, *Notes on the State of Virginia,* 227.
5. Sinha, *Slave's Cause,* 205–6; Walker, *Walker's Appeal,* quotations, 31, 14, 58, 79; Jefferson quotation, *Notes on the State of Virginia,* 198.
6. Chambers, *Lynchburg An Architectural History,* 45, 50; Yancey, *Lynchburg,* "nabob" quotation, 18; Chambers, *Poplar Forest,* 96–98, Jackson dinner; Fairfax Harrison, ed. *The Harrisons of Skimono* , 53 and following; Thomas Jefferson to Hugh Chisholm, Aug. 31, 1817, Jefferson papers, Founders Online/National Archives, brickwork quotation; John W. Eppes to Jefferson, April 28, 1817, grandson quotation.
7. Elson, *Lynchburg Virginia,* 17, Lynch description; Brown, *Pioneer Quakers,* 104; Bell, *Quaker Friends,* 72, 91; Bedford County, Va. Deed Book 7, 334; Worrall, *The Friendly Virginians,* 213.

8. Rhodes, *Campbell County Abstracts,* unpaginated.
9. Brown, *Lynchburg's Pioneer Quakers,* 99–100, 82, 85, quotations, 82–85; Tyler-McGraw, *At the Falls,* 68; Worrall, *Friendly Virginians,* 226–27; Tyler-McGraw, *An African Republic,* 83–103.
10. Tyler-McGraw, *At the Falls,* 67.
11. Bell, *Our Quaker Friends, 117–28,* author's compilation; Cabell, *Sketches,* 18–19.
12. Irons, *Proslavery Christianity,* denomination percentages, 6; Guyatt, *Bind Us Apart,* 61–63; Bell, *Our Quaker Friends,* 117–28; Cabell, *Sketches,* 18–19.
13. Christie and Dumond, *George Bourne,* 14–16; Guyatt, *Bind Us Apart,* 166–68, quotations, 166, 168; Sinha, *Slave's Cause,* 172–73; *Presbyterian Minutes 1789–1820,* 582, 610, 618, 626, 628, 682.
14. Mary Robinson Morton to her husband, June 6, 1806, Letters of Mary Robinson Morton, 1805–1806, Box 1, Haverford College Special Collections.
15. Jackson, "Negro Churches," 181–203; Early, "Diary," 237–51.
16. Thomas Jefferson to Charles Willson Peale, May 8, 1816, Jefferson papers, Founders Online/National Archives; Chambers, *Poplar Forest,* 99.
17. Von Briesen, *Letters of Elijah Fletcher,* 36; Rainville, *Invisible Founders,* 21–54; McDonald, *Poplar Forest,* 56–64.
18. Jefferson to John Lynch, Jan. 21, 1811, Jefferson papers, Founders Online/National Archives; *The first annual report of the American Society for Colonizing the Free People of Color . . .* Washington: Printed by D. Rapine, 1819, LOC.
19. Cabell, *Sketches,* 300, quotation; *African Repository* 19 (1843), 36.
20. Humphreys to Jefferson, Jan. 23, 1817, enclosure, Jefferson papers, Founders Online/National Archives, quotations.
21. Ibid.
22. Dew, *Making of a Racist,* 161–62.
23. Tyler-McGraw, *African Republic,* 41, 63–66; Eric Burin. "Envisioning Africa: American Slaves' Ideas about Liberia," *Liberian Studies Journal* 27 (2002), 1–17; Alan Neely, "Teague, Colin," *Biographical Dictionary of Christian Missions* (New York: Macmillan Reference USA, 1998), 115, 660. Boone, *Liberia,* 26.
24. Sinha, *The Slave's Cause,* 160–68.
25. Clegg, *The Price of Liberty,* 22–25, 37–38.
26. Ashmun, Jehudi. *History of the American Colony in Liberia, from December 1821 to 1823,* Washington City: Way & Gideon, 1826.
27. Ashmun, *Brief History,* quotations, 6–7.
28. Ashmun; Burrowes, *Kola Forest,* 318; Tyler-McGraw, *African Republic,* 130.
29. Ashmun, *Brief History,* 24–25, 29, quotations; Page, *Black Resettlement,* 30; Murray, *Atlantic Bonds,* 78.

30. Ashmun, *Brief History,* 24, quotation; Clegg, *Price of Liberty,* 103; Mills, Brandon, "Situating African Colonization with the History of U.S. Expansion," in *New Directions,* 166–83.
31. Von Briesen, *Letters,* 97nn2–4.
32. "Public Meeting," *Daily Virginian,* Aug. 29, 1825, quotations.
33. "Public Meeting," *Daily Virginian,* Aug. 29, 1825, quotations; "Fourth of July, 1825," *Daily Virginian,* July 4, 7, 1825.
34. *Daily Virginian,* Sept. 25, 1825, "few advantages" quotation. *Daily Virginian,* July 4, 1825, "hemisphere" quotation.
35. Library of Congress, J.B. Harrison papers in Burton Norvell Harrison family papers, 1812–1926, LOC, Boxes 1, 5, 6, first quotation, box 1, folder 7; *African Repository* 3 (1827–28) 193–208, 331–37, second quotation, 337; Elson, *Lynchburg, Virginia,* 76–78; Page, *Black Resettlement,* 3–4; Scruggs, *History of Lynchburg,* 40.
36. *African Repository* 3 (1827–28) 193–208; "Mr. Toler's Address," *African Repository* 9 (1833–34), 298.
37. Kearn, *Court Street,* 6–7; The Southern Review, Vol. XIX No. 37, 234, quotation about Early; "Colonization," Daily Virginian, Sept. 1, 1825.
38. Colhouer, *Sketches,* 357–59; "William H. Holcomb Diary and Autobiography, 1855 and 1892," University of North Carolina Libraries, Wilson Special Collections.
39. Slaughter, *Virginian History of African Colonization,* 13, quotations; Von Briesen, *Letters of Elijah Fletcher,* 75n1, 97nn2–4, 288; Rainville, "African American History," unpaginated.
40. Cabell, *Sketches and Recollections,* 214–219. Chambers, *Lynchburg Architectural History,* 33; Thomas Jefferson to Newhall, Sept. 1817, Jefferson papers, Founders Online/National Archives; Lisa Francavilla, "That Time When Thomas Jefferson Bought 'Ready-Made' Shoes," Research and Education blog, Monticello; *African Repository* 2 (1826), 221.

3. The First to Leave

1. Congressional Serial Set, *Harriet* ship's list, 192; "On board the ship Harriet, Norfolk Harbour," *Christian Advocate* 185–87; Thomas A. Holcombe, Lynchburg, to Ralph Gurley, Jan. 8, 1829; Jackson, *Early Strivings,* 31.
2. Royall, *Southern Tour,* 100, quotation.
3. George Erskine to Ralph Gurley, April 2, 1829, first quotation; George Erskine to Ralph Gurley, July 30, 1829, second quotation.
4. Guyatt, *"Rethinking Colonization in the Early United States," New Directions,* 339, quotation.
5. Tyler-McGraw, *African Republic,* 83–103, first quotation, 84; *African Repository* 5 (1829), 32; Blight, *Frederick Douglass,* 35–47, Douglass quotation, 46.

6. John Kennedy to Ralph Gurley, Jan. 14, 1830. Staudenraus, *African Colonization,* appendix; Huberich, *Political History,* 435; Page, *Black Resettlement,* 30. (No one really knows how many Africans were in pre-Liberia, but Page's figure of 250,000 seems reasonable.) Schwarz, *Migrants,* 72.
7. Capt. W. E. Sherman to Thomas C. James, June 4, 1830, Sherman to Edward Hallowell, May 10, 1830, Capt. Nicholson to Henry Clay, March 17, 1828, in *Pennsylvania Colonization Society,* appendices; Burrowes, *Kola Forest,* 47. Clegg, *Price of Liberty,* 77–92; Lugenbeel, *Sketches,* 27–28.
8. *African Repository* 6 *(1831),* 275; Navy Department to Ralph Gurley, Dec. 7, 1829; Joseph Mechlin Jr. to Ralph Gurley, Jan. 10, 1830, Elliott Cresson to Ralph Gurley, Dec. 4, 1829, quotation.
9. Tyler-McGraw, *African Republic,* 130, first quotation.
10. *African Repository* 6 (1830–31), 61, quotation; Burrowes, *Kola Forest,* 47; Dunn, *Historical Dictionary,* 219; Holsoe, *Manding,* 1–12.
11. Richard Randall letter extracted in "The Cabinet of Instruction, Literature and Amusement" (New York: Theodore Burling, 1829), 608; *African Repository* 5 (1829–30), 6–7, 281; *African Repository* 6 (1831) 61, quotation. Holsoe, Manding, 1–12.
12. *African Repository* 5 (1831), 50; Huberich, *Political History,* 384–85.
13. Benjamin Brand to Ralph Gurley, Nov. 18, 1829; Mechlin letter, March 20, 1830, in Huberich, *Political History,* 384–85; *African Repository* 8, 130.
14. Tyler-McGraw, *African Republic,* 132; William Crane to Ralph Gurley, March 30, 1829, quotation.
15. *African Repository* 4 (1829–29), 380; "Religious Intelligence," *Christian Advocate,* 186; David Burr to Ralph Gurley, Jan. 7, Feb. 20, 1829.
16. "Emigrants to Liberia," *Daily Virginian,* Feb. 9, 1829, extract of Jan. 18 letter from "Williamsburg Plough-Boy," first quotation; Benjamin Brand to Ralph Gurley, Jan. 20, 1829, second quotation.
17. *African Repository* 4 (1829) 380, first quotation; Anthony Williams to Ralph Gurley, June 19, 1830, in *African Repository* 6 (1830–31), 211.
18. John McPhail to Ralph Gurley, Jan. 24, 1829; Tyler-McGraw, *African Republic,* 63–67.
19. C. C. Harper to Ralph Gurley, Jan. 19 and Jan. 26, 1829; Cooper, *Sugar Beach,* 13, 116; Alford, *Prince Among Slaves;* Congressional Serial Set, *Harriet* ship's list, 191–94.
20. Innes, *Liberia,* 24, first quotation.
21. Joseph Shiphard to ACS, April 1829; Shiphard to Joseph E. Cooke, no date, and to pastor of First Presbyterian Church, Richmond, March 8, 1830; Connecticut Colonization Society, *Annual Report,* unpaginated appendix, quotations.
22. [Illegible] to Ralph Gurley, June 26, 1829, quotation.

23. "Lynchburg Colonization Society," *Daily Virginian,* Aug. 1, 1829, quotation; Harriet 1829 ship's list and 1843 Liberian Census, *Congressional Serial Set,* 1843.
24. *African Repository* 5 (1829), 280–82, quotations; "Late from Liberia," *Genius of Liberty,* June 1829, final quotation.
25. Tyler-McGraw, African Republic, 140–41; David Burr to Ralph Gurley, Feb. 11, 1830.
26. Burr to Gurley, Feb. 11, 1830; Tyler-McGraw, *African Republic,* 41.
27. Jefferson County, TN, Deed Book N, Jan. 11, 1816, 103–4; Dunn, *Abolitionist,* 46, 159n; Rankin, A.T., *Truth Vindicated and Slander Repelled.* Ironton, Ohio: The Register Press, 1883, quotation, 5–6.
28. George Erskine to Ralph Gurley, Jan. 1, 1829, quotation. *African Repository* 6 (1830), 264–65; *African Repository* 5 (1830), 30, quotation.
29. George Erskine to Ralph Gurley, Feb. 27, 1829, quotations, LOC, ACS domestic letters, Series I, incoming.
30. George Erskine to Thomas Balch, June 5, 1829. quotations; Richard Toler to Ralph Gurley, Dec. 17, 1829.
31. Richard Toler to Ralph Gurley, Dec. 17, 1829; George Erskine to Ralph Gurley, June 22, 1829, quotation.
32. George Erskine to Ralph Gurley, June 26, July 30, 1829, quotations.
33. Elijah Fletcher to Ralph Gurley, Nov. 4, 1829; George Erskine to Ralph Gurley, Nov. 27, 1829.
34. William Atkinson to Ralph Gurley, Dec. 19, 1829.
35. John Kennedy to Ralph Gurley, Jan. 7, 1830, quotation; J.W. Anderson to Ralph Gurley, Jan. 14, 1830; John McPhail to Ralph Gurley, Jan. 14, 1830, March 29, 1830.
36. Capt. W.E. Sherman to Thomas C. James, *African Repository* 6 (1830), 142–44, quotation 142.
37. George Erskine to "a gentleman in Richmond," March 9, 1830, American Colonization Society, *A Few Facts* pamphlet, 15, quotation.
38. Ibid., 15, first two quotations; George Erskine to Ralph Gurley, April 3, 1830, *African Repository* 6 (1830), 121, third quotation.
39. *A Few Facts,* 15–16, quotations.
40. Jeremiah Osborne to Ralph Gurley, July 12, 1830, incl. Bacon's letter.
41. Clegg, 86.
42. Tyler-McGraw, "The Prize I Mean," 355–74.
43. George Erskine to Ralph Gurley, April 3, 1830, *African Repository* 6 (1830), 121; A.D. Williams to Ralph Gurley, AR 6 (1830), 273–75.
44. *African Repository* 6 (1830–31), 274–75, quotation.
45. Shick, Liberian Census Data, 1843; Congressional Serial Set, *Liberia* ship's list, 194–95.

4. The Graveyards Always Look Fresh

1. Jackson, *Free Negro Farmer,* 392. Woodson, *Free Negro,* 173.
2. Richard Toler to Ralph Gurley, Feb. 15, 1830; John Kennedy to Ralph Gurley, March 23, 1830.
3. Royall, *Southern Tour,* 110–14, quotations, 114; "Brief View of Lynchburg by A Stranger," [Elisha Bates], *Daily Virginian,* Feb. 1, 1830.
4. Richard Toler to Ralph Gurley, Dec. 17, 1829, quotations.
5. Heinegg, *Free African Americans,* 149; Woodson, 142; Virginia Marriages, 1785–1940, Family Search database; Library of Virginia, Franklin County, Va., "Personal Property Tax Lists, 1804–1821;" Emigrants Database, *Virginia Emigrants to Liberia,* UVA.; Jackson, "Virginia Free Negro Farmer," 391, quotation.
6. Richard Toler to Ralph Gurley, Dec. 17, 1829; Asante, "Martin Delany," quotation.
7. *African Repository* 6 (1830–31), 130, quotation; Cabell, *Sketches and Recollections,* 204, 358; Delaney and Rhodes, *Free Blacks,* 69.
8. John Kennedy to Ralph Gurley, April 21, 1830; Latrobe to Gurley, April 23, 1830, quotation.
9. Brendan Wolfe, "Slavery by the Numbers (redux)," Encyclopedia Virginia blog, encyclopediavirginia.org; Congressional Serial Set, Carolinian ship list, 202–4; Montgomery ship list, 196–97; Benjamin Brand to Gurley, Oct. 21, 1830; John McPhail to Ralph Gurley, Oct. 17, 1830.
10. J. Mechlin Jr. to Ralph Gurley, Dec. 11, 1830, *Arican Repository* 7 (1831), 18–21; James Forten to William Lloyd Garrison, Oct. 20, 1831, Boston Public Library, Anti-Slavery collection, digital commonwealth.org.
11. *African Repository* 7 (1831), 25, first quotation; 340, 158, 258, second quotation. Orangutan, *African Repository* 7 (1831), 17–18.
12. Sinha, *Slave's Cause,* 164–65, first quotations; James Forten to William Lloyd Garrison, Oct. 20, 1831; Winch, 249–51, 422n6, final quotation, 250.
13. Winch, 249–51; *African Repository* 7 (1831–32), 341; "Mortality at Liberia," *Liberator,* Nov. 26, 1831; *Liberator,* March 31, 1832, quotation.
14. American Anti-Slavery Society, "Examination of Mr. Thomas C. Brown," 5, first quotation; 8, second quotation.
15. Chambers, *Architectural History,* 199. Dunaway, *African American Family,* 29. Delaney and Rhodes, *Free Blacks,* 31.
16. "The Insurrection," *Daily Virginian,* Aug. 25, 1831, quotation; *Liberator,* Oct. 22, 1831, 2; Withers, *Autobiography,* 39–42; Asante, *100 Greatest African Americans.*
17. "An Address . . . By Charles L. Mosby," *Daily Virginian,* Aug. 25, 1831, quotations; Richard Toler to Ralph Gurley, Aug. 22, 1853, final quotation.

18. J. B. Pinney to Ralph Gurley, March 10, 1834, *African Repository* 10 (1834), 47–58, quotation, 56; *African Repository* 10 (1834), 13, 99.
19. P. F. Voorhees to Levi Woodbury, Dec. 14, 1843, *African Repository* 10 (1834), 20–22; *African Repository* 10 (1834), 20–22, quotation, 21.
20. *African Repository* 10 (1834), 118, first quotation. *African Repository* 9 (1833–34), 236, final quotation.
21. *African Repository* 10 (1834), 21.
22. Garrison, *Thoughts On African Colonization,* 5, quotation.
23. *Liberator,* March 1, 1834, quotations from Holcombe's Dec. 28, 1833, letter to *New York Evangelist.*
24. *Liberator,* Aug. 2, 1834, Bourne quotations; *Liberator,* Sept. 20, 1834.
25. Slaughter, *African Colonization,* 70, first quotation; *African Repository* 10 (1834), 42, second quotation.
26. Brown, "Postal Campaign," 229; *Daily Virginian,* Aug. 10, 1835, quotation.
27. "Anti-Abolition Meeting," *Daily Virginian,* Aug. 31, 1835.
28. *Daily Virginian,* Aug. 10, 1835; Brown, *Lynchburg's Pioneer Quakers,* 88; *Daily Virginian,* Sept. 17, 1835; "A Small Affair," *Liberator,* Sept. 19, 1835; "Another Arrest," *Daily Virginian,* Aug. 31, 1865; *Liberator,* Sept. 19, 1835.
29. *Daily Virginian,* Aug. 31, 1835, first quotation; *Liberator,* Oct. 5, 1835, quotation from *Lynchburg Democrat;* Grimsted, *American Mobbing,* 116.
30. *Daily Virginian,* Sept. 3, 1835, quotations.
31. John Early to Ralph Gurley, Sept. 5, 1835; *African Repository* 11 (1835), 184, quotations 226–25; Davis, *Wills of Amherst County,* 96; Early to Gurley, Sept. 5, 1835; *African Repository* 11 (1835), 184.
32. Sinha, *Slave's Cause,* 335, first quotation; Staudenraus, *African Colonization Movement,* appendix, receipts; *African Repository* 16 (1840), 52–53; "Colonization and Abolition Contrasted," *African Repository* 16 (1840), 28, pamphlet quotation.
33. "The Garland Family," Yancey, *Lynchburg,* 310–14.
34. Schwartz, *Migrants Against Slavery,* 72; *African Repository* 14 (1838), 43–47, quotations.
35. 1843 Census of Liberia, Serial Set 458, U.S. Congress, Senate Document 150, 2nd Session, 28th Congress; Clegg, *The Price of Liberty,* 210–11; Tyler-McGraw, *An African Republic,* 137.

5. Holding On Against the Odds

1. Tyler, McGraw, *African Republic,* 179; *African Repository* 32 (1856), 271 (Martha Harris); Zion Harris to Ralph Gurley, May 26, 1851; *African Repository* 40 (1864), 137, and 42 (1866), 148 (W. H. Lynch); *African Repository* 40 (1864), 137, 37 (1861), and 27 (Hopkins Erskine).

2. *African Repository* 18 (1842), 242–53, quotation 242; McKee, *Sherbro Mission,* 71–72.
3. Lindsay, *Atlantic Bonds,* 87, quotation; 95.
4. Miller, ed., *"Dear Master,"* 76n2; *African Repository* 19 (1843), 71; Dunn, *Historical Dictionary,* 45; "Notes on Liberia," *Baptist Missionary Magazine* XXIII, 54, quotation.
5. *African Repository* 15 (1839), 277, quotation.
6. Miller, *Dear Master,* n1, 73–74 (citing Huberich, *Political and Legislative History,* 638–65); *African Repository* 15 (1839), 276–85, quotation, 283.
7. Martha Erskine to Ralph Gurley, May 16, 1839, quotations.
8. *African Repository* 15 (1839), 291–94, reprinted from *African Luminary,* quotation, 291.
9. *African Repository* 15 (1839), 291, 294, quotations.
10. *African Repository* 15 (1839), 291–94, first quotation, 294, second quotation, 291, reprint from *African Luminary; New York Journal of Commerce* in *African Repository* 16 (1840), 194–97, extracts of letters from Sion and Martha Harris.
11. Sion Harris to Ralph Gurley, April 16, 1840, quotation; Thomas Buchanan to Samuel Wilkeson, *African Repository* 16 (1840), 176–88. *New York Journal of Commerce* in *AR* 16 194–97, quotation, 196.
12. Sion Harris to Ralph Gurley, April 16, 1840; *African Repository* 17 (1841), 127; *African Repository* 34 (1858), 340.
13. Martha Harris to Ralph Gurley, April 16, 1840, quotation; *African Repository* 18 (1842), 300; *African Repository* 16 (1840), 197, quotation.
14. Murray, *Atlantic Passages,* 183–89, quotation 187.
15. Levi Walker to William McClain, Sept. 1, 1841, quotations. The Walkers were living in Millsburg by 1843, per the 1843 Liberian census (Shick).
16. Murray, *Whiteness in Africa,* 55–56; Zion Harris to Ralph Gurley, May 26, 1851, transcript in Hale, *Liberia,* 254, quotation.
17. Levi Walker to Ralph Gurley, May 10, 1842; *African Repository* 18 (1842), 258–63.
18. Samuel Cornelius to Elisha Whittlesey, April 8, 1842; Oct. 25, 1842, quotations.
19. Samuel Cornelius to Elisha Whittlesey, Oct. 25, 1842, quotations, with enclosed "Statement for the Rev. Cornelius" signed by Wm. Lynch, same date; *African Repository* 43: 36, 77, 100, 127, 201, 220; Cabell, *Sketches,* 22, 23n.
20. City of Lynchburg, Va., Will Book A, will 131–33, inventory 193.
21. Congressional Serial Set, *Barque Globe's Company,* 312–13; Tyler-McGraw, *African Republic,* 126.
22. Cabell, *Sketches,* 20–22; Santos and Bowman, *Rot, Riot and Rebellion,* 119.

23. "Jefferson's University . . . the early life (JUEL)," *Journals of the Chairman of the Faculty, 1827–1827; Minutes of the Faculty of the University of Virginia, 1825–56,* quotations.
24. Cabell, *Sketches,* 20–23.
25. Cabell, *Sketches,* 22–23, quotations.
26. *African Repository* 19 (1843), 201; William Lynch to John McClain, Nov. 21, 1842.
27. *African Repository* 19 (1843), 36, 77, 127, 200; *Maryland Colonization Journal,* vol.1, no. 19, 1.
28. *African Repository* 19 (1843), 126–27, reprinted from *Maryland Colonization Journal,* quotations.
29. *African Repository* 19 (1843), 265.
30. *African Repository* 19 (1843), 122–23, transcript of Aug. 29, 1842, letter from emigrant George S. Brown to Brother Chase; Missionary Report, *Methodist Episcopal Church,* 23, 29.
31. Will of William Lynch Jr., Lynchburg, Va., Will book C, 136, inventory 210–16, 238; Cabell, *Sketches of Lynchburg,* 23, quotation.
32. *African Repository* 23 (1847), 307; Murrell family papers, University of Virginia Special Collections, MSS 6740; Reeves, *From Tally-Ho,* 79–81.
33. Sion Harris to William McClain, June 5, 1848, first quotation; Hale, *Liberia,* 253, transcript of Sion Harris to Ralph Gurley, May 26, 1851, quotation.
34. George W. Leyburn to William McClain, Feb. 22, 1849, *African Repository* 25 (1849), 121.
35. George W. Leyburn to William McClain, Feb. 22, 1849; *African Repository* 26 (1850), 137–41, first quotation, 138; *AR* 25, 1849, 36, second quotation.

6. The Era of Washington Copeland

1. Sinha, *Slave's Cause,* 240–46, 335–38; Davis, *Problem of Slavery,* 121; Staudenraus, *African Colonization,* appendix.
2. Washington Copeland to William McClain, Sept. 29, 1859, LOC, ACS domestic letters, Series I, incoming, first quotation; Asante, "Martin Delany," unpaginated, second quotation. After he purchased his freedom, Copeland wrote several letters to the ACS between 1859 and 1861. Most of the details about his life are drawn from these letters and are confirmed by census and emigration records as well as other letters from the ACS, his apparent former owner, and Lynchburg acquaintances.
3. Davis, *Problem of Slavery,* 114, quotation.
4. Washington Copeland to William McClain, Oct. 14, 1860, quotation; Copeland to McClain, Sept. 29, 1859.

5. Copeland to McClain, Sept. 3, 1861, Jacob D. Mitchell to William McClain, Oct. 8, 1859; Copeland to McClain, Sept. 29, 1859, quotation.
6. Chambers, *Architectural History,* 202.
7. "Miller's Executor," 109, quotations 266. Miller's illegitimate children in "Page vs. Rives," 296–306.
8. Elson, *Lynchburg,* 183–86; Samuel Miller papers MS2037, 1833–72, Brock Collection, Box 103, Huntington Library.
9. "Miller's Executor," 291–93, 576, quotations
10. Link, *Roots of Secession,* 30–34, quotation, 33, from *Richmond Whig;* Chambers, *Architectural History,* 34, 119, 131.
11. Link, *Roots of Secession,* 30, first quotation, 29, third quotation; Elijah Fletcher to Calvin Fletcher, Dec. 28, 1850, Von Briesen, *Fletcher letters,* 226, second quotation.
12. Link, Roots of Secession, 107–10; Christian, *Lynchburg and Its People,* 148; "Southern Demands," *The National Era,* Aug. 23, 1855, final quotation.
13. "Slavery," *Daily Virginian,* Nov. 28, 1842, quotation.
14. Link, *Roots of Secession,* 156, "amputation;" Tyler-McGraw, *An African Republic,* 57–60.
15. William Valentine to William McClain, April 24, 1850, quotation; McClain to Valentine, April 29, 1850.
16. James Winn to William McClain, Sept. 6, 1850.
17. Lugenbeel, *Sketches,* 30–35; William McClain to William Valentine, Sept. 19, 1850.
18. William McClain to Samuel Miller, Sept. 19, 1850. McClain to Ambrose Rucker, March 25, 1850.
19. Ambrose Rucker to William McClain, Sept. 14, 1850.
20. Chambers, *Architectural History,* 133; Delaney and Rhodes, *Free Blacks of Lynchburg,* 31; "Anti-Slavery Sentiment in the South," *The National Era,* Dec. 30, 1847, quotation.
21. *Boston Medical and Surgical Journal,* vols. 27–28 (1843), 445; Gustavus Rose to William Waller, Dec. 21, 1835; "Virginians in Indiana," *William and Mary Quarterly* v10, Second Series (Oct. 1930): 313.
22. Link, *Roots of Secession,* 150–51.
23. "Horrible," *Frederick Douglass' Paper,* Nov. 3, 1854, quotation; Sinha, *Slave's Cause,* 353, 564–75; *New-York Daily Tribune,* Dec. 17, 1842.
24. "Virginia and the Tribune," *Vincennes Gazette,* Dec. 17, 1859. quotation; Dunn, *Civil War,* 94–95.
25. "Old Virginia—Her Statesmen Needed at Home," *New York Times,* Oct. 3, 1856. Review of "Memorial Discourse, on the Occasion of the Death of Bishop John Early, D.D.," The Southern Review 19 (Jan. 1876), 234–37.
26. Miller, *Dear Master,* 131; Washington Copeland to William McClain, Feb. 17, 1860.

7. A Freedom Odyssey

1. Washington Copeland to William McClain, Sept. 29, 1859; Copeland to McClain, Feb. 17, 1860, quotation. "Miller's Executors," 34.
2. Copeland to McClain, Sept. 29, 1859, first quotations; Copeland to McClain, Oct. 14, 1860, "rob us" quotation. Martin Delany, "Political Destiny of the Colored Race on the American Continent (1854)", in Newman, et al., *Pamphlets of Protest*, 228, quotation.
3. Jacob Mitchell to William McClain, Oct. 8, 1859.
4. Washington Copeland to William McClain, Feb. 17, 1860, quotation; Copeland to McClain, Sept. 29, 1859; Copeland to McClain, Oct. 14, 1860.
5. Washington Copeland to William McClain, Oct. 14, 1860. quotation. McClain to Copeland, Oct. 20, 1860.
6. *African Repository* 36 (1860), 365, total emigrants; *African Repository* 37 (1861), 117, quotation.
7. Hall's "An Address to the Free People of Color of the State of Maryland, 1859," in "From Slavery to Freedom: The African-American Pamphlet Collection, 1822–1909," LOC, American Memory Collection.
8. *African Repository* 36 (1860) 365; Clegg, *Price of Liberty*, 98, quotation.
9. Ericson, David F. "The American Colonization Society's Not-So-Private Colonization Project," in *New Directions*, 111–24.
10. *African Repository* 37 (1861), 281–82, quotations.
11. *African Repository* 36 (1860), 83; Isaac Snowden to ACS, Jan. 29, 1861.
12. Lugenbeel, *Sketches*, 21; *African Repository* 37 (1861), 145–46, from the *Liberia Herald.*
13. *African Repository* 39 (1863), 25–26.
14. Washington Copeland to William McClain, Sept. 3, 1861. William Helm to William McClain, July 10, 1860.
15. Copeland to McClain, Sept. 3, 1861, quotations; *African Repository* 38 (1862), 237.
16. *African Repository* 39 (1863), 27, "money" quotation; Martha Erskine Ricks to William McClain, Aug. 20, 1859; *African Repository* 39 (1863), 27–29.
17. Tyler-McGraw, *African Republic*, 169; *African Repository* 39 (1863), 29, quotation.
18. M. A. Ricks to Ralph Gurley, Aug. 12, 1862, in *African Repository* 39 (1863), 29–30, quotation 30; H. W. Erskine to ACS, Aug. 24, 1860; *African Repository* 36 (1860), 5–6.
19. Martha A. Ricks to Ralph Gurley, Aug. 20, 1859, quotation; Copeland to McClain, Sept. 3, 1861.
20. M. A. Ricks to Ralph Gurley, Aug. 12, 1862, in *African Repository* 39 (1863), 29–30, quotations.

21. *Daily Virginian*, Feb. 15, 1860, A.B. Rucker advertisement; Washington Copeland to "Doctor Hall," Sept. 3, 1861. Copeland to McClain, Sept. 3, 1861, quotations.
22. *African Repository* 39 (1863), 23–26.
23. *African Repository* 38 (1862), 243, transcript of May 5, 1862, note from Lincoln to Crummell and another commissioner; Burin, *Peculiar Solution*, quotation 162.
24. Congressional Serial Set, 39th Congress, Senate Executive documents, vol. 2, Ex. Doc. 55, "Transportation, Settlement and Colonization of Persons of the African Race," 31–32.
25. Washington Copeland to James Hall, Sept. 3, 1861; Copeland to McClain, Sept. 3, 1861, second quotation.
26. Wright, *They Left*, 7, 13, 47, 78, 98; "Political Meeting at Second Baptist Church," The Historical Marker Database.

8. Banished from Old Virginny

1. *African Repository* 34 (1858), 185, 301.
2. McLeroy, *Strangers in their Midst*, 259, quotation.
3. Library of Virginia, Chancery Records Index, Nelson County, index no. 1888-026, Executors of Nicholas Dettor vs. John Dettor, etc.
4. John Paxton to William McClain, July 31, 1858.
5. Sollors, Werner, et al., eds. *Blacks at Harvard*, 24, 28–30; Nercessian, "Nineteenth-Century Black Graduates . . ." 88–89; *African Repository 30* (1854), 172,19, 214–19.
6. *African Repository* 32 (1856), 260, extracts from June 2, 1856, Isaac H. Snowden letter, first quotation; *African Repository* 34 (1858), 205, extracts from March 28, 1858, Snowden letter, "Saratoga" quotation; Snowden to ACS, July 31, 1858.
7. African Repository 30 (1854), 189; "Attempted Outrage by Negroes" and "A Slave Whipped to Death," *Liberator*, Sept. 22, 1854.
8. *African Repository* 41 (1865), 161, 175, 251, 332; *African Repository* 35 p. 164, quotation; "Message of the President of Liberia," *Vincennes Gazette*, Vincennes, Ind., March 19, 1859; Burrowes, *Kola Forest*, p. 186; *African Repository* 35 (1859), 166.
9. *African Repository* 34 (1858), 93, quotation.
10. Randy Saylor's "Timothy Rogers Junior: Quaker to Slavemaster," contains a wealth of documentation and description of the Rogerses' court cases and I am indebted to him for many of the details in this account.
11. *African Repository* 36 (1860) 36; Saylor, depositions; Maris-Wolf, *Family Bonds*, 140.

12. Jacob Mitchell to William McClain, April 25; May 3, "unwilling" quotation; Saylor, citing the *Friend,* vol.23 (1850), 298–99.
13. Jacob Mitchell to William McClain, May 28, 1850, quotation.
14. Maris-Wolf, *Family Bonds,* 124, 139, 140, 253–54nn95–99.
15. *African Repository* 35 (1859), 172–73, quotation, 383; *African Repository* 34 (1833), 117; *Vincennes Weekly Western Sun,* Oct. 3, 1857, reprint from *New York Commercial Advertiser,* quotations; Dunn, *Historical Dictionary,* 153.
16. *African Repository* 35 (1859), 170–73, 378–79. First quotation, 170; second quotation, 171.
17. William McClain to Jacob Mitchell, Oct.1, 1859, quotation; John Sale to McClain, Oct. 18, 1859.
18. *African Repository* 35, 1859, 379; *African Repository* 36 (1860), 11, 205, 330. John M. McCalla Jr. handwritten journal in "John McCalla family papers, 1754–1917 and undated," David M. Rubenstein Rare Book & Manuscript Library, Duke University, 60–81.
19. H. J. Roberts to William McClain, April 2, 1860.
20. H. J. Roberts to McClain, April 2, 1860.
21. *African Repository* 30 (1854), 194, 214–17, 340; Virginia Colonization Board Journal of Proceedings, June 6, 1854, Library of Virginia; McLeroy, *Strangers in Their Midst,* 119; Amherst County, Va., Will Book 13, 51, from Davis, *Wills of Amherst County; New York Times,* Sept. 21, 1852, quotation.
22. Virginia Colonization Board Journal of Proceedings, 1853–54, Library of Virginia, part 3, p5 quotation; William McClain to Henry S. Davis, Amherst, April 20, 1854.
23. William McClain to ACS offices, May 12, 1854; *African Repository* 30 (1854), 30, 78, 123, 177, 189, 193–94, 201, 203, 340; *African Repository* 32 (1856), 111, Gurley quotation.
24. *African Repository* 32 (1856), 105; *African Repository* 30 (1850), 347.
25. Blassingame, *Slave Testimonies,* 555–59; *Cincinnati Tribune,* June 17, 1923.
26. *African Repository* 30 (1854), 21; [signature illegible] to William McClain, Nov. 12, 1853, quotation.
27. Will of John Cheatwood, Will Book 7, Bedford County, Va., 115–16.
28. G. W. Leyburn to Ralph Gurley, Aug. 3; *African Repository* 30 [1854], 47.
29. G. W. Leyburn to William McClain, April 9, 1850, first quotation; "Report of the [Virginia] Colonization Board for the Years 1854 & 1855," 5, second quotation; Marie Tyler-McGraw, *An African Republic,* 57, 60.
30. *African Repository* 30 (1854), 19–24, ship's list; J.W. Lugenbeel to Ralph Gurley, Oct. 31, 1853. *African Repository* 30 (1854), 21; Lugenbeel to Gurley, Nov. 3, 1853.
31. William McClain to ACS office, Nov. 8, 1853, quotation; Staudenraus, *African Colonization,* appendix.

32. H. W. Dennis to William McClain, Jan. 18, 1854, *African Repository* 30 (1854), 133–34; William C. Burke to William McClain, Jan. 16, 1854, *African Repository* 30 (1854), 133, 189.
33. *African Repository* 31 (1855), 37.
34. Oldfield, "Protestant Episcopal Church," 32; *African Repository* 30 (1854), 36, "handmaid" quotation; E. W. Stokes, et al., to ACS, June 3, 1853.
35. Will Book 13, Amherst County, Va., 448; "Emancipated Slaves," *New York Times,* Oct. 24, 1859.
36. "Departure of Emancipated Negroes—Don't Want to Leave," *Staunton Vindicator,* Oct. 14, 1859, reprinted from *Lynchburg Republican,* quotation; "Our Colored Population," *Liberator,* Nov. 18, 1859, citing the Columbus, Ohio newspaper.

9. The More Things Change . . .

1. Christian, *Lynchburg,* 177.
2. The Lynchburg News, April 22, 1900; *Historic Southern Monuments.* New York and Washington: Neale Publishing, 1911, 422; Smith, *Managing White Supremacy,* 25–26.
3. Keehn, *Knights,* 47, 58, 106, 134; "Arrest of Gen. Bickley," *Vincennes Gazette,* July 25, 1863; *New York Times,* Dec. 16, 1860, quotation; *Daily Virginian,* June 27, 1859.
4. R. A. Hunt, Lynchburg, Va. to Abraham Lincoln, Jan. 18, 1861. Abraham Lincoln papers, Series 1. General Correspondence, 1833 to 1916, Manuscript/Mixed Material, LOC; Mary F. Blackford to William McClain, Jan. 21, 1861; Tyler-McGraw, African Republic, 103.
5. Letter to the editor, *Daily Virginian,* August 15, 1856, first quotation; Tripp, N. Wayne, "Lynchburg during the Civil War," *Encyclopedia Virginia; Daily Virginian,* May 3, 1865, reprinted from *Washington Chronicle;* Charles Blackford, *Annals,* 149–51; *African Repository* 23 (1847), 307; Susan Blackford, *Memoir,* second quotation.
6. Editorial, *Daily Virginian,* June 28, 1859, quotation.
7. Library of Virginia, "Slavery in Virginia: A Selected Bibliography;" Delaney, *Free Blacks,* 31; *African Repository* 41 (1865), 361, 369, 370; Berlin and Gutman, "Natives and Immigrants," 1175–1200; *Daily Virginian,* April 3, 1861, quotation.
8. Jackson, *Negro Office-holders,* 28–29; Tripp, *Yankee Town, Southern City,* 17, 166, 183, 185.
9. Perdue, *Weevils In the Wheat,* 323. Hargrove advertisement, *Lynchburg Republican,* June 3, 1863; Bancroft, *Slave-Trading,* 92–93. Chambers, *Architectural History,* 132–33, quotation; Nicholas Guyatt, "How Proslavery Was the Constitution?" *New York Review of Books,* June 6, 2019, 46.

10. Perdue, *Weevils in the Wheat,* 325–26.
11. Ramsey, Suzanne. *Appetite for History,* "In his own words: the Story of Lynchburg Freedman Charley Mitchell." https://appetite4history.com/2016/09/07/in-his-own-words-the-story-of-lynchburg-freedman-charley-mitchell/.
12. Stinnett, Joe. "For good and bad, Civil War editor was man of his times," *The News & Advance,* Lynchburg, Va., April 18, 2015.
13. Editorial, *Daily Virginian,* Jan. 7, 1863.
14. Editorial, *Daily Virginian,* Jan. 7, 1863; Egerton, *Wars of Reconstruction,* 190; Burin, *Slavery and the Peculiar Solution,* 160–65; Jordan and Thomas, *19th Virginia Infantry,* 27; *Liberator,* Aug. 22, 1862.
15. Advertisements, *Daily Virginian,* Feb. 17, March 22, 1865. *The Daily Virginian* ceased publication around this time and did not resume until a few weeks after the April surrender; Scruggs, *Lynchburg Virginia,* 113.
16. Nicholas, *Sheridan's Campaign,* 24–27; News story, *Daily Virginian,* July 6, 1865.
17. Mack Nuckles to William McClain, Lynchburg, July 10, 1865, quotations. This letter was signed "Mack Nuckles" and Mosby wrote in an enclosed note that it was dictated by "some Yankee here."
18. Editorial, *Daily Virginian,* May 19, 1865; Editorial, *Daily Virginian,* June 1, 1865, quotation.
19. "General Orders No. 2 and 7," *Daily Virginian,* May 23, 1865; News story, *National Anti-Slavery Standard,* July 8, 1865, extract from *Rochester Democrat.*
20. "General Order No. 10," *Daily Virginian,* May 27, 1865; "General Order No. 15," *Daily Virginian,* June 1, 1863.
21. News story, *Daily Virginian,* June 29, 1865; Editorial, *Daily Virginian,* July 19, 1865; "General Order No. 38," *Daily Virginian,* July 18, 1865.
22. "General Order No. 15," *Daily Virginian,* June 1, 1863; Commentary, *Daily Virginian,* May 29, 1865; Editorial, *Daily Virginian,* July 19, 1865, quotation.
23. Egerton, *Wars of Reconstruction,* 178; New story, *Daily Virginian,* June 2, 1865; Dennett, *The South As It Is,* 53, quotation.
24. *Daily Virginian,* June 16, 1865, quotations; Dennett, *The South As It Is,* 44, 51.
25. Editorial, *Daily Virginian,* July 7, 1865, *New York Herald* quotations; Folkerts, "Bennett's New York Herald," 667; Dennett, *The South As It Is,* 35; "Founding Prospectus," *The Nation,* ca. July 6, 1865, final quotation.
26. Dennett, *The South As It Is,* first quotation, 48; Egerton, *Wars of Reconstruction,* 123, second quotation; Tripp, *Yankee Town,* 166–67, 169.
27. Dennett, *The South As It Is,* 46–47, first quotations; 56, second quotation.
28. Dennett, *The South As It Is,* 72–74, quotation.

29. Dennett, *The South As It Is,* 67, first quotation; *Daily Virginian,* Aug. 21, 1865, final quotations.
30. Dennett, *The South as It Is,* 74–85, quotations, 78.
31. "A Trip to Lynchburgh," *New York Times,* April 29, 1866; Dennett, *The South As It Is,* 78.
32. Dennett, The *South As It Is,* 79–83, quotations.
33. *Daily Virginian,* Nov. 3, 4, 17, 1865, quotation, Nov. 4.
34. *Daily Virginian,* Sept. 26, 1865.
35. News story, *Daily Virginian,* Feb. 13, 1866; James Garland to William Coppinger, Lynchburg, Feb. 12, 1866.

10. Coming Into the New Country

1. Mac Knuckles to Charles L. Mosby, Nov. 6, 1865, reprinted in *Daily Virginian,* Nov. 13, 1865.
2. John Mack Nuckles and Levi M. Norvell to William McClain, Jan. 5, 1866; H. W. Dennis to William McClain, June 1, 1867; Tyler-McGraw, *African Republic,* 152.
3. Daniel Laing to William Coppinger, Feb. 12, 1866.
4. Tyler McGraw, *African Republic,* 158; Daniel Warner obituary, *New York Times,* March 13, 1881.
5. Daniel Warner to William Coppinger, Jan. 6, 1866, first two quotations; Alexander Crummell to Coppinger, July 4, 1866; Murray, "Whiteness in Africa," 23; Clegg, *Price of Liberty,* 97–98.
6. Murray, *Atlantic Passages,* 195–201, quotation, 201.
7. *Daily Virginian,* Feb. 6, 1866; Daniel Warner to William Coppinger, Jan. 6, 1866, Charles Deputie to William Coppinger, March 19, 1866; *African Repository* 42 (1866), 40.
8. *African Repository* 41 (1865), 44–46, extract from *Liberia Herald;* William [Eu]banks to William Coppinger, Careysburg, Liberia, April 22, 1866.
9. Levi M. Norvell to William Coppinger, Careysburg, Liberia, Sept. 4, 1866; H. W. Dennis to William Coppinger, Careysburg, Liberia, Sept. 5, 1866.
10. "Sketch of the Careysburg Road by William Douglass," December 1867, LOC; "Location of Careysburgh," John Seys, undated hand-drawn map, LOC; John Mack Nuckles and Levi M. Norvell to William McClain, Careysburg, Liberia, Jan. 6, 1866; Charles Deputie to William Coppinger, March 19, 1866. Woodson McNuckles to William McClain, April 21, 1866, first quotation; *African Repository* 41 (1865), 332–33, second quotation.
11. Sollors, et al., *Blacks at Harvard,* 24, 28–30; *African Repository* 31 (1855), 40.
12. Daniel Laing to William McClain, Feb. 18, 1863, LOC, ACS letters from Liberia, Series I, incoming, quotation.

13. *African Repository* 42 (1866), 86–88; Judith P. Rives to William Coppinger, Feb. 7, Feb. 21, 1866; William Douglas to "friend", Jan. 29, 1866; Terrell papers, UVA Library Special Collections; Freeman, *Careysburg,* 43–55; *African Repository* 44 (1868), 47, 337.
14. "The Liberia Mission Field," *African Repository* 42 (1866), 160–77, quotation, 168; Tyler-McGraw, p. 165; Burrowes, *Kola Forest,* quotation, 76–77. "Message of the President of Liberia," *Vincennes Gazette,* March 19, 1859.
15. Woodson McNuckles to William McClain, April 21, 1866, quotations; *African Repository* (1868), 313; William [Eu]banks to William Coppinger, April 22, 1866; Daniel Laing to Coppinger, April 22, 1866; *African Repository* 42 (1866), 253; "Visit to Careysburg" (J. J. Roberts); *African Repository* 35 (1859), 247–50; *African Repository* 37 (1861), 7; *African Repository* 41 (1865), 332.
16. *African Repository* 33 (1857) 219, quotations; William [Eu]banks to William Coppinger, April 22, 1866.
17. William C. Burke to Mary C. Lee, Feb. 20, 1865, in Wiley, *Slaves No More,* 204, quotation.
18. *African Repository* 42 (1866), 253; H. W. Dennis to William Coppinger, Sept. 5, 1866; John Mack Nuckles and Levi M. Norvell to William McClain, Jan. 5, 1866, quotation.
19. John Mack Nuckles and Levi M. Norvell to William McClain, Careysburg, Liberia, Jan. 5, 1866, longer letter; *African Repository* 42 (1866), 157, and *Daily Virginian,* April 16, 1866, shorter letter; John McNuckles to Mr. Editor, March 1, 1866; William Coppinger to McNuckles, Washington, D. C., April 30, 1866.
20. H. W. Dennis to William Coppinger, Monrovia, Liberia, Sept. 5, 1866; William [Eu]banks to William Coppinger, April 22, 1866; *Daily Virginian,* June 16, 1866, summary of April 22, 1866, Norvell letter, quotations.
21. William Coppinger to J. D. Mitchell, Washington, D.C., March 9, 1866; Mitchell to Coppinger, Lynchburg, Va. March 19, 1866.
22. John Orcutt to William McClain, Lynchburg, Va., April 6, 1866; J. D. Mitchell to William Coppinger, March 19, 1866; John Averitt to William Coppinger, June 1, 1866, quotation.
23. William Coppinger to C. W. Button, April 9, 1866; Egerton, *Wars of Reconstruction,* 199, 215.
24. William Coppinger to H. B. Latrobe, April 30, 1866; William Coppinger to Alexander Crummell, April 30, 1866; William Coppinger to Thomas S. Malcom, April 28, 1866.
25. William Coppinger to Alexander Crummell, April 30, 1866, first quotations; William Coppinger to John Averitt, April 19, 1866.
26. John Averitt to William Coppinger, June 1, 1866.

27. William Coppinger to Alexander Crummell, April 30, 1866; Alexander Crummell to William Coppinger, Monrovia, Liberia, July 4, 1866; John Averitt to William Coppinger, June 1, 1866.
28. *Daily Virginian*, June 16, 1866; H.W. Dennis to William McClain, April 25, 1866, quotation.
29. Woodson McNuckles to William McClain, Careysburg, April 21, 1866; Daniel Laing to William Coppinger, April 22, 1866.
30. John R. Freeman to William Coppinger, note to "Dr. L," attached to letter of April 14, 1866.
31. Charles Deputie to William Coppinger, April 22, 1866; Woodson McNuckles to William McClain, April 21, 1866. Freeman attributed McNuckles's death to "typhoidal apoplexy;" Daniel Laing to William Coppinger, Careysburg, Liberia, April 22, 1866.
32. John Freeman to William Coppinger, April 14, 1866. LOC, ACS letters from Liberia, Series I, incoming, quotations. *African Repository* 42 (1866), 253.
33. Daniel Warner to William Coppinger, July 6, 1866, first quotation; William [Eu]banks to William Coppinger, Careysburg, Liberia, April 22, 1866, second quotation; John Averitt to William Coppinger, Lynchburg, Va., June 1, 1866, third quotation; William Coppinger to John R. Freeman, June 23, 1866, final quotation.

11. The Not-as-Promised Land

1. Woodson McNuckles to William McLain, April 22, 1866, first quotation; William McLain to Woodson Mack Nuckles, June 20, 1866, second quotation.
2. William [Eu]banks to William Coppinger, April 22, 1866; Charles Deputie to William Coppinger, April 22, 1866.
3. H. W. Dennis to William Coppinger, April 25, 1866.
4. Daniel Laing to William McLain, Careysburg, April 22, 1866; H. W. Dennis to William Coppinger, Monrovia, Oct. 13, 1866. Daniel Laing to H. W. Dennis, Feb. 7, 1867; Daniel Laing to William McClain, Feb. 8, 1867.
5. William Coppinger to John Orcutt, June 20, 1866; William Coppinger to John Averitt, June 23, 1866.
6. William Eubanks to William Coppinger, Aug. 31. 1866, quotation.
7. William Eubanks to William Coppinger, Aug. 31, 1866, first quotation; Charles Deputie to William Coppinger, Careysburg, Sept. 6, 1866, second quotation.
8. *African Repository* 42 (1866), 279, first quotation; *African Repository* 43 (1867), 86; Charles Deputie to William Coppinger, April 30, 1867;

H. W. Dennis to William Coppinger, Sept. 5, 1866; D.B. Warner to William Coppinger, Sept. 6, 1866, 'gold' quotation; H. W. Dennis to W.M. McClain, Oct. 13, 1866.

9. Jonas Carey to William McClain, Oct. 12, 1866, quotation.
10. William Coppinger to John Averitt, Aug. 18, 1866, quotation.
11. Frederick Hyde to William Coppinger, Jan. 10, 1867; AR 43, p. 86.
12. George Wheaton to William Coppinger, Feb. 7, 1867, quotations; William [Eubanks] to William Coppinger, Feb. 7, 1867, quotation.
13. Charles Deputie to William Coppinger (two letters), April 30, 1867, quotations; Daniel Laing to William McClain, Feb. 8, 1867; John D. Moore to William Coppinger, Monrovia, Feb. 9, 1867.
14. Daniel Laing to William Coppinger, Feb. 7, 1867; John Freeman to William Coppinger, Jan. 7, 1868.
15. Sanderfer, *Tennessee Emigration Movements*, 270–74; *Memorial of the Semi-centennial Anniversary of the American Colonization Society* (1867) 25, 101; William Coppinger to H. W. Erskine, Sept. 12, 1866; William Coppinger to S. D. Denison, Sept. 17, 1866.
16. H. W. Erskine to William Coppinger, Aug. 14, 1866, first and second quotations; Erskine to McClain, Aug 23, 1866; Erskine to William McClain; Sept. 8, 1866, "ruling class" and "arduous labors" quotations; Erskine to Coppinger, Sept. 22, 1866; *African Repository* 29 (1853), 286; *African Repository* 40 (1865), 137.
17. Sanderfer, *Tennessee Emigration Movements*, 274; "Interesting Ceremony," *Voice of Masonry and Tidings from the Craft, Volume 5* (Chicago: John C.W. Bailey, Publisher, 1867), 14; *Daily Virginian*, Oct. 3, 1866, 'put to shame' quotation; "Special dispatch to N.Y. Tribune," *National AntiSlavery Standard*, Sept. 1, 1866, final two quotations.
18. *Richmond Daily Dispatch*, front page, Oct. 6, 1866, reprinted from *News* (Lynchburg); "Lecture on Liberia," *Daily Virginian*, Oct. 4, 1866, quotations.
19. H. W. Erskine to William Coppinger, Monrovia, Jan. 10, 1867.
20. William Evans to William Coppinger, Feb. 9, 1867, quotation. Charles Deputie to William Coppinger, Feb. 4, 1867, ACS letters.
21. Charles Deputie to William Coppinger, April 30, 1867; George W. Rose to William Coppinger, May 27, 1867, quotation; *African Repository* 33 (1857), 210.
22. William Eubanks to William Coppinger, May 27, 1867, quotation; George W. Rose to William Coppinger, May 27, 1867; Charles Lewis to William Coppinger, Aug. 18, 1867.
23. William Douglass to William Coppinger, Feb. 7, 1867; William Douglass to William Coppinger, Aug. 14, 1867, 'Did not know me' quotation;

H. W. Dennis to William McClain, June 1, 1867; Daniel Laing to William Coppinger, Feb. 12, 1867.

24. Charles Deputie to William McClain, Monrovia, June 1, 1867, quotation.
25. Lorenzo Norvell to William McClain, Dec. 13, 1867; Miss Murrell to William Coppinger, Oct. 20, 1867; T.H. Ivey to William McClain, Nov. 27, 1867.
26. *Staunton Spectator,* April 16, 1867, reprinted from the *Lynchburg Republican; News* (Lynchburg), Oct. 2, 3, 4, 1866.
27. *News* (Lynchburg), Oct. 2, 1866, quotation; "Affairs in Virginia," *New York Times,* April 7, 1867; New York Times, June 2, 1867, reprinted from *Daily Virginian.*
28. "Affairs in Virginia," *New York Times,* April 7, 1867, quotation.
29. "Through the South," *New York Times,* June 10, 1867.
30. "A Trip to Lynchburgh," *New York Times,* April 29, 1866.
31. Brent Tartar, "African Americans and Politics in Virginia," Dec. 20, 2020; Tartar, "Disenfranchisement," July 19, 2016; Tartar & Dictionary of Virginia Biography, "Samuel F. Kelso (ca. 1825–1880)," Dec. 22, 2021, all in *Encyclopedia Virginia.* "Result of Registration in Virginia," New York Times, Aug. 15, 1867; H.W. Dennis to William McClain, June 1, 1867, Monrovia.
32. "Through the South," *New York Times,* June 12, 1867, quotations.
33. *New York Times,* June 7 and June 29, 1867.
34. John Freeman to William Coppinger, Jan. 7, 1868; "Lynchburg Timeline 1700–2009", compiled by Ken Morrison for Lynchburg Public Library; *Alexandria Gazette,* March 20, 1868, quotation.

12. Those Who Carried On

1. George Rose to William Coppinger, Jan. 12, 1869.
2. "Liberia," *West African Record,* April 1870.
3. George Rose to William Coppinger, Jan. 12, 1869, quotation; Rose to Coppinger, Aug. 21, Sept. 3, and Oct. 12, 1871.
4. George Rose to William Coppinger, May 12, 1875, quotation. Rose to Coppinger, March 15, 1873, and July 22, 1873.
5. Williams, *Liberian Exodus,* 29.
6. George Wheaton to William Coppinger, Feb. 7, 1867; Wheaton to Coppinger, March 11, 1869.
7. Brown, "Barclay Women," 31–32.
8. Levi M. Norvell to William Coppinger, Sept. 4, 1866, quotation.
9. Tripp, *Yankee Town, Southern City.* 174–75, 236, 247 (Klan), 248, "personal servant" quotation 174; Ferguson, *Negro in Politics,* 12–13; "Government Property," *Valley Virginian,* Jan. 16, 1868, musket quotation.
10. Anderson, *Journey to Musardu,* 6, quotation.

11. Anderson, *Journey to Musardu,* 40, 46–47, quotation, 33.
12. Anderson, *Journey to Musardu, 56,* 82–84, drawing, 82.
13. *African Repository* 46 (1870), Akpan, M. B. "Black Imperialism: Americo-Liberian Rule over the African Peoples of Liberia, 1841–1964." *Canadian Journal of African Studies / Revue Canadienne Des Études Africaines* 7, no. 2 (1973). 217; Leopold, *History of the Loma,* 6–7; *African Repository* 46 (1870), 316–17.
14. *Daily Virginian,* June 30, July 2, 3, 1869; quotations, July 2.
15. "The Argument Closed," *Daily Virginian,* July 3, 1869, quotations.
16. *Daily Virginian,* July 8, 9, 10, 1869; William Whitley, "John Warwick Daniel (1842–1910)," *Dictionary of Virginia Biography/Encyclopedia Virginia;* Bennett Minton, "The lies our textbooks told my generation of Virginians about slavery," *Washington Post,* July 31, 2020; Joe Stinnett, "Founder of public education in Virginia finally gets recognition in Lynchburg," *Cardinal News,* Feb, 15, 2022.
17. *Daily Virginian,* July 8, 9, 10, 1869, July 8 quotations.
18. "Despicable," July 13, 1869, *Daily Virginian,* first quotation; Charles L. Mosby, July 12, 1866 public letter published July 15, 1866, in *Daily Virginian,* all other quotations.
19. Withers, *Autobiography,* quotations 248–49.
20. Ferguson, *Negro in Politics,* quotation, 14.
21. Taylor-McGraw, *African Republic,* 174–75; Clegg, *Price of Liberty,* quotation, 263; *African Repository* 6 (1830–31), 142.
22. Lynch, *Blyden,* 52 and n69, quoting Erskine to J. C. Lowry in Presbyterian Board of Foreign Missions papers, vol. 9.
23. Martha A. Ricks to Ralph Gurley, April (no date), 1865, *African Repository* 42 (1866), 24, quotations.
24. Tyler-McGraw, *African Republic,* 169; Jeffrey Green, "The African President's Widow in London," jeffreygreen.co.uk, no date.
25. Lynch, *Blyden,* 52, 217; Nemata Blyden, "The Search for Anna Erskine," 31–43, first quotation, 279n9; Williams, *Liberian Exodus,* 55, final quotation.
26. *Daily Virginian,* June 18, 1866.
27. W. H. Lynch to William Coppinger, April 26, 1873.
28. Williams, *Liberian Exodus,* 44, first quotation; 31, other quotations.

Afterword

1. Obituary of Willis D. Knuckles Jr., *Liberian Observer,* liberianobserver.com, July 2014; "President Sirleaf pays tearful tribute to Willis Knuckles," *Liberian Observer,* no date; Freeman, Careysburg, 68 (photograph), 115–17, 135–39.

2. Tyler-McGraw, *African Republic*, quotation, 170.
3. Center for Global Development, "Liberia's Recovery from Devastation," https://www.cgdev.org/page/liberias-recovery-devastation.
4. Burin, *Peculiar Solution*, 166, first quotation; *African Repository* (1887–88), 35, second quotation.
5. Cooper, *Sugar Beach*, 113, 116; Emigrant Database, Virginia Center for Digital History, http://virginians-to-liberia.iath.virginia.edu.

BIBLIOGRAPHY

Primary Archival Sources

American Colonization Society (ACS) records, 1792–1964: Manuscript Division, Library of Congress, MS10660. These were donated to the LOC in 1964 and include 190,000 items in 717 containers, including the Letters of the American Colonization Society: Series I: Incoming Correspondence, 1819–1917; Series II: Outgoing Correspondence, 1839–1912; Series III: General Correspondence, 1909–1965; Series IV: Financial Papers, 1818–1963; Series V: Business Papers, 1816–1963; Series VI: Subject File, 1792–1964; and Series VII: Miscellany, 1835–1935. (Unless otherwise indicated, all letters cited are from these collections.)

The African Repository and Colonial Record: Periodical issued bi-monthly, 1835–1892, by the American Colonization Society from its offices in Washington, D.C.

Congressional Serial Set: "Information relative to the operations of the United States squadron on the west coast of Africa, the condition of the American colonies there, and the commerce of the United States therewith," 28th Congress, 2d. Session, S. Doc. 150, serial 458. (This is the chief source of early ships' lists.)

Emigrants Database, *Virginia Emigrants to Liberia,* Virginia Center for Digital History, University of Virginia http://virginians-to-liberia.iath.virginia.edu.

Federal Census Population Schedules, 1790–1870, US Census for Virginia, and Lynchburg and Amherst, Bedford, Campbell (incl. Lynchburg pre-1810) counties, and "Historical, Demographic, Economic, and Social Data: The United States, 1790–1970," Ann Arbor, MI: Inter-university Consortium for Political and Social Research.

Archival Collections

Accessible Archives collections of nineteenth century newspapers, accessible-archives.com.

Bureau of Refugees, Freedmen and Abandoned Lands/Freedmen's Bureau records, Lynchburg subdistrict, 1865–66, National Archives.

Cabell Family Papers, Special Collections Research Center, Swem Library, College of William and Mary.

Chronicling America, Library of Congress, page images from digitized US newspapers 1777–1963.

James Hunter Terrell papers, Special Collections, University of Virginia Library.

John McCalla family papers, 1754–1917 and undated, David M. Rubenstein Rare Book & Manuscript Library, Duke University, personal papers, Box 6, diary of John McCalla Jr.

Jones Memorial Library, Lynchburg, Va. Rare books, manuscripts, enslavement records, census data.

Papers of Thomas Jefferson, *Founders Online,* National Archives. Original source: *The Papers of Thomas Jefferson,* Retirement Series. Princeton: Princeton University Press, 2006.

Published Sources

Allen, William E. "Liberia and the Atlantic World in the Nineteenth Century: Convergence and Effects." *History in Africa* 37 (2010): 7–49.

American Colonization Society. *A Few Facts Respecting the American Colonization Society and the Colony at Liberia.* Way and Gideon, 1830. African American Pamphlet Collection, Library of Congress.

Alexander, Archibald. *A History of Colonization on the Western Coast of Africa.* William S. Martien, 1846.

Alford, Terry. *Prince Among Slaves: The True Story of An African Prince Sold Into Slavery in the American South.* Oxford University Press, 1977.

American Colonization Society. *Memorial of the Semi-centennial Anniversary of the American Colonization Society, Celebrated at Washington, January 15, 1867.* The Society, 1867.

Anderson, Benjamin. *Narrative of a Journey to Musardu, the Capital of the Western Mandingoes.* S. W. Green, 1870.

Asante, Molefi Kete. *100 Greatest African Americans: A Biographical Encyclopedia.* Prometheus Books, 2003.

Ashmun, Jehudi. *History of the American Colony in Liberia, from December 1821 to 1823.* Way & Gideon, 1826.

Balch, T. B. *Reminiscences of Georgetown, D.C.* Henry Polkinhorn, Printer, 1859, Library of Congress website.

Bancroft, Frederick. *Slave Trading in the Old South.* University of South Carolina Press, 1996 reprint of 1931 original.

Bell, James P., ed. *Our Quaker Friends of Ye Olden Time.* J.P. Bell Publishers, 1905.

Berlin, Ira, and Herbert G. Gutman. "Natives and Immigrants, Free Men and Slaves: Urban Workingmen in the Antebellum American South." *American Historical Review* 88, no. 5 (Dec. 1983): 1175–1200.

Blackford, Charles Minor. *Annals of the Lynchburg Home Guard.* John W. Rohr, printer, 1891.

Blackford, Susan Leigh. *Memoir. (Chapter One of Life In and Out of the Army in Virginia during the War between the States.)* Madison Heights, Va: Percy Press, 1959, reprint of 1894 original.

Blassingame, John W., ed. *Slave Testimonies: Two Centuries of Letters, Speeches and Interviews.* Louisiana State University Press, 1977.

Blight, David W. *Frederick Douglass: Prophet of Freedom.* Simon & Schuster, 2018.

———. *American Oracle: The Civil War in the Civil Rights Era.* Belknap Press of Harvard University Press, 2011.

Blyden, Nemata. "The Search for Anna Erskine," In *Stepping Forward: Black Women in Africa and the Americas.* Ohio University Press, 2002: 31–43.

Boone, Clinton C. *Liberia As I Know it,* Richmond: 1929. No publisher listed.

Brown, Bertram Wyatt. "The Abolitionists' Postal Campaign of 1835." *The Journal of Negro History* 50, no. 4 (Oct. 1965): 229.

Brown, Douglas Summers. *Lynchburg's Pioneer Quakers and Their Meeting House, Bicentennial Edition.* Lynchburg: H. E. Howard, 1986 reprint of 1936 first edition.

Brown, Thomas C. *Examination of Mr. Thomas C. Brown: A Free Colored Citizen of S. Carolina as to the Actual State of Things in Liberia.* New York: American Antislavery Society, 1834.

Burin, Eric. "Envisioning Africa: American Slaves' Ideas about Liberia." *Liberian Studies Journal* 27 (2002): 1–17.

———. "A Manumission in the Mountains: Slavery and the African Colonization Movement in Southwestern Virginia." *Appalachian Journal* 33, no. 2 (Winter 2006): 164–86.

———. *Slavery and the Peculiar Solution: A History of the American Colonization Society.* University Press of Florida, 2008.

Burrowes, C. Patrick. *Between the Kola Forest and the Salty Sea, A History of the Liberian People Before 1800.* Know Your Self Press, 2016.

Cabell, Margaret A. *Sketches and Recollections of Lynchburg by the Oldest Inhabitant (Mrs. Cabell). 1858.* Lynchburg Historical Foundation, 1974 reprint.

Chambers, S. Allen, Jr. *Lynchburg An Architectural History.* University Press of Virginia, 1981.

———. *Poplar Forest and Thomas Jefferson.* Forest, Va: The Corporation for Jefferson's Poplar Forest, 1993.

Christian, W. Asbury. *Lynchburg and Its People.* Lynchburg, Va.: J. P. Bell Co., 1967, reprint with index of 1900 original.

Christie, John W., and Dwight L. Dumond. *George Bourne and The Book and Slavery Irreconcilable.* Historical Society of Delaware, 1969.

Clegg, Claude A., III. *The Price of Liberty: African Americans and the Making of Liberia.* The University of North Carolina Press, 2004.

Coke, Thomas. *Extracts of the journals of the late Rev. Thomas Coke L.L.D.; comprising several visits to North America and the West-Indies.* R. Napper, 1816.

Cooper, Helene. *The House on Sugar Beach.* Simon and Schuster, 2008.

Davis, Bailey F. *The Deeds of Amherst County, Virginia, 1761–1807 and Albemarle County, Virginia, 1748–1763.* Southern Historical Press, 1979

———. *The Deeds of Amherst County, Virginia, 1807–1827. Books L–R.* Southern Historical Press, 1985

———. *The Deeds of Amherst County, Virginia, 1827–1852. Books S–Z.* Southern Historical Press. 1985

———. *Lynchburg and Nelson County Virginia Wills, Deeds and Marriages 1807–1831.* Southern Historical Press. 1985.

———. *The Wills of Amherst County, Virginia 1761–1865.* Southern Historical Press. 1985.

Davis, David Brion. *The Problem of Slavery in the Age of Emigration.* Vintage Books, 2014.

Davis, Jefferson. *The Rise and Fall of the Confederate Government.* D. Appleton and Co., 1881.

Delany, Martin. *The Condition, Elevation, Emigration and Destiny of Colored People.* 1852. Project Gutenberg ebook, 2005.

Delaney, Ted, and Phillip W. Rhodes. *Free Blacks of Lynchburg Virginia 1805–1865.* Warwick House Publishing, 2001.

Dennett, John Richard. *The South as It Is: 1865–1866.* Viking Press, 1965.

Dew, Charles B. *The Making of a Racist / A Southerner Reflects on Family, History, and the Slave Trade.* University of Virginia Press, 2016.

———. *Bond of Iron: Master and Slave at Buffalo Forge.* W. W. Norton, 1994.

———. *Apostles of Disunion: Southern Secession Commissioners and the Causes of the Civil War.* University of Virginia Press, 2001.

Du Bois, W. E. B. *Black Reconstruction in America, 1860–1880.* The Free Press, 1992.

Dunaway, Wilma A. *The African American Family in Slavery and Emancipation.* Cambridge University Press, 2003.

Dunn, Durwood. *An Abolitionist in the Appalachian South: Ezekiel Birdseye on Slavery, Capitalism, and Separate Statehood in East Tennessee, 1841–1846.* University of Tennessee Press, 1997.

———. *The Civil War in Southern Appalachian Methodism.* University of Tennessee Press, 2014.

Dunn, D. Elwood, Amos J. Beyan, and Carl Patrick Burrowes. *Historical Dictionary of Liberia, Second Edition.* African Historical Dictionaries 83. Scarecrow Press, 2001.

Dunn-Marcos, Robin, Konia T. Kollehon, Bernard Ngovo, and Emily Russ. *Liberians, an Introduction to their History and Culture.* Center for Applied Linguistics, 2005.

Dunn, Susan. *Dominion of Memories / Jefferson, Madison and the Decline of Virginia.* Basic Books, 2007.

Dunn, William R., and T. Gibson Hobbs Jr. *Historical Sketches from the Iron Worker.* Lynchburg Historical Foundation, 1984.

Early, John. "Diary of John Early, Bishop of the Methodist Episcopal Church, South (Continued)." *The Virginia Magazine of History and Biography* 34, no. 3 (1926): 237–51.

Early, Jubal. *Narrative of the War Between the States.* Reprint with introduction by Gary Gallagher. Da Capo Press, 1989.

Early, R. H. *Campbell Chronicles and Family Sketches.* Lynchburg, Va.: J. P. Bell Co., 1927.

Egerton, Douglas R. *Wars of Reconstruction / The Brief, Violent History of America's Most Progressive Era.* Bloomsbury Press, 2014.

———. *Gabriel's Rebellion: The Virginia Slave Conspiracies of 1800 and 1802.* University of North Carolina Press, 1993.

Elson, James M. *Lynchburg Virginia: The First Two Hundred Years 1786–1986.* Warwick House Publishers, 2004.

Ferguson, Harry S. *The Participation of the Lynchburg, Virginia Negro in Politics. 1865–1900.* Thesis, Virginia State College, 1950: 12–13.

Folkerts, Jean. "Bennett's New York Herald and the Rise of the Popular Press," review, *The Journal of American History* 77, no. 2 (Sept. 1990): 667.

Franklin, John Hope, and Loren Schweninger. *Runaway Slaves: Rebels on the Plantation.* Oxford University Press, 1998

Freeman, Benjamin G. *Careysburg.* Outskirts Press, 2014.

Garrison, William Lloyd. *Thoughts On African Colonization: Or an Impartial Exhibition of the Doctrines, Principles And Purposes of the American Colonization Society. Together With the Resolutions, Addresses And Remonstrances of the Free People of Color.* Garrison and Knapp, 1832.

Gates, Henry Louis, Jr. *Stony the Road: Reconstruction, White Supremacy, and the Rise of Jim Crow.* Penguin Press, 2019.

Grimsted, David. *American Mobbing, 1828–1861: Toward Civil War.* Oxford University Press, 1998.

Guyatt, Nicholas. *Bind Us Apart: How Enlightened Americans Invented Racial Segregation.* Basic Books, 2016.

Hale, Sarah J., ed. *Liberia: or Mr. Peyton's Experiments.* Harper & Brothers, 1853.

Hall, Richard L. *On Afric's Shore: A History of Maryland in Liberia, 1834–1857.* Maryland Historical Society, 2003.

Harrison, Fairfax, ed. *The Harrisons of Skimono.* Privately printed, 1910.

Heinegg, Paul. *Free African Americans of North Carolina, Virginia, and South Carolina from the Colonial Period to about 1820, Vol. 1.* Baltimore: Genealogical Publishing Co., 2005.

Hine, Darlene Clark, ed. *Crossing Boundaries: Comparative History of Black People in Diaspora.* Indiana University Press, 2001: 225–27.

Holsoe, Svend E. "The Manding in Western Liberia: An Overview." *Liberian Studies Journal* 7 (1976–77): 1–12.

Huberich, Charles H. *The Political and Legislative History of Liberia Vol. 1.* Central Book Co., 1947.

Innes, William. *Liberia; or the Early History & Signal Preservation of the American Colony on the Coast of Africa.* Waugh & Innes, 1832.

Irons, Charles F. *The Origins of Proslavery Christianity: White and Black Evangelicals in Colonial and Antebellum Virginia.* University of North Carolina Press, 2009.

Jackson, Luther Porter. "The Early Strivings of the Negro in Virginia." *The Journal of Negro History* 25, no. 1 (Jan. 1940): 25–34.

———. *Free Negro Labor and Property Holding in Virginia.* New York: Atheneum, 1969.

———. *Negro Office-holders In Virginia, 1865–1895.* Guide Quality Press, 1945.

———. "The Planting of Negro Churches." *The Journal of Negro History 16,* no. 2 (April 1931): 181–203.

———. "The Virginia Free Negro Farmer and Property Owner, 1830–1860." *The Journal of Negro History* 24, no. 4 (1939): 390–439.

James, Winston. *The Struggles of John Brown Russwurm: The Life and Writings of a Pan-Africanist Pioneer, 1799–1851.* NYU Press, 2010.

Jefferson, Thomas. *Notes on the State of Virginia.* Cary and Lea, 1825, original published 1787.

Keehn, David C. *Knights of the Golden Circle: Secret Empire, Southern Secession, Civil War.* LSU Press, 2013.

Kendi, Ibram X. *Stamped from the Beginning—The Definitive History of Racist Ideas in America.* Bold Type Books, 2016.

Leopold, Robert. "A Brief History of the Loma People." *Liberian Studies Journal 31,* 2 (2006): 5–30.

Lindsay, Lisa A. *Atlantic Bonds: A Nineteenth-Century Odyssey from America to Africa.* University of North Carolina Press, 2017.

Link, William A. *Roots of Secession: Slavery and Politics in Antebellum Virginia.* University of North Carolina Press, 2003.

Lowe, Richard. *Republicans and Reconstruction in Virginia, 1856–70.* University Press of Virginia, 1991.

Lugenbeel, J. W. *Sketches of Liberia.* C. Alexander, Printer, 1850.

Lynch, Hollis R. *Edward Wilmot Blyden: Pan-Negro Patriot, 1832–1912.* Oxford University Press, 1967.

McDonald, Travis C. *Poplar Forest, Thomas Jefferson's Villa Retreat.* University of Virginia Press, 2023.

McKee, William. *History of Sherbro Mission, West Africa.* United Brethren Printing House, 1874.

McLeRoy, Sherrie S. and William R. *Strangers in Their Midst: The Free Black Population of Amherst County Virginia.* Heritage Books, 2007, revised edition.

Maris-Wolf, Ted. *Family Bonds: Free Blacks and Re-enslavement Law in Antebellum Virginia.* The University of North Carolina Press, 2015.

Martin, Joseph. *New and Comprehensive Gazetter of Virginia and the District of Columbia.* Charlottesville, 1835.

Miller, Armistead. *Liberia Described. A discourse embracing a description of the climate, soil, productions, animals, missionary work, improvements, &c. With a full description of the acclimating fever.* Joseph M. Wilson, 1859.

Miller, Randall M., ed. *"Dear Master" Letters of a Slave Family.* Cornell University Press, 1978.

Miller's executor v. the Board of the Literary fund, &c. And Ro. W. Davidson, &c., privately printed 619-page bound transcript of proceedings in lawsuits over Samuel Miller's will, formerly owned by Jubal Early. Jones Memorial Library, Lynchburg, Va.

Minutes of the General Assembly of the Presbyterian Church, 1789–1820. Presbyterian Board of Publication, n.d.

Morgan, Phillip D. *Slave Counterpoint: Black Culture in the Eighteenth-Century Chesapeake and Low Country.* University of North Carolina Press/Omohundro Institute, 1998.

———. "Slave Life in Piedmont Virginia, 1720–1800" in *Colonial Chesapeake Society.* University of North Carolina Press, 1988.

Morgan, Phillip D., and Michael L. Nicholls. "Slaves in Piedmont Virginia, 1720–1790." *William and Mary Quarterly* 46, no. 2 (April 1989): 211–51.

Moses, Wilson Jeremiah. *Liberian Dreams: Four Back-To-Africa Narratives from the 1850s.* Penn State University Press, 1998.

Murray, Robert. *Atlantic Passages: Race, Mobility and Liberian Colonization.* University Press of Florida, 2021.

Nercessian, Nora N. "Nineteenth-Century Black Graduates of Harvard Medical School." *Journal of Blacks in Higher Education* 47 (Spring 2005): 88–89.

Page, Sebastian N. *Black Resettlement and the American Civil War.* Cambridge University Press: Cambridge and New York, 2021.

Pollard, Edward A. *The Lost Cause: A New Southern History of the War of the Confederates.* New York, E.B. Treat & Co., 1867.

Perdue, Charles, and Thomas E. Barden, eds. *Weevils in the Wheat: Interviews with Virginia Ex-Slaves.* Charlottesville: University Press of Virginia, 1976.

Neely, Alan. "Teague, Colin," in *Biographical Dictionary of Christian Missions,* ed. Gerald H. Anderson. New York: Macmillan Reference USA, 1998.

Newman, Richard, Patrick Rael, and Phillip Lapsansky, eds. *Pamphlets of Protest—An Anthology of Early African American Protest Literature, 1790–1860.* New York: Routledge, 2001.

Nicholas, Richard L. *Sheridan's James River Campaign of 1865 through Central Virginia.* Charlottesville: Historic Albemarle, 2012.

"Notes on Liberia." *The Baptist Missionary Magazine* XXIII. Press of John Putnam, 1843: 52–54.

Oldfield, J. R. "The Protestant Episcopal Church, Black Nationalists, and Expansion of the West African Missionary Field, 1851–1871." *Church History* 57, no. 1 (1988): 31–45.

"Page vs. Rives." US Circuit Court, Western District of Virginia, at Lynchburg, March 1877, 296–306 in *Reports of Cases Decided in the Circuit Courts of the United States for the Fourth Circuit* 1. Washington, DC: W. H. and O. H. Morrison, 1877: 296–306.

Powell, C. A., B. T. Kavanaugh, and David Christy. "Transplanting Free Negroes to Ohio from 1815 to 1858." *The Journal of Negro History* 1, no. 3 (June 1916): 302–17.

Rainville, Lynn. *Invisible Founders: How Two Centuries of African American Families Transformed a Plantation into a College.* Berghahn Books, 2022.

Reeves, William D. *From Tally-Ho to Forest Home: The History of Two Louisiana Plantations.* AuthorHouse, 2005.

Reid, Whitelaw. *After The War: A Southern Tour (May 1, 1865 to May 1, 1866).* Samson Low, Son, & Marston, 1866.

Report of the Board of Managers of the Pennsylvania Colonization Society. Philadelphia: Thomas Kite, 1830.

Rhodes, Phillip Wayne. *Campbell County, Virginia Deed Book I Abstracts.* Friends of the Campbell County Public Library, 1976.

Robert, Joseph C. *The Tobacco Kingdom: Plantation, Market, and Factory in Virginia and North Carolina, 1800–1860 (1938).* Duke University Press, 1965 reprint of 1938 original.

Rose, Gustavus to William Waller, Dec. 21, 1835, "Virginians in Indiana," *William and Mary Quarterly* 10 Second Series (Oct. 1930): 312–13.

Royall, Anne. *Mrs. Royall's Southern Tour Vol. 1.* Washington: 1830.

Sanderfer, Selena. "Tennessee's Post Civil War Black Emigration Movements." *Tennessee Historical Quarterly* 73, no. 4 (Winter 2014): 254–79.

Sanneh, Lamin. *Abolitionists Abroad / American Blacks and the Making of Modern West Africa.* Harvard University Press, 1999.

Schwarz, Phillip J. *Migrants Against Slavery: Virginians and the Nation.* The University Press of Virginia, 2001.

Shick, Tom W. *Behold the Promised Land: A History of Afro-American Settler Society in Nineteenth-Century Liberia.* Johns Hopkins University Press, 1980.

Sherman, Mary Antoinette Brown. "Barclay Women in Liberia—Two Generations: A Biographical Dictionary." *Liberian Studies Journal*, vol. 30, no. 1 (2005): 28–38.

Sinha, Manisha. *The Slave's Cause, a History of Abolition.* Yale University Press, 2016.

Sirleaf, Amos Mohammed D. *Visionary Liberian Leader: Ellen Johnson-Sirleaf.* Authorhouse, 2009.

Slaughter, Phillip. *The Virginian History of African Colonization.* Macfarlane & Ferguson, 1855.

Smith, J. Douglas. *Managing White Supremacy: Race, Politics and Citizenship in Jim Crow Virginia.* University of North Carolina Press, 2002.

Southern Historical Society Papers. Richmond: Southern Historical Society, 1876.

Staudenraus, P. J. *The African Colonization Movement 1816–1865.* Columbia University Press, 1961.

Tarter, Brent. *Virginians and Their Histories.* University of Virginia Press, 2020.

———. "African Americans and Politics in Virginia (1865–1902)," "Disfranchisement," "Samuel F. Kelso (ca. 1825–1880)," Encyclopedia Virginia/Virginia Humanities, encyclopediavirginia.org.

Thomas, Hugh. *The Slave Trade: The Story of the Atlantic Slave Trade, 1440–1870.* Simon & Schuster, 1997.

Tomek, Beverly C., and Matthew J. Hetrick, eds. *New Directions in the Study of African American Colonization.* University Press of Florida, 2017.

Tripp, Stephen E. *Yankee Town, Southern City.* New York: New York University Press, 1997.

Tyler-McCraw, Marie. *An African Republic: Black and White Virginians in the Making of Liberia.* The University of North Carolina Press, 2007.

———. *At the Falls: Richmond, Virginia and Its People.* University of North Carolina Press, 1994.

Tyler-McGraw, Marie. "The Prize I Mean Is the Prize of Liberty: A Loudoun County Family in Liberia." *The Virginia Magazine of History and Biography* 97, no. 3 (1989): 355–74.

Underwood, Thomas A., Caldwell Titcomb, and Werner Sollors, eds. *Blacks at Harvard: A Documentary History of African American Experience at Harvard and Radcliffe.* NYU Press, 1993.

Von Briesen, Martha. *The Letters of Elijah Fletcher.* University Press of Virginia, 1965.

Walker, David. *Walker's Appeal in Four Articles . . . Third edition.* Boston: David Walker, 1829.

Wiley, Bell, ed. *Slaves No More: Letters from Liberia, 1833–1869.* University of Kentucky Press, 1980.

Williams, Alfred Brockenbrough. *The Liberian Exodus. An Account of Voyage of the First Emigrants in the Bark 'Azor' and Their Reception at Monrovia.* The News and Courier Book Presses, 1878.

Winch, Julie. *A Gentleman of Color: The Life of James Forten.* Oxford University Press, 2002.

Withers, Robert E. *Autobiography of an Octogenarian.* Stone Printing & Mfg. Co. Press, 1907.

Wolf, Eva Sheppard. *Race and Liberty in the New Nation—Emancipation in Virginia from the Revolution to Nat Turner's Rebellion.* Louisiana State University Press, 2006.

Woodson, Carter G. *Free Negro Heads of Families in the United States in 1830.* The Association for the Study of Negro Life and History, 1925.

Works Progress Administration. *The Negro In Virginia.* John F. Blair, 1994, originally published in 1940.

Worrall, Jay, Jr. *The Friendly Virginians / America's First Quakers.* Iberian Publishers, 1994.

Wright, Deborah L. *They Left Their Mark: The Enforcement Acts of 1870.* Deborah Lowe Wright: 2003, second edition 2017.

Yancey, Rosa Faulconer. *Lynchburg and Its Neighbors.* J.W. Ferguson & Sons, 1955.

Online Resources

Asante, Molefi Kete. "Martin Delany: The First Transformationist." Essay based on 2012 speech, in "William Still: An African American Abolitionist" in Still Family Library exhibit, Temple University, http://stillfamily.library.temple.edu/stillfamily/exhibits/show/william-still/historical-perspective/martin-delany--the-first-trans.

Gates, Henry Louis. "The Truth Behind '40 Acres and a Mule,'" 2013 blog post originally published on *The Root.* https://www.pbs.org/wnet/african-americans-many-rivers-to-cross/history/the-truth-behind-40-acres-and-a-mule/.

Janney, Caroline E. *The Lost Cause,* Encyclopedia Virginia, Virginia Humanities/Library of Virginia. https://encyclopediavirginia.org/entries/lost-cause-the/.

Jefferson's University—The Early Life Project (JUEL). Early records of the University of Virginia. http://juel.iath.virginia.edu/home.

Monticello website, Thomas Jefferson Encyclopedia, *Physical Descriptions of Jefferson.* https://www.monticello.org/research-education/thomas-jefferson-encyclopedia/physical-descriptions-jefferson/.

Murray, Robert P. "Whiteness in Africa: Americo-Liberians and the Transformative Geographies of Race," Dissertation, University of Kentucky, Theses and Dissertations—History. 23. (2013) https://uknowledge.uky.edu/history_etds/23.

Saylor, Randy. "Timothy Rogers Junior: Quaker to Slavemaster." Canadian Friends Historical Association: 2019. https://cfha.info/TimothyRogersJr.pdf.

Shick, Tom. *Emigrants to Liberia, 1820–1843: An Alphabetical Listing.* https://archive.org/details/emigrants-to-liberia-1820-1843.

INDEX